Financial Statement
Fraud Casebook

Financial Statement Fraud Casebook

BAKING THE LEDGERS AND COOKING THE BOOKS

Edited by
Dr. Joseph T. Wells

WILEY

John Wiley & Sons, Inc.

Published by John Wiley & Sons, Inc., Hoboken, New Jersey.
Published simultaneously in Canada.

For general information on our other products and services or for technical support, please contact our Customer Care Department within the United States at (800) 762-2974, outside the United States at (317) 572-3993 or fax (317) 572-4002.

Wiley also publishes its books in a variety of electronic formats. Some content that appears in print may not be available in electronic books. For more information about Wiley products, visit our web site at www.wiley.com.

Library of Congress Cataloging-in-Publication Data:

Financial statement fraud casebook: cooking the books/edited by Joseph T. Wells.
     p. cm.
  Includes index.
  ISBN 978-0-470-93441-8 (hardback); 978-1-118-07704-7 (ebk); 978-1-118-07705-4 (ebk); 978-1-118-07706-1 (ebk)
  1. Misleading financial statements. 2. Fraud. I. Wells, Joseph T.
  HV6768.F565 2011
  363.25^{1}963–dc22

Printed in the United States of America.
10 9 8 7 6 5 4 3 2 1

To the Gregor family, with love

Contents

Preface

Enron. Tyco. WorldCom. The South Sea Bubble. Ivar Kreuger. Equity Funding. While the first three of these infamous financial statement frauds may be burned into your memory, chances are the rest of them are not. Even so, efforts by executives and insiders to cook the books have a long and storied history. Let's take a closer look.

The South Sea Company was formed in England in 1711 by Lord Treasurer Robert Harley and a shady character named John Blunt. Because of Harley's political influence, the company was granted a monopoly for trading rights in Spanish South America. But his main purpose was an attempt to help his government pay for an enormous debt it had incurred during the War of the Spanish Succession, which did not end until 1713.

The essence of the deal was for the South Sea Company to assume nearly all of England's debt in exchange for stock. Since audited financial statements did not exist at the time, the company's insiders simply talked up the value of the stock and individual citizens put their life savings into the scheme. When the bubble eventually burst, it nearly bankrupted a proud nation.

Ivar Kreuger (1880–1932) was so rich that he also loaned money to countries — France, Spain, Romania and Poland — to help them rebuild the wreckage of the First World War. Although born in Sweden, Kreuger immigrated to the United States in the early twentieth century and made his fortune in matches. Before his death by suicide, Kreuger's corporation, the Swedish Match Company, owned four-fifths of the entire world supply. This was made possible by essentially the same method used by the South Sea Bubble: Kreuger, one of the richest men in the world at the time, made loans to nations in exchange for monopoly rights for match production.

However, all that glitters is not gold; Kreuger was a ruthless crook, not simply a monopolist. Money to fund wars was not cheap so the Match King raised additional capital by selling shares on the New York Stock Exchange until the Great Depression caused by the market crash. Only then — when Kreuger desperately needed cash — was it revealed that Ivar had created a dizzying maze of nearly 400 interconnected companies all with one common element: phony balance sheets and income statements at a time when audits were rare. Ivar Kreuger's response was to end his life with a 9mm pistol shot to the heart.

And at the heart of financial statement fraud is usually the corporate structure. By the late 1700s, there were only about 40 operating in the United States. By 1800, that had risen to 300. Today there are nearly 6 million corporations, which include about 17,000 public companies.

Although America's Black Friday uncovered a plethora of crooked corporate wrongdoing, the Securities and Exchange Acts of 1933 and 1934 addressed the problem head-on by requiring companies listed on the stock exchange to have certified audits. For a few decades, that strategy seemed to work.

But then came Stanley Goldblum (1927–) and the Equity Funding scandal that set public accounting on its ears. The company was formed in 1960 by Gordon McCormick to pool individual life insurance policies and to resell them to investors. His principal hire was a muscled, 6'2" Goldblum who had both a personal and business credo: to get as big as possible. Stanley acquired the company in late 1961 and soon went public. Because the concept of repooling insurance policies was new, it quickly became a Wall Street darling, with stock prices nearly doubling year-over-year. But there was one more reason the market price was so high: In order to sustain growth, Stanley wasn't just cooking the books; he was microwaving them.

To show his outrageous profits, all Goldblum really needed were phony insurance policies to fool the auditors. He even arranged for a few of the fake policy holders to "die" periodically so that the actuarial tables would not send out red flags. But once fraud starts in the executive suite, it's very hard to stop — much like a freight train with no brakes. The more phony policies created, the more Goldblum had to come up with. His solution? Create a department off-site whose sole duty was to create fake paperwork.

The auditors were among the biggest fools in this scam. By dutifully ticking and footing phony policies, they completely missed in 1972 that a full third of Equity Funding's $2.5 billion in assets didn't even exist. The fraud was finally unraveled when a former employee ratted out Goldblum's gang of thieves to a Wall Street reporter. Equity Funding went broke, Stanley Goldblum went to prison, and the international audit firm (which loudly protested that it was not responsible for detecting fraud) went back to work, shy of several hundred million dollars because of civil damages. Yes, Stanley and Equity Funding accomplished Goldblum's goal of getting big. But a bubble full of hot air is predestined to burst.

In response to the Equity Funding fraud, the American Institute of Certified Public Accountants (AICPA) formed the Commission on Auditor Responsibilities (referred to as the Cohen Commission) in 1974 and issued its final report in 1978. The Commission — and much subsequent auditing literature — had great difficulty in using the word "fraud," preferring instead the term "irregularities." But the report did grudgingly concede that the auditor should at least have some fraud-detection role and so the profession issued Statement on Auditing Standards (SAS) 16.

The external auditors have had a long and tortured history over their responsibilities, or lack thereof, in detecting fraud. The subject was first addressed in authoritative literature in the latter part of the nineteenth century with the publication of *Auditing: A Practical Manual for Auditors* by Lawrence R. Dicksee. He and other authors at the time took the position that the detection of fraud and errors was the main responsibility of auditors. That began to change when Robert H. Montgomery published the first edition of his seminal work, *Montgomery's Auditing* in 1912. (Montgomery was one of the original founders of what has now morphed into PriceWaterhouseCoopers.)

For several decades, the profession inched away from fraud detection and became more engrossed in reporting issues. It attempted to lay the responsibility for fraud on management, which is akin to asking the fox to guard the chicken house. The reason for the auditing industry's reluctance to accept a larger role in fraud detection can be described in one word: liability. The latter part of the twentieth century was littered with lawsuits over audit failures, many of them in the hundreds of millions of dollars.

The response of the profession was curious. Instead of educating itself about fraud detection, it decided that the public needed to be informed on what an audit could and couldn't accomplish. In 1988, the Auditing Standards Board issued nine Statements on Auditing Standards on what it termed "expectation gap" issues. Among them was SAS 53, which superseded SAS 16. This new standard still did not embrace the term "fraud" but it gradually inched up the auditor's duties. It wasn't until 1997, with the issuance of SAS 82, *Consideration of Fraud in a Financial Statement Audit,* that "the other F-word" was used in official literature. Once again, the profession begrudgingly took more responsibility.

The final statement as of this writing, SAS 99, was issued in 2002. It provided specific guidance for auditors in fulfilling their fraud-related responsibilities. So in about a quarter of a century, four fraud-related statements were released. For a profession that is oft criticized for moving at the speed of glaciers, that's lightning-quick action. But then came Enron, which cost investors hundreds of billions of dollars. The public and the U.S. Congress were outraged. That anger soon boiled over when WorldCom's Bernie Ebbers and Tyco's Dennis Kozlowski looted their corporate treasuries for hundreds of millions of dollars.

Congress decided, among other things, that the accounting profession had done a poor job in policing itself so it took away that responsibility with the passage of the Sarbanes-Oxley Act in 2002, which transferred auditing standards to the newly created Public Company Accounting Oversight Board (PCAOB), a creature of the SEC.

From the headlines around the world, one could conclude massive accounting frauds are the rule; not the exception. But that would be wrong. In the following pages, you will be exposed to the real world of financial statement frauds and quickly see that they come in all shapes and sizes — large, medium, small. And they are not the exclusive domain of the United States but rather occur in nearly every corner of the globe. These scams happen in public and private companies, nonprofits and even charities. Still, they have two common elements. First is that they are almost always committed by those in ultimate charge of their organizations. Second, nearly all were once legitimate entities but changed for the worse when they attempted to conceal poor financial performance.

These cases were not written by academics or historians viewing the situation from afar, but rather those directly involved in the investigation of the financial statement frauds. They are all members of the Association of Certified Fraud Examiners (ACFE), the largest antifraud organization in the world. The coauthors contributed their time and talent solely so that others could learn from their experiences. To protect privacy, key names have been changed. No one, including me, received a dime; all profits go to the ACFE Foundation, which provides scholarships to deserving students. They will become tomorrow's fraud fighters and need all the help we can give them.

Thanks go first to the coauthors of this book; we are all deeply indebted to them. Then comes the ACFE staff, especially Laura Hymes, who acted as project manager and principal editor. John Gill, Andi McNeal, Dawn Taylor and Amy Adler of the research department deserve special recognition. Finally, I'd be amiss if I didn't thank ACFE President and CEO Jim Ratley, Vice President Jeanette LeVie and Assistant to the Chairman Lindsay Fassauer. Their assistance has been invaluable.

What will happen next in financial statement fraud? If the past is any indication, we may be in for a rough ride. One unmistakable trend is that we have gone from investing in stocks to speculating on them. Current share price, not a company's future, is frequently king. That brings even more pressure on executives to meet short-term goals. Enforcement by regulatory agencies, while necessary, is inadequate and probably will remain so. Moreover, our population will continue to age until about the mid-twenty-first century. That means more investment in the market of retirement funds. Or put another way, the pool of money subject to manipulation will get bigger. A final unmistakable trend is that financial statement frauds over the past hundred years have gotten larger and more frequent. Don't expect that to change soon. But keep fighting the good fight; it does make a difference.

Dr. Joseph T. Wells, CFE, CPA
Austin, Texas
June 2011

Financial Statement
Fraud Casebook

Keep On Trucking

RALPH WILSON

Jenny Baker was viewed by her associates as a brilliant CFO. She was known for her ability to predict the outcome of future uncertainties with startling accuracy. She was also known to be very demanding, even intimidating at times. Many of her staff had experienced one of her famous outbursts; consequently, they didn't always feel comfortable asking her many questions. She had started her career as a staff auditor for one of the Big Four accounting firms, where she specialized in the transportation industry and was well regarded for her understanding of the nuances of sometimes complex financial transactions.

Using her experience as a launching pad, Jenny had taken a job in regulatory accounting for a regional trucking firm and had moved quickly through the ranks to become the CFO. Not content with a regional firm, she had made several strategic career moves that finally landed her a job as vice president of finance at a national transportation company. During her tenure there, Jenny had gained the confidence of those around her, including the CEO and many of the directors on the company's board.

While pursuing her career, Jenny had also found time to marry and have two children; she even had three grandkids. When she wasn't working, she loved to spend time with her grandchildren; she would even plan her vacations as family events so that she could include them. She was in her mid-fifties, had a nice home, a country-club membership and was no longer driven to advance in her career. She was satisfied with where she was in life. Her long-term plan was to retire early and enjoy all of the things she had worked so hard to earn.

Atkins Trucking

Atkins Trucking Company had been founded in the late 1930s as the economy began to recover somewhat from the Great Depression. The company began as a local trucking firm in a major metropolitan area in the northeast. The founder, Daniel Atkins, had prided himself on delivering high-quality service and always pleasing the customer. Over the years, the company had acquired a reputation for integrity.

After World War II, the transportation industry really began to grow and Atkins Trucking expanded from a local operation to a regional firm and eventually became a national player in the field of transportation. As a result of the expanded transportation market and to recognize new service lines, the company had changed its name to Atkins Transportation Services. Because of family influence, however, the company remained closely held. The only public financing of company activities came from the debt markets. The company made regular use of commercial paper and occasionally issued bonds for long-term capital investments. Atkins Transportation employed 3,500 people concentrated at corporate headquarters, as well as in strategic transportation hubs located throughout the United States.

Always Learning

I was the internal audit director for Atkins Transportation Services. My department consisted of six employees, one of whom was designated as a special projects auditor. One of the things we liked to do was proactively look for fraud. We often undertook data mining to look for improper expenditures or unusual vendor relationships. Sarah Harrington, the special projects auditor, routinely brainstormed with me about new approaches for finding fraud. One day we received a brochure describing a forensic accounting class focusing on financial statement analysis. Since neither of us had taken such a class before, we signed up for it. It turned out to be a wise investment.

Forensic financial statement analysis typically includes techniques involving horizontal and vertical relationships among the basic financial statements — the balance sheet, the income statement, and the statement of cash flows. I remember the instructor specifically telling us to focus on "time-sensitive interdependencies" to identify possible manipulation. In other words, look at what happens over time, not just the current year or the previous year. He also said the most important indicator of earnings manipulation is the correlation of reported earnings with reported cash flows from operations. After completing the class, we had lots of new tools at our disposal to look for fraud.

Armed with this information, I downloaded ten years of company financial data into a spreadsheet and began the process of selectively graphing the relationships we had been taught in class. This was a tedious process, but it began to reveal some unusual patterns. For the early years on the graph, the reported earnings did correlate well with the cash flows from operations; however, the most recent five years showed a remarkable divergence in correlation. Moreover, an analysis of the allowance for doubt-ful accounts showed entirely unexpected results. For example, during a pe-riod of strong revenue growth, the allowance had increased dramatically. According to what I had heard, the company was doing a great job at col-lecting accounts receivable. What I was seeing painted a different picture.

This was all new territory to me. We weren't quite sure what to do next. However, I remember thinking, "This is exciting . . . this stuff really works!" Almost every day, I would call in Sarah or one of the other auditors to show them what I had found. "Look at this," I said. "Do you understand why this is happening?" No one had any explanations.

As I continued my analysis, Sarah began to download journal entries from the company's accounting system. She organized the entries and looked into some of the accounts that didn't make sense. One day Sarah came into my office and said, "I found some journal entries with the nota-tion 'Jenny's entry' as the explanation for the transaction." I asked, "Is there any other information about the purpose of the entry?" "No, that's all there is," she said.

Sensing that we had found something significant, we began to discuss what to do. Soon a consensus emerged that we should talk to our external audit firm. They were already onsite with only six more weeks until the annual report was completed. We scheduled a meeting and showed the engagement partner and the auditor in charge our financial statement analysis. Then we talked about the transactions we had found with the unusual notations. They seemed interested in our work, but their initial response was, "We need to finish the engagement . . . our opinion is due by the 30th of next month." This didn't sound promising, but they said they'd get back to me.

After a few days, I received an e-mail from the engagement partner say-ing they were not going to pursue the issue this year. They had looked at their work papers and they were satisfied with the explanations they had received from management. However, they suggested that we look more closely at the issues. I thought, "Great . . . what do we do now?"

Management by Intimidation

"Why can't the controller explain these entries?" I asked. Sarah and I had just come from a meeting with the company controller and the director of accounts receivable. Rather than take a more direct approach in our investi-gation, we had decided to initiate an audit of accounts receivable. That way, we could gather more information and not raise too much concern.

Our meeting had started off well, but soon became uncomfortable when we asked about some of the entries that had been made to the allow-ance for doubtful accounts. We showed the controller, Stewart Wood, some of the journal vouchers with the notation "Jenny's entry" and asked if he could explain them. He responded, "If you want to understand those entries, you'll have to go and talk to Jenny." "Why is that?" I said, "Don't you know the reason for these entries?" At that point, Stewart became defensive and said, "Those entries are communicated to me by management; you'll need to talk to them."

Not wanting to concede so easily, I changed tactics and said, "These entries are affecting our bottom line, Stewart. Some of them increase the bottom line and some of them decrease it. What do you think management is trying to do here?" Stewart was unwilling to respond, so Jack, the director of accounts receivable, intervened and said, "I've worked in this industry for a long time and this kind of thing is not unusual. Management is just trying to smooth out the peaks and the valleys. This is fairly common; you shouldn't be too concerned about it."

Next we turned our attention to some of the bad debt accounts related to the allowance for doubtful accounts. Jenny was very exacting in her demands for information, so the controller had set up several accounts to keep track of bad debts by service line. There was a bad debt account for short-haul service, one for long-haul service and one for international service. There was even an account called "Bad debt — NA." I showed this to Stewart and asked him what "NA" meant. He responded, "It means 'not assigned.'" "What do you mean by that?" I said. Stewart explained, "This account is not assigned to any of our service lines; management uses this account to make occasional adjustments to bad debt expense." "Is this part of your normal monthly process?" I asked. "No," Stewart replied. "Management decides when we make entries to this account."

I asked Stewart to explain the methodology for determining the amounts to book to the NA account. He said he didn't know the methodology. I then asked to see the substantiation for some of the entries. He said he didn't have any. I asked him who approved the entries to this account and he told me that no one approved them. "These entries are made at Jenny's direction," he said. "No one needs to approve them."

This was astounding to me. There were absolutely no controls over some very material accounting entries. How could the external auditors have missed this? I knew from prior audits that the monthly process for estimating bad debts was well substantiated and that all entries were required to be approved. We had apparently stumbled into a dark closet and we soon discovered that no one appreciated us trying to shine some light in there.

Before proceeding further though, Sarah and I decided to dig into the accounting records some more. We downloaded all the entries made by Stewart over the past five years and then performed text searches looking specifically for the words "Jenny's entry" in the description field. We learned that Jenny concentrated her unusual activities in two areas: accounts receivable and regulatory reserves. We already knew what was happening in accounts receivable so we began to focus on the regulatory reserves.

Regulatory reserves were contingent liabilities established for settling accounts with various taxing authorities. In the transportation industry, licensing fees and taxes were subject to audit and sometimes the taxing authorities would make adjustments to what the company had already paid. The reserve accounts were established to estimate potential audit adjustments.

Next, I charted the balance in the reserve accounts over ten years to see what was there. Not surprisingly, I saw the same unusual pattern of increasing and decreasing balances that seemed unrelated to underlying business conditions. "Those must be some of the peaks and valleys," I thought.

Sarah scheduled a meeting with the director of regulatory accounting to see if he could help explain the regulatory reserve transactions. Soon after scheduling the meeting, Sarah received an e-mail from the director explaining that he was headed away on vacation and he would like to delay the meeting until after he returned. That seemed strange; he knew about his vacation when he scheduled the meeting. Why did he want to delay it? Soon we learned that Jenny had ordered him not to meet with us until he returned.

The next morning, I received a call from the CEO, Todd Martin. He wanted me to know that he had received a call from Jenny Baker. She had complained that I was being unprofessional in dealing with her staff. She said that I had told her staff that she was manipulating the accounting records. I told Todd that all we had done was ask questions about some accounting entries that didn't make sense. We didn't know what was happening and the only way to find out was to ask questions. Todd replied, "Just be aware that Jenny isn't happy about what you're doing. Watch your step."

Later that day I received an e-mail from Jenny telling me that she wanted to know the scope and objectives of our audit. She said her people were busy doing their work and didn't have time for all of the questions we were asking. I replied that we had sent a memo to the director of accounts receivable announcing the audit and that she had been copied. I also explained to her that once we began collecting information, we had found some entries that didn't make sense. I stated, "As auditors, we have the responsibility and the authority to follow the trail wherever it leads." I copied the CEO on my response. Jenny didn't reply.

After the director of regulatory accounting returned from his vacation, we succeeded in scheduling a meeting. Sarah met with him and got the same story we had already heard. The director kept track of all of the known regulatory liabilities, but Jenny directed him to create reserves for unknown liabilities. The director couldn't explain the methodology for estimating these reserves. The amounts were determined by Jenny based on her years of experience in the transportation industry. He had no reason, nor desire, to question Jenny about the reserves. If we wanted to know more about them, then we'd have to ask Jenny.

After talking it over with Sarah, we decided to go directly to Jenny for answers. We scheduled a meeting for the following Monday. When we arrived, we noticed several of her high-ranking staff members arriving in the conference room as well. We had expected to be meeting with Jenny alone. Perhaps this was an intimidation tactic — Jenny was famous for intimidating her own employees. Now it was our turn. I leaned over to Sarah and whispered, "Looks like this is going to be a big meeting."

Once the meeting got started, we proceeded to explain our concerns about the accounting entries we had found. We reported that internal controls over certain transactions were nonexistent and asked Jenny if she could explain what was happening. Her response was unusual. Rather than discuss the specific transactions, she began by talking about the complexity of the transportation industry. She talked about all of the regulatory and economic uncertainty and how it affected financial reporting. She then reviewed all of the experience that she and her staff had and said they were more than qualified to account for all of that uncertainty by including reserves in the company's financial statements. We, conversely, didn't have the same experience that she had; we were not experts in the industry. I admitted to her that we didn't have the same experience that she had, but we could understand the accounting if someone explained it to us.

Although she didn't say it, her message to us was that we had to rely on her experience rather than normal accounting rules. That's where I turned my attention next. Prior to the meeting, I had brushed up on internal controls over accounting estimates as well as the rules for recording contingent liabilities. I asked her, "So, you're telling me that with all of the uncertainty in the transportation industry, it's hard to estimate things like bad debts and tax liabilities?" "Yes," she replied. "It's almost impossible to estimate things like bad debts or regulatory reserves. We look at our financial statements each month and if the numbers don't look right, we make adjustments as needed based on our experience. We try to reflect the underlying business."

I informed her that according to FASB No. 5, *Accounting for Contingencies*, contingent liabilities may be recorded only if it is probable that an asset has been impaired or a liability has been incurred. Moreover, any contingency must be capable of reasonable estimation. If those criteria aren't met, then the proper accounting treatment is to disclose the contingency rather than to record it. She then stated firmly, "Our financial statements have been audited by our external auditors and they had no problems with any of the entries." I told her that we planned to talk to the external auditors, but any further information she could provide might be helpful. After some additional comments by Jenny, the meeting concluded.

Before contacting the auditors, however, I told Sarah that we needed more information. "Let's dig through the accounting records and see what we can find," I said, so Sarah headed over to the accounting department to begin looking at the suspicious journal vouchers and making copies of any supporting documentation. When she got back, we began to review the vouchers. After looking at a number of documents, Sarah suddenly exclaimed, "Look at this!" She handed me a voucher with a copy of an e-mail from Jenny attached to it. It was written to the controller instructing him not to report some extra income the company had received that quarter. It stated, "Don't book this as income. Put it in the reserve accounts." That was all we needed to make our case. I immediately called the CEO's office to schedule a meeting.

Dreading the News

The CEO was out of town, so our meeting had to wait until the following Friday. The delay allowed us plenty of time to put together a solid presentation. We had examples of journal entries with no support and no approval; we had graphs showing the ups and downs in the allowance for doubtful accounts, as well as the regulatory reserves. We had a graph showing the reported bottom line and what it would have been without "Jenny's entries." And to top it all off, we had Jenny's e-mail ordering the controller not to report income.

All of this painted a clear picture of improper earnings management, the goal of which is to smooth reported earnings. Jenny accomplished this by increasing contingency accounts like the allowance for doubtful accounts and other reserves when business was good and decreasing the accounts when business was bad. Within generally accepted accounting principles, management has the ability to influence reported earnings, but only within reasonable limits. Jenny was clearly out of bounds.

When I arrived at the CEO's office on Friday, he was anticipating me like someone anticipates a trip to the dentist. He knew it needed to happen, but he wasn't looking forward to it. Once I showed him our presentation, he asked, "Why is Jenny doing this? I don't understand it. Atkins Transportation already has a strong financial position." "I think it's the debt rating," I replied. "Bondholders and ratings agencies like to see stable earnings. Greater earnings volatility means greater risk; greater risk means higher interest rates. Stability lowers our debt costs."

The CEO leaned back in his chair, thought for a few minutes, and said with a sense of resignation, "I need to call the chairman of the board; why don't you go call our audit firm and get them over here." I agreed and left the room. I wasn't happy about any of this, but it was my job. Atkins Transportation Services had built an excellent reputation. This kind of behavior could permanently damage that reputation. These practices needed to be stopped.

During the next few days, there was a flurry of activity. I had meetings with the audit committee, a meeting with the chairman of the board and a meeting with our audit firm. The audit firm formulated a plan to restate earnings; we hired consultants to help with the process, and my staff was enlisted to provide assistance. Our legal counsel began the process of contacting the SEC and our debt underwriters to inform them of the situation and what we planned to do about it. No one knew what the repercussions would be, but we believed we were doing the right thing to protect our reputation.

Rather than being fired, Jenny was given the option to retire. She gladly accepted the opportunity to "spend more time with her family." I believe it was the right outcome. Jenny's departure would allow her to spend time with her grandkids, and she would no longer be under the pressure she felt to achieve a certain level of financial performance. I was certain her employees would be relieved.

Lessons Learned

When Sarah and I first considered taking a forensic accounting course, we had high hopes, but we weren't sure how valuable the material would be. After all, we had already been to quite a few auditing courses in our careers and studied published resources as well. What we learned, however, was a different approach to investigation. Forensic accountants must be very thorough because their reports typically end up in court where they will be attacked by the opposing side.

Preparing for this type of encounter requires a highly disciplined approach to an investigation. For example, the auditor must acquire a very strong knowledge of the company's financial statements. This can be achieved only by reading the statements thoroughly and analyzing the numbers using horizontal and vertical techniques that include graphical depictions. The minimum suggested analytical horizon is the previous five years, but in this case we needed to go back ten years to see the unusual relationships that existed. If we had not taken the time to do this, we would not have uncovered the improper activities. The forensic accounting course gave us the tools we needed to be successful.

We also realized the importance of corporate culture. Jenny was known for intimidating her employees and that environment allowed the accounting scheme to sprout and grow without opposition or detection. After a while, everyone considered the unusual entries to be a part of the normal routine. No one questioned why the entries were being made. The culture made it possible for the scheme to take place.

(continued)

Although it seems like an elementary concept, we also saw the importance of basic internal controls. If controls such as requiring substantiation for every entry and requiring approval for every entry had been followed, then it would have been far more difficult for someone to start and perpetuate the kind of activities we found during our audit.

We also found that we needed a thorough grasp of basic accounting rules. For example, we had to review the definition of a *liability* and we also had to understand accounting for contingencies. We found it was most helpful to go back and read the original accounting statements from the Financial Accounting Standards Board. Textbooks were helpful, but the original pronouncements included discussions that were right on point and helped us make our case. In fact, those resources were indispensable in overcoming opposing viewpoints.

Then there was the issue of becoming discouraged. When undertaking this type of audit, it is possible that feathers will be ruffled or careers will be threatened. Sarah and I found it helpful to read about similar situations as described in educational materials from the Association of Certified Fraud Examiners. These books and videos confirmed for us that we were finding real problems, not misunderstandings. We also found encouragement by reading books like *Extraordinary Circumstances* by Cynthia Cooper, who recounted what happened to her while investigating the WorldCom scandal. We knew if she could fight through to the end, we could do it also. It made the obstacles easier to overcome because we knew what was coming and could prepare for it in advance. These resources made a big impact on our audit.

Recommendations to Prevent Future Occurrences

Pay Attention to Significant Transactions

Auditors, both internal and external, sometimes get in the habit of focusing on routine accounting transactions while ignoring nonroutine transactions. This is true because most accounting transactions are routine in nature. They happen on a regular basis and are well understood. Nonroutine transactions, however, have a much higher risk because they fall outside the normal accounting process.

(continued)

(*continued*)

More audit effort should be expended to identify nonroutine transactions and determine the purpose of those entries. Moreover, nonroutine accounting entries should be evaluated throughout the reporting period, not simply the entries made near the end of the year. Manipulation of accounting records can occur at any time.

Apply Controls to All Transactions

Internal controls do not work if they are not applied to all transactions. There should be no special class of transactions that are controlled differently than others. The same principle applies to transactions originated by higher levels of management; the same controls should apply regardless of who requests an entry. Controlling 99% of the accounting entries is insufficient. That remaining 1% is more than enough to misstate financial results.

Increase Board Involvement

Sarbanes-Oxley requires that qualified financial experts serve on the boards of publicly traded firms; however, not all companies are publicly traded. Therefore, it is important for those firms to compensate in some way if there is no qualified financial expert on the board. One way is to hire a board consultant whose job it is to interact with company financial executives, understand what they are doing and advise the board on matters of significance related to financial reporting. Regardless of the type of firm, financial reporting should be a priority for all board members, and audit committees should be very engaged in the financial reporting process.

Don't Tolerate Abusive or Defiant Behavior

There is often a tendency at the higher levels of an organization to tolerate behavior that is otherwise unacceptable. There are many reasons for this, but regardless of the reasons, there should be an understanding that deviations from behavioral standards promote an environment where other standards also may be violated. Behavioral issues involving high-ranking financial personnel should not be viewed in isolation but should be considered a weakness in the control environment that can have a real impact on financial reporting. Boards and CEOs need to evaluate this risk and auditors need to consider it in planning their audits.

(*continued*)

Improve Auditor Awareness and Training

An auditor is only as good as the tools at his or her disposal. Training is an essential ingredient for success. There is always new fraud research being conducted, new audit techniques being developed and new fraud schemes being hatched. Auditors must remain current with these new developments if they wish to remain effective. Without adequate training, auditors might overlook issues that have the potential to cause serious harm to the public, to employees and to company reputations. Training is always a wise investment.

About the Author

Ralph Wilson, CFE, CPA, is a graduate of Liberty University and the University of Virginia. He has approximately 25 years of professional audit and compliance experience in a number of industries, including financial services, education, healthcare, not-for-profit and governmental. Mr. Wilson also teaches graduate auditing and fraud examination courses.

CHAPTER

Too Good to Be True?

CAROLYN CONN

Terry Burns was living the good life. Most people would have said he had already achieved the American dream, and he was only 55 years old. Burns lived in a 6,000-square-foot mansion on the Alabama Gulf Coast, spent summers in exotic places (including his summer home in the Bahamas) and was married to a former beauty queen. After nearly 30 years in real estate development, he was elected president and chairman of the board (with the controlling interest) of Monarch Group, a residential development and construction company. Not long after he was chosen to head the company, Monarch was reported by several financial services as "a stock to watch."

Burns knew he had *earned* his success. He graduated from Plains University in the panhandle of Oklahoma with a degree in accounting. With a near-perfect GPA and a résumé full of accomplishments (including president of the accounting club), Burns was recruited by several national accounting firms and the largest regional accounting firms in both Oklahoma and Texas. He was determined to leave what he described as his "backwater" hometown, certain he would find financial success in the "big city." Burns accepted a lucrative offer from one of the large national accounting firms in their Dallas office. He lost no time in passing all parts of the exam to become a Certified Public Accountant, holding a license in both Texas and Oklahoma. He was an active member of several professional associations.

Burns quickly moved up the ranks and became a senior auditor, specializing in cash-flow management for a variety of clients, ranging from small proprietorships to Fortune 500 companies. After four years with the accounting firm, Burns took a position as vice president of a real estate developer in the Dallas/Fort Worth area. He had primary responsibility for all aspects of the financial operations, but he also managed product development, construction and marketing of single-family homes and multi-family complexes, as well as subdivision development. Burns was surprised at how much he loved the construction business. He told his friends, "Who would have thought a numbers guy could be so good at the creative aspects of my job . . . like marketing?!" During the next nine years, his employer's revenues grew to $30 million annually and Burns was recruited to join Monarch Construction.

Even though it meant moving to Alabama where Monarch was headquartered, Burns eagerly accepted their offer. His new responsibilities included land acquisition and development, financing, home construction, marketing and sales. He told his wife, "I know neither one of us want to leave our family and friends in Dallas, but Monarch's poised for a major expansion and they want me as CEO. Instead of VP, I'll be at the top! In addition to a $200,000 annual salary, I'll get stock in the company. It's the opportunity of a lifetime." His wife was persuaded to make the move when he described the people of Alabama as being a lot like them and their current circle of friends — conservative with strong family values and religious principles.

Steve Knight was all too familiar with the unpredictable nature of the "oil patch" of West Texas. He was born and grew up in Midland, where oil *was* the economy. When things were good in the oil industry, it trickled down and out — affecting oil-service companies as well as every employer and business owner in the region. And, when things were bad in the oil industry, it had the same negative effect on everyone in the region, including Knight's own CPA practice.

He had worked summers during his college years in the oil field, driving a truck to deliver pipe and other supplies to oil rigs. Knight drove hundreds of miles per day in 100-degree temperatures over dusty, unpaved roads in trucks with little or no suspension and no air conditioning. When he arrived home each night, he was coated in dust that had swirled into the open windows of his truck. He never complained because the pay was good and the money paid for college. Knight's parents were farmers who had always struggled financially. When he was a sophomore in high school, his father told him, "I'm real sorry, son. But, if you want to go to college, you're going to have to earn your own way."

Not long after that, Knight told his mother, "I *won't* spend my life on this farm. I'm getting a degree in something where I can work in an office . . . with air conditioning!" During his sophomore year at Mountainview University, he took the required introductory accounting class and really enjoyed it. He changed his major from undecided business to accounting and kept his minor in agricultural business, to appease his dad. After completing his bachelor's degree, Knight went to work for an independent oil exploration company headquartered in nearby Odessa. Two years later he passed the CPA exam. He stayed with the independent oil company for six years and then became a partner in a local CPA firm.

After a few years, he bought out the other partners and became a sole practitioner focused on tax and auditing work.

Anyone who worked with or for Knight described him as "one in a million . . . the nicest guy you'll ever meet." He was intelligent and hardworking. Even if a client brought in the documents for their tax return extremely late, he worked through the night to assure the return was filed on time. He pitched in and helped lower-level employees get their work done and meet deadlines. His longtime assistant often marveled at his good nature. "I've never heard Mr. Knight say a cross word or speak badly of anyone."

In the second year after he "went solo," Knight's firm was hired by the parent company of Monarch to perform their annual audit. He developed a strong working relationship with the top executives of Monarch and was asked to serve on their board of directors. It was an easy decision for Knight when Monarch asked him to become CFO three years later. He had confidence in the company's leadership and in their financial viability. Knight felt that working for a CEO like Terry Burns would be ideal. Because Burns was also a CPA, it would be easy to discuss financial results and accounting issues with him. In all his dealings with Burns, Knight had found him to be honest and straightforward, someone whose word was his bond. Knight was only 49 years old when he joined Monarch as CFO. His new six-figure salary was considerably higher than the earnings from his CPA practice. He was glad to leave the oil patch. He looked forward to deep-sea fishing in the Gulf of Mexico and playing golf on the challenging courses in Alabama.

Simon Fitch knew early in his teens that he wanted to major in business and be involved in mergers and acquisitions. His father worked on Wall Street as a corporate attorney and Fitch was enthralled with the descriptions of his father's work. His college fraternity brothers kidded him about being a geek when he excitedly told them about things he learned in his business law and accounting principles classes. He took their kidding goodnaturedly. "You guys may be right. But, you ought to hear my dad talk about hostile takeovers and tense negotiations. It's never boring and he makes some big bucks!"

Fitch grew up in the Hamptons, accustomed to what his father's money could buy: private schools, weekends on Cape Cod and the family's summer home in the Poconos. He went straight through college, first earning a bachelor's degree in general business and completing an M.B.A. one year later. His résumé looked like the perfect preparation for a well-mapped-out career.

After earning his master's degree, he was hired in the research department of a nationally recognized real estate research firm in New York City. He worked there for two years and then spent three years as a senior consultant with a regional management consulting firm. He specialized in business start-ups and corporate mergers with a specialty in real estate. Fitch subsequently enrolled in accounting classes at night and earned enough hours to sit for and pass the CPA exam in New York. He was then hired as a senior manager with a large national accounting firm, where he stayed for four years. He was persuaded to leave the accounting firm to become the CFO of Astral Productions, a multimedia production company. Fitch stayed with Astral for five years, with responsibilities for all accounting and administrative functions. During his time there, Astral had annual revenues of nearly $150 million and almost 400 employees.

Thomas Nathan was a chameleon who fit in regardless of the environment. He easily went from wearing a hard hat and steel-toed work boots alongside subcontractors on a job site to wearing a tuxedo and rubbing elbows with top politicians and venture capitalists. Nathan had a story for every occasion and was always the life of any party. Nathan's reputation as a former football star, coupled with his rugged good looks and charm made him both a man's man and a ladies' man.

He was born in northwestern Alabama "in the sticks," as Nathan described his hometown. He was not a good student in high school, but kept his grades high enough to stay on the football team. He knew football was his ticket out. "I'm getting away from this one-horse town and I'm going to be *somebody*." His plan worked. Nathan played for a powerhouse college football team. He was named All-American in both his junior and senior years. But injuries from a motorcycle accident during the spring of his senior year kept him from a professional football career.

After college graduation, Nathan and his three brothers started Nathan Brothers Construction Company. Their first jobs were minor remodeling projects and they did all the work themselves. As their firm grew, they became the general contractor on much larger jobs and hired subcontractors. Each brother managed one aspect of the business — one worked with residential clients to develop specifications and plans, another handled bids from subs, another did the financing and accounting — and, Thomas was the CEO and front man. He did marketing and sales and was the face of the business. His brothers were amazed at his sales abilities. They often kidded him, "It may be corny to say but, Tom, you could sell ice cream to Eskimos."

Ever the risk-taker, Thomas Nathan persuaded his brothers to expand their business into high-end residential properties to become developers in Alabama and other nearby states. They changed their firm's name to Alabama Resort Developers, a private corporation. The firm acquired options to buy a few tracts of pristine property in areas generally regarded as untouchable for development. Some of the tracts were heavily wooded and adjoined national and state forests or conservation areas. Others were on the Gulf coast, along beaches that were carefully monitored and protected by environmentalists. Through Thomas's political connections and possibly a few "financial incentives," he obtained state and local permits for their firm to develop some of the properties.

Monarch

Monarch Group, Inc. (MG), was originally incorporated under the name Black Gold Exploration (BGE) in the early 1970s in California. For decades, BGE's primary business was oil and gas exploration, until Ronald Topper, founder and primary shareholder of BGE, wanted a change. "I love the excitement of oil and gas exploration, but the highs and lows are wearing me out. I want something equally exciting but a bit more predictable." In December of that year, BGE ceased all operations in the oil and gas industry and disposed of its assets. That same month, the company made a dramatic change when it acquired Monarch Construction, Inc., and several related entities with the goal of concentrating on the construction business. Monarch Construction had operated along the Alabama Gulf Coast as a developer of residential subdivisions and a construction firm for single-family homes (primarily entry-level homes). A year after the acquisition, BGE bought out Ronald Topper's interest and changed the name to Monarch Group. Shortly after Topper left, Terry Burns was elected as president and chairman of the board.

Consistent with the corporation's strategic plan to expand into more exclusive segments of the market, Monarch acquired Alabama Resort Developers (ARD). The acquired company was a developer of five-star resorts and upscale homes (both single-family and condominiums), owned by Thomas Nathan and his three brothers (all of whom were actively involved in the company). Monarch's upper management and board of directors were thrilled about their acquisition of ARD, primarily because of that firm's reported ownership of options to purchase numerous large parcels of property for development. In his remarks in the board meeting when the ARD acquisition was finalized, Burns told the group: "In addition to having options on some of the most beautiful and sought-after undeveloped property in the southeast, ARD has already obtained all regulatory approvals to develop these properties. This is truly a coup for Monarch."

Monarch's CEO, Terry Burns, and CFO, Steve Knight, signed the corporation's Form 10-K filed the year ARD was acquired. Note 1 of that filing stated: "The company's consolidated subsidiaries include Monarch Group, Inc., and its subsidiary, Monarch Mortgage, Inc., and Alabama Resort Development, Inc., and related entities." The note explained further that the financial statements included activities "carried on directly and/or through other entities which are majority owned or controlled through acquisition options." There is also a reference to "nonrevocable options" to purchase ownership interest in various entities.

Note 2 of Monarch's 10-K described the buyout of Ronald Topper, former CEO. Monarch disposed of all remaining oil and gas assets along with some sand and gravel properties, transferring title to Topper in exchange for all of his shares of Monarch's common stock. Topper's stock had constituted a significant percentage of the voting shares of Monarch.

Steve Knight left his position as Monarch's CFO early the following spring. He moved back to his hometown and opened his own CPA firm, working again as a sole practitioner. Simon Fitch was hired to replace him. Burns and Fitch signed that year's quarterly filings with the SEC. In those reports, the "Summary of Accounting Policies" described the "consolidated financial statements" as including the accounts of "Monarch and its subsidiaries, including Alabama Resort Developers and its related entities." The explanatory notes for both fiscal years were clear about the consolidation of ARD into the Monarch Group.

Acquisition of ARD was effected with the issuance of 5 million shares of Monarch's common stock to the Nathan brothers in exchange for their 100 percent ownership of ARD. Note disclosures in Monarch's year-end report indicated ARD's historical cost of total assets was just over $40 million with total liabilities of $43 million, leaving negative equity of approximately $3 million. However, the "fair values" of total assets was stated at more than $70 million, total liabilities of $50 million and net equity of $20 million. ARD was described in this note as being involved in development, design and construction of resort properties with *options* to acquire several large real estate projects along the entire Gulf Coast (ranging from Texas to Florida). The value of those options comprised just over $50 million of the total assets of ARD and 30 percent of the firm's total inventory of properties.

In a note about their Land and Home Inventory, Monarch Group reported they held *options* to purchase land, with the options reported at the excess of the fair market value over the option price. The options were obtained as part of the acquisition of ARD. Monarch stated their intentions to exercise all the options during the next fiscal year (unless future circumstances influenced them not to do so).

One stipulation of the ARD acquisition was that Thomas Nathan and all three of his brothers would become employees of Monarch, while continuing their previous ARD responsibilities.

Surprise from the SEC

"The SEC is doing what?!" Terry Burns was shocked at what his CFO, Simon Fitch, was telling him. That morning Fitch received a registered letter from the SEC stating the agency was investigating Monarch for allegations of filing fraudulent financial statements. "Simon, we've always done everything squeaky clean. That's the only way I do business. What on earth can this be about? Did they give you any details?"

Fitch had no other information except that the SEC investigator would be at Monarch headquarters the following week to begin the investigation. When the SEC investigator arrived, she concentrated on the annual financial report and the following two quarterly filings after ARD was acquired. Her concern was over the manner in which the consolidation had been reported and the ownership of the options for development of a number of ARD properties. During their first meeting with her, Burns and Fitch were surprised by how familiar she was with details of the ARD acquisition.

They suspected Thomas Nathan had filed an anonymous complaint with the SEC and provided behind-the-scenes details of the acquisition. He was not happy at Monarch. Within a month of joining the firm, he began trying to undo their deal. Burns observed, "We don't do business like Thomas does — fast and loose. I wish we had known he was such a wheeler-dealer before we brought him on board." Two months later, Fitch reported to Burns that ARD had fraudulently recorded unauthorized and improper mortgages on property owned by Monarch. Burns confronted Thomas Nathan and his brothers and fired all of them.

Burns and Fitch could not figure out how the Nathans had obtained enough details about Monarch's holdings to attempt the fraudulent mortgages for property they did not own. The day after the brothers were fired, Fitch tried to retrieve information from Thomas' office computer but realized the hard drive was missing. He knew the drive contained a significant amount of confidential financial data. A subsequent and thorough analysis of the firm's database by an IT specialist revealed someone had accessed even more of Monarch's electronic files without permission. Burns and Fitch suspected it was Thomas Nathan.

"I knew he was a slick salesman, but I never would have expected him to know enough about technology to hack into our system," was the first reaction from Burns when he got the IT report. Fitch surmised, "He probably didn't do it himself. He could have brought somebody in here at night, or maybe they did it remotely."

The Monarch Group filed a complaint with the circuit court in Alabama against Thomas Nathan for return of the hard drive. Because other litigation had been filed by both Monarch and ARD against each other, the court ordered the hard drive be copied so that both Monarch and Nathan could have access to the information on it. Monarch did not take action against Nathan for what they suspected to be his unauthorized access to the company's database.

An Inexperienced Investigator and Bungled Due Diligence

To Burns and Fitch, it seemed like the SEC investigator was on-site forever. She scrutinized the contracts for Monarch's acquisition of ARD and the option contracts for ARD's development properties. She interviewed the Nathan brothers and all of Monarch's board members. She also interviewed Burns (CEO), Knight (former CFO), Fitch (current CFO) and their external auditor.

Monarch's auditor had issued an unqualified opinion for the annual report under question. The auditor provided copies of his firm's work papers for the annual audit and the two quarterly reviews after the ARD acquisition. Both his firm and Monarch showed the SEC investigator documentation from their discussions with other accountants about how the ARD consolidation should be recorded. Burns told the investigator, "We even went the extra mile and hired a second CPA firm with a national reputation for specializing in consolidations to ensure it was reported correctly." He did not say it out loud to her, but Burns had serious concerns about the investigator's inability to understand the intricacies of the consolidation. She appeared uncertain and inexperienced.

The SEC investigator gave the impression that she believed Burns, Knight and Fitch conspired to overstate Monarch's total assets by at least $50 million (the value of ARD's options). It did not help that Monarch's stock price increased significantly during the time period under investigation and that Burns had sold a considerable amount of his own holdings in the company's stock. His position was that he reinvested most of those proceeds back into Monarch. However, the SEC investigator did not attempt to prove or disprove his assertion. It was also problematic that some of the properties the Nathan brothers said they owned and brought into the consolidation as ARD assets were not owned by them individually or by their company.

Burns did his best to convince the SEC investigator the options were being renewed and they should not have been written off at the end of the fiscal year. "It's just a technicality that the ink wasn't dry on our option contracts when the annual report was filed. It was a timing issue. I've done business all my life on a handshake. The people who owned those properties *knew* we had a deal.[1] Why can't you understand that?!" He explained further that Monarch did write off some of the options in the next year when it was determined they definitely would not be renewed.

A Few Unhappy Executives

It took almost three years from the time Monarch received the SEC notice about their investigation until the agency's formal report was issued. The two major findings were: (1) Monarch overstated its assets because some of ARD's options had expired when the annual financial report was filed, and (2) when Monarch wrote off the most significant expired options, they improperly reallocated the acquisition cost of ARD such that the adjustments were minimized. The SEC took action against Burns, Knight and Fitch ordering them to "cease and desist" from causing violations of SEC rules. Burns was ordered to disgorge $30,000 and pay $6,000 in interest related to the sale of his Monarch stock. All three men consented to the issuance of the SEC's order without admitting or denying any of its findings.

The SEC took a separate action against Monarch's external auditor. The firm and the engagement partner were found to have failed in conducting one annual audit and two quarterly reviews in accordance with generally accepted accounting principles (GAAP). The partner was prohibited from practicing before the SEC for six months. He consented to the SEC's order without admitting or denying the findings.

Administrative actions were also taken by the state boards of accountancy against all the men who held CPA licenses: Burns, Knight, Fitch and the external audit partner. They were reprimanded without losing their licenses and most of them paid nominal administrative penalties and costs.

Lessons Learned

For Terry Burns, the lessons learned in this situation were, "*Never* take a company public." He remains convinced the SEC investigator was inexperienced and did not understand the real estate development industry or the complexities of Monarch's consolidation with ARD. "We spent millions of dollars defending ourselves, as if we were common criminals. I'd never take a company public . . . never again."

In hindsight, Terry says, "We probably should have written off the options sooner. But we were actively working to renew them. I was certain they would all be renewed, so I thought it was okay to keep them on the books." The lesson here seems to be to stick to the letter of the law when it comes to GAAP. It might have been better to write off the options when they expired near the end of the fiscal year. If the option contracts had all been renewed subsequent to year-end, the financials could have been restated at that time.

An oft-repeated phrase can describe another lesson from this case: "If it sounds too good to be true, it probably is." Thomas Nathan represented his company as owning and having options to buy properties that were regarded as almost unobtainable for development. He also convinced Monarch's management that he had regulatory approval to develop all the properties. If other developers had not been able to get such approvals and access to the properties, it was unlikely Nathan's company had done so. As a result of the SEC investigation, Monarch's management learned that ARD did not have ownership of, or even options to buy, some properties they reported as assets.

The most important lesson learned, according to Burns, is to perform a more thorough background check on people you bring into your business. "We thought we'd done adequate due diligence in checking out the Nathans. We hired a professional to investigate them; but, what we did was obviously not enough. Right now if you do

(*continued*)

(continued)

an Internet search on Thomas Nathan's name, you'll find stories about other people he's conned. It turns out he was involved in flipping property in another state and reportedly defrauded several banks."

Recommendations to Prevent Future Occurrences

This was a situation in which Murphy's Law seemed at work — everything that could go wrong did go wrong. Even though Monarch's management consulted with several accounting professionals, including a nationally recognized CPA firm with expertise in consolidations, the SEC investigator did not agree with their advice. Ultimately, the SEC has legal authority to establish accounting principles. Monarch executives might have avoided the situation if they consulted with the SEC on the front end . . . before they filed their financial reports.

Monarch's CEO, two CFOs and the external audit manager — all of whom were CPAs with reputations as honest, hard-working professionals — were duped by a confident and likeable fraudster. Thomas Nathan fits the description of a predatory fraudster (someone who actively searches for opportunities to steal), and the most effective prevention method against predators is to perform extensive background checks. The investigator Monarch hired to perform a background check on ARD and its owners was not thorough enough, evident in how easy it was (several years after Monarch's acquisition of ARD) to find news and reports of wrongdoing by Thomas Nathan *years* before Monarch bought his company.

If you were buying a new house or a car, you would shop around. If you were about to have surgery, you would seek more than one medical opinion. That same modus operandi should be followed in business dealings. When the stakes are high and the risk of loss is great, it could be well worth the cost of hiring more than one investigator to perform background checks on potential business partners or associates. In addition to performing more extensive background investigations, if Monarch's management had hired forensic accountants prior to buying ARD, they might have determined the Nathans did not own or have options to buy all the properties they claimed as assets.

If you cannot afford an investigator to perform background checks, *do it yourself.* With the Internet, there is no excuse not to do

(continued)

searches on individuals and firms you plan on bringing into your company. A five-minute online search would have revealed an authoritative source citing past fraudulent acts by Thomas Nathan.

Another recommendation relates to financial reporting. Whether operating as a public or a private company, financial reporting decisions must be made in such a way that they cannot be called into question. When the options Monarch acquired as part of the ARD deal expired, they should have been written off immediately. It did not matter that renewal negotiations were ongoing.

Keeping those options on the books as assets would not have passed the "newspaper test." Think about what a particular business decision will look like as a headline on the front page of the newspaper (or a website). For Monarch, "Expired Options Reported as Assets" would not generate good press. If a decision cannot be easily explained and understood by someone reading the newspaper, don't do it.

It is also important to remember that almost anyone can raise doubts about you and your business. Even ill-founded accusations by unscrupulous individuals can cost significant amounts of time and financial resources to defend against. Reminding ourselves how easily such situations can occur reinforces our need for making "squeaky clean" business decisions and performing adequate due diligence.

About the Author

Carolyn Conn, CFE, CPA, is an accounting faculty member in the School of Management and Business at St. Edward's University with areas of interest in fraud examination and ethics. She has held several administrative positions in the nonprofit sector with responsibilities that included investigating occupational fraud.

Note

1. Later on, Burns learned this was not entirely correct. He had directed Monarch to make a large payment to Thomas Nathan for the purpose of renewing the expiring real estate options. However, Nathan took the money for himself and did not renew the options.

Trust Us . . . We Wouldn't Lie to You

INDEPENDENTLY AND OBJECTIVELY RESEARCH EVERY NEW CLIENT

STEPHEN PEDNEAULT

I nland Distributors was a new client of Shipman Calabrese, a regional public accounting firm where I worked as a manager. Josh Addison, a well-respected banker with Family Bank and a good friend to Shipman Calabrese, had recommended that the owners of Inland, who were seeking new auditors, contact our firm. Shipman Calabrese had a great reputation with Josh and Family Bank. According to Josh, the owners of Inland Distributors, a large distributor of machinery with annual revenues of approximately $25 million, were in discussions with him to restructure the company's financing and potentially move their borrowing and banking relationships over to Family Bank. Leading Inland was Sam Forde — a primary shareholder who was also the president and chief executive officer. Brad Crossman was Inland's chief financial officer and, working under Brad, Evan Bowers was the controller.

My role at Shipman Calabrese was one of a utility player with significant experience. When there were risky or new engagements, our engagement partner would frequently add me to the traditional audit team, to complement the skills and experience brought by the other firm members. Frequently the firm would have a scheduling need and place me on a traditional audit team simply to ensure an engagement was adequately staffed, even if it was an engagement outside of my specialty, the forensics field.

Growing Distribution

Inland Distributors maintained one primary headquarters with a large warehouse for receiving and shipping machinery. A second satellite warehouse was maintained about five miles from the main building, and many orders shipped directly to the customer or end user from the satellite warehouse. The company enjoyed an almost exclusive distributorship throughout a multistate region, with few true competitors. According to information provided by Josh, past sales were strong, and Inland was growing. Inland's management was seeking additional financing due to their growth in sales.

The New Client

Based on the recommendation from Josh, Shipman Calabrese accepted Inland as a new audit client late in the year. Little independent due diligence was performed by David Kirkham, the partner in charge at Shipman Calabrese, and, because Inland had a December year-end, an audit team was quickly assembled by Kirkham to begin planning for the upcoming audit. I was asked to help out the audit team. Kirkham held a planning meeting at Inland with Sam, Brad and Evan. One of Kirkham's biggest concerns was coordinating the physical inventory that had to be conducted by Inland's staff at the end of the year, because Inland's financing was collateralized in large part by its inventory.

Inland's executives identified their need for audited financial statements to obtain financing from Family Bank and informed us that they needed the completed statements within 60 days of their year-end close (December 31). That timing would be tight even for a recurring client with a history at our firm. A brand new audit client with a known reliance on financing completed within 60 days during tax season — the busiest time for any accounting firm — was insane. Still, Kirkham scheduled the audit, met with our team and we proceeded with the audit.

Sam instructed Brad and Evan to plan, schedule and oversee the physical inventory and ensure procedures were followed to provide sufficient audit evidence to meet our standards. Shortly after our planning meeting, the inventory was scheduled, and our firm received a copy of the inventory instructions provided to Inland's staff.

On the day of the inventory I drove to Inland's main location with another auditor, Jeff Coyle, to observe the inventory and perform test counts. I knew little about the company or its inventory, but learned what I needed on the ride out. As we pulled onto Inland's property, Jeff told me to park in the front visitor's lot. Jeff said Kirkham instructed him to park in front and use Inland's main entrance, where someone would meet us.

We entered and, after signing in, were escorted to a large conference room. Shortly after, Sam, Brad and Evan joined us, introduced themselves and began discussing Inland's physical inventory, which they said was underway.

I asked three questions of them, as follows:

- Is any of the inventory obsolete?
- Is any of the inventory owned by anyone other than Inland?
- Will there be any movement of inventory (shipping or receiving) while the counting is being performed?

We were assured that the entire inventory was owned by Inland, that machines turned every three to four months (resulting in no obsolete inventory) and that there was no inventory movement until the counts were completed. Brad provided us with an internal Inland memo instructing the staff not to ship or receive any machinery until the count was completed and he provided the green light to resume normal operations. It was just what an auditor would want to hear from their client.

As Jeff and I headed out to the warehouse, we saw another meeting going on in a conference room down the hall. It looked like another team of auditors was in a meeting with Sam and Brad. We entered the warehouse to find staff counting and tagging machines and other inventory. I asked one of the employees where we should start observing the counting, and I was told the inventory directly in front of me didn't belong to Inland, but to the other company. The question that popped into my head as I looked over at Jeff was, "What other company?" Senior management had just told me that the entire inventory was owned by Inland. Strike one.

The individual told me the counting had just started, and it would be more efficient if we started observing and performing our test counts at the remote warehouse first. He said the staff across town had started much earlier in the morning and, given the smaller size of the warehouse, they might even be finished with their counts.

It sounded like a good plan, so Jeff and I headed across town. As we walked in, we noted the satellite warehouse was segregated into areas designated with letters, starting with A and going through K. When we walked through the warehouse we noted the count teams were working in the G area and tags were fixed on the inventory in the A through G sections. We went over to talk with the staff and asked about their progress. They told us they started their counting in section D and figured they needed another hour or so to finish through area K. I asked why the items in sections A–C had inventory tags on them if the staff members didn't count them. An employee said section C contained items that hadn't moved in the past year, that section B had items that had been there for several years, and that section A had items that never moved. They laughed when they told us the inventory tags were from prior years and only the dates were updated. Once again I looked at Jeff, and thought back to the senior management's assertions that the entire inventory was current and none was obsolete. Strike two.

The counting was well documented, our test counts revealed no exceptions and, other than the fact that sections A–C contained obsolete items, the inventory looked well conducted. We headed back to Inland's headquarters, and when we arrived on the property I decided to drive around the back of the building. Jeff was not happy with my decision to circumvent Kirkham's instructions, but I had to know why management wanted to control how and where we entered the building. Behind the warehouse we immediately observed a flatbed tractor-trailer loading machinery from the shipping area. I parked and we walked over to the truck driver. I asked him where the machines were heading, and he gave me the customer's name. He said a similar truck left about an hour earlier. I asked him what he thought the approximate value was of the machines on his truck, and he estimated it was about $150,000. I asked him about the earlier truck, and he said it was about the same. I thought about senior management's statement and memo that there was to be no product movement in or out during the inventory. I even had the memo indicating the same. Now I knew why they wanted to control where we went on their property. Strike three.

Whom Can You Trust?

I looked at Jeff, the audit manager for this engagement, who was directly responsible to Kirkham, and wondered what he wanted to do, knowing that senior management basically lied in response to every question I asked them. I asked Jeff how much he knew about Inland, their financial situation and their need for an audit. I also asked Jeff if he knew why Inland needed a new auditor this year, which led them to our firm. Jeff did not have the answers, as Kirkham had been the primary contact for Inland's leadership.

I decided we needed to have another meeting with Sam, Brad and Evan to see firsthand their reactions to our discoveries and their inaccuracies. First, we summoned Brad to the shipping area. Surprised to see us there, he acted flabbergasted that there was any activity in the shipping area. He quickly pulled out his memo instructing Inland's staff to conduct no shipping and receiving, and told us he would get to the bottom of it. I had never seen such acting by a client — it was worthy of an Emmy. Our next encounter was with Evan, who asked that we join Sam, Brad and him in the conference room. Walking back past the second conference room, I could clearly tell the other individuals were also auditors, just not from our firm.

After about 15 minutes alone in the conference room, Jeff and I were joined by Sam, Brad and Evan. Each had a long look on his face and seemed unable to make eye contact. I started by asking them why there was well-known obsolete inventory at the warehouse across town, and yet this morning they stated there was none. Sam's response was that he didn't take into account the machines and parts in those areas because that was inventory they were planning on disposing from the warehouse as part of the audit. Sam was rationalizing his lying with a plan they just hatched in response to our discoveries to discard inventory that, according to the warehouse staff, had been on hand for years. I didn't believe him, and I knew they could tell.

I asked them whose inventory was immediately outside in the main warehouse — the same inventory they claimed was entirely owned by Inland this morning. Again Sam responded, saying that there was a second, related company whose inventory was commingled within the machines and parts throughout the warehouse. He stated the inventory I was referencing should not have been part of our observations, as there was a second group of auditors from another firm present who should have been observing those areas of the inventory. Once again I shot a look over to Jeff — what other company, and what inventory belongs to whom? I asked Sam how we would be able to differentiate what inventory belonged to Inland, which would be part of our audit, versus what inventory belonged to this other related company we had never heard about. Sam said he and Brad would be able to show us what belonged to each entity. I thought to myself, sure, of course I can trust these guys. They were *completely* honest with us this morning, upon our first interaction with them as a new audit client of the firm, so *certainly* whatever they provide us will be accurate. I knew we had no independent way of determining what inventory belonged to which entity, and worse, no way of knowing if the same inventory was being double counted for inclusion on both entities' financial statements.

Sam asked us where we would go from there to finish the inventory and proceed with the audit. I left that question for Jeff, as my opinion was that we should gather our files, walk back to our car and drive away from Inland as fast as possible, regretting spending any time with them. Jeff, however, recognized that was not our call, and suggested that we speak with Kirkham about how to proceed. Sam, Brad and Evan left us, and from the looks on their faces, they were all too happy to get out of that uncomfortable meeting after being caught in their lies.

Jeff called Kirkham and shared the issues we discovered at Inland. For reasons unbeknownst to me, Kirkham identified procedures for us to perform to complete our audit requirements over the inventory observation. Amazed that we didn't simply withdraw from the engagement, I spent the remainder of the day watching staff members count items and performing test counts of their work. I didn't have any idea if I was observing and counting Inland's inventory or someone else's.

At one point later that day I walked out the back door of the warehouse and saw close to a dozen trailers parked in the lot, along with two out-buildings. I wondered what they contained and walked out for a closer look. Each trailer and both buildings were locked. I told Jeff I was going to get Brad and Evan, and that if they wouldn't open each trailer and building for our review I would have to cut the locks. Otherwise, I was leaving and would inform Kirkham that there could be a material amount of inventory stored in the trailers and buildings that the client refused to open. Brad met us at the loading area and stated the trailers were empty, but there were older machines being stored in the buildings. I thought to myself — great, more old inventory they never told us about. I told Brad my plans if the trailers were not opened and, although I could tell he no longer liked me, he did find someone who had a key to open the trailers. They were indeed empty, just as he had described. Finally we were provided a true statement, a first for this new client.

Justice Is Not Always Served

As best as possible, given the conditions, Jeff and I completed the day's observations as directed by Kirkham. I documented everything that occurred, including our observations and the client's inaccurate responses regarding inventory. On the way out, I saw the other auditors in the second conference room working away at their computers.

In the car I asked Jeff what he thought of his new audit client; he was much more understanding than I was and tried to find explanations for the inaccuracies. The next morning we met with Kirkham and shared our experiences with him, providing more details in person than over the phone the day before. Kirkham thanked me for my efforts in assisting Jeff with the inventory and told me I could return to my regular forensic work. Kirkham said he and Jeff would complete the audit and meet with Sam, Brad and Evan to get a better understanding of what happened.

Later that day Jeff told me Kirkham called Josh at Family Bank to determine how well Josh knew the company and each individual, as well as how much due diligence had been performed by Family Bank prior to the referral. Josh indicated little due diligence was performed, and that both the company and the three executives had little to no experience with the bank.

Over the course of the next few weeks, Jeff led his audit team through the required audit procedures — as identified in large part by Kirkham — and created a preliminary draft of Inland's financial statements. Jeff confided in me that he felt the firm should withdraw from the engagement without issuing a financial statement for Inland. During the course of fieldwork Jeff learned that two companies commonly owned by Sam were working out of Inland's main building. The inventory we observed at Inland's main location was divided between the two companies and, despite management's assertions as to ownership, there was no independent and objective way to corroborate what portion of the inventory was owned by each company. The other auditors we saw during our inventory observation were at Inland to conduct their initial procedures over the second company. The fact that Sam retained separate audit firms for each commonly owned company operating out of the same location, using the same inventory and the same personnel, should have been reason enough for Kirkham and the firm to withdraw from the engagement. I surmised Sam's motive for hiring separate firms was that they would not be able to match audit records to show that the inventory — and possibly other activity — was redundant on both company's books.

Kirkham met with Sam to discuss the issues. Sam knew that Kirkham might withdraw from the engagement, so he threatened Kirkham and

Shipman Calabrese with a lawsuit. Sam told Kirkham that if the financial statements were not completed and issued by the agreed-upon date, Inland would not be able to obtain financing and could suffer a devastating financial loss.

After performing a few additional procedures, Kirkham issued Inland's financial statements. As a compromise, a small inventory reserve was added to the balance sheet for obsolete inventory, but nowhere near the amount that should have been added — if Inland even owned the inventory to begin with. The reserve was small enough to not interrupt any calculated ratios, and so Kirkham, fearing the lawsuit Sam had threatened, took the risk and issued the financial statements. Inland successfully obtained the financing and, within a few short months, sold off the second company along with its inventory, whatever portion that may have been. Shipman Calabrese did not retain Inland or Sam as a client and, to the best of my knowledge, nothing negative ever came of the actions of Sam, Brad and Evan. No successor accounting firm called Shipman Calabrese or Kirkham to ask why Inland was no longer a client, something I highly recommended when contemplating a new client. Kirkham failed to perform this step before he accepted Inland's engagement. It is likely that Sam simply found yet another audit firm for yet another first-year engagement — a pattern he likely had been perpetrating for years.

Lessons Learned

- Nothing replaces good due diligence prior to accepting a new client, especially one with a tight deadline and pending financing that is dependent on the audit outcome. Although Sam and Inland were referred by Josh at Family Bank, Kirkham should have performed background and reference checks on Inland, Sam, Brad and Evan. A public records search would have revealed Sam's second company, which likely would have led Kirkham to ask Sam about the second company's audit, revealing that Sam intended to engage a second firm.
- Kirkham should have obtained copies of Inland's prior financial statements and tax returns, which would have revealed that Inland retained a different accounting firm each year. He also should have obtained personal and business references for Sam, Brad and Evan, one of whom might have revealed Sam's plans to sell off the second company. Plans were in the works to sell the company once the financial statements were issued, because the buyers were waiting for them to make their purchase decisions.

(continued)

(*continued*)

- It should be standard procedure to contact a potential new client's past accountants to learn about their experience. If he had done so with the Inland engagement, Kirkham could have, at a minimum, learned whether the prior accounting firm was paid, and why the firm was replaced after only one year of service.
- Spontaneous, unplanned, surprise audit procedures often reveal transactions and activity that would have gone undetected if the client knew your plan or, worse, dictated the procedures you performed. Ignoring the instructions to park in front and enter through the front door revealed Sam's deception. The surprised look on Sam's and Evan's faces at the time showed that they never expected us to go around back, let alone talk with the truck driver. It was apparent to me that Inland's management controlled previous audits and was shocked that we deviated from the expected procedures.

Recommendations to Prevent Future Occurrences

- *Perform Due Diligence.* Regardless of how a potential new client is introduced to your firm, perform independent due diligence procedures *prior* to accepting the client. If no reliable independent information can be obtained, don't accept the client, regardless of the level of service you're being asked to provide and the associated fees.
- *Remain Objective.* While you want to respect your client's requests, first and foremost you have to remain loyal to professional standards designed to minimize risks and exposure to you and your firm. Sometimes clients lie to their auditors. Remain skeptical, objective and unbiased during an audit and independently corroborate any information provided by your client.
- *Don't Let Clients Control Your Procedures.* Be wary of the clients who control and limit your procedures and the information they provide. Many frauds go undetected simply because the accountants didn't stand up to a client's evasiveness. Insist on executing the procedures that you objectively designed for an engagement — you might hit the tip of the iceberg.
- *Design Unplanned and Unexpected Procedures to Find Fraud.* The steps and measures that accountants generally undertake are

(*continued*)

somewhat predictable, especially for recurring client engagements. Clients with financial personnel who came from public accounting are very knowledgeable of the procedures the outside accountants will perform, and can hide fraudulent activity if they want to. By performing unexpected procedures, you might uncover evidence of potential fraudulent activity.

- *Remain Vigilant.* Unfortunately no one is above the ability to commit fraud when sufficient pressure is in place. Many frauds have been perpetrated through violations of friendship and trust, and the least suspicious individual is often the perpetrator. When things do not make sense or add up to an independent and objective eye, consider fraud as an explanation regardless of your relationship with the individual or entity.

About the Author

Stephen Pedneault, CFE, CPA/CFF, is the principal of Forensic Accounting Services, LLC, a local CPA firm in Glastonbury, Connecticut, specializing only in forensic accounting, fraud investigation and litigation support matters. Steve is also an adjunct professor at the University of Connecticut and is the author of three recent books (Wiley).

Rotten from the Core

PAUL POCALYKO AND COLLEEN VALLEN

Often the driving force behind a business, even a large one, rests with a core group of people. These are the people with the vision and the foresight to enthusiastically grow and push the business in new directions, which are often directly tied to the values, needs, wants and focus of the core group. The power of that core can be significant and have positive results. But when the personal needs and wants of a company's leaders become the primary driver in the business, the result often has disastrous financial outcomes. Business headlines have illustrated these failures time and again — occupational fraud, bankruptcy and corruption.

CBA Construction was a company dominated by a core group. CBA specialized in the engineering, design and construction of power, governmental, transportation, civil and industrial projects. Like many large construction companies, CBA was international with various divisions and focuses. As a complex company, CBA needed dynamic leadership to be successful. At CBA, that was driven by senior managers who understood the company, its clients and its markets. At the heart of CBA's leadership team were Jason Cunningham and Mark Nicholas.

Cunningham had served as CBA's CEO for several years. Although relatively new to the position, he had a powerful influence on the company. He recognized immediately that his personal success was tied to CBA and quickly took the reins of his new position and immersed himself in his role.

Cunningham's focus was financial success — his and the company's. He was intuitive and quickly identified threats to the organization and developed a new vision for CBA's future. To carry it out, Cunningham surrounded himself with people he considered both knowledgeable and loyal to the company, in particular Mark Nicholas, who became his second in command. Together, they would implement Cunningham's strategy.

Mark Nicholas was the CFO and Cunningham's trusted advisor. He had been with CBA for 30 years and understood the financial aspects of the business, along with the day-to-day operations. Nicholas had risen up through the ranks and was knowledgeable about CBA's history, business model, market and competitors. He was committed to the company and was well respected by employees. His personal success was also tied to CBA's, both financially and emotionally. Cunningham knew that Nicholas' passion and position would be essential to earning support for his new company plans, from both staff and the market.

As soon as he began as CEO, Cunningham developed a relationship with Nicholas by engaging him as an advisor, a sounding board and a resource, and the relationship evolved into a strong, dominant team.

Industry Trends

CBA was incorporated in Delaware in 1929 and focused on the energy industry. Over time, the company became a leader in constructing power plants for U.S. utility companies. Unfortunately the success enjoyed during most of its long history did not continue indefinitely. CBA's high stock price in its best year of operation was $87.50 but dropped to a low of $52 as its business model and market conditions began to change.

CBA's success during its growth was driven by significant market demand for new energy facilities combined with often-used cost-plus or time-and-materials contracts. These paid CBA a markup, which almost guaranteed a profit and a return to the shareholders. There was minimal risk and CBA saw no need to implement controls over its costs. In fact, the more the contract cost, the greater profit CBA earned.

As CBA moved into a new decade, there was a slowdown in construction of energy facilities. Capital spending on energy projects declined, and demand slowed as people began evaluating different types of energy production. Some of CBA's clients merged and others developed a new direction for their operations.

In addition, the market began to demand fixed-fee, lump-sum contracts so project owners could predict the outcome associated with an investment in a new facility. These contracts shifted all the risk to CBA, and the agreed-upon fee at the start of the project meant cost control was now imperative to profitability — bad news for a management team that had not been able to effectively control costs. As a result, the company began experiencing diminishing profits and ultimately lost all profit margins. This failure was apparent to CBA's board of directors and the outside audit firm.

Although CBA's management understood the problem, they were able to mask some of the deteriorating financial conditions through asset sales and the absorption of an overfunded pension plan. Stock analysts watched with concern as cash flow continued to drop and profits eroded. This was the situation when Cunningham took over as CEO, and he was aware that it was time for bold strategies.

A Redirection of Energy

Cunningham realized that to get the stock price up, the company desperately needed significant backlog. *Backlog* is a term in the construction industry for the value of the projects that a contractor expects to be completed in the near future. Analysts and investors use backlog as a measure of a contractor's health. Cunningham and Nicholas devised a plan to increase CBA's reported backlog by monumental proportions. Together they sold their master plan to their management team with a clear message — with more backlog the company would surely experience stronger earnings and improve its perception with the stockholder group. More earnings were imperative if Cunningham, Nicholas and the management team were to maintain their jobs, six-figure salaries and bonus plan, and extract any value from their stock options.

To increase backlog, CBA's management focused on securing large projects. Since the market appeared saturated with domestic customers, they began attempts to sell to the far reaches of the globe. At the time, the available larger projects were fixed-fee contracts in developing nations. Although CBA did not have the experience or track record to effectively manage and execute these, Cunningham pushed forward in an effort to strengthen the financial outlook and ramp up backlog.

With the new philosophy and approach established, CBA's management entered negotiations with a large overseas consortium of companies to build an energy facility in Southeast Asia. PI Industries was under the leadership of Soartu Todie, its president. The PI project was to be the largest single contract CBA had ever bid — approximately $700 million, with the potential to exceed $1 billion. These kinds of numbers were what CBA needed in its backlog to impress the most critical analysts and shareholders.

As Cunningham began negotiations with PI, he also applied for three years of professional liability insurance for CBA from The Insurance Partners (TIP). Obtaining appropriate insurance coverage was a key part of CBA's ability to do business because potential clients considered insurance coverage, along with experience, financial health and other factors, when deciding who to hire.

As part of the application process for insurance, CBA was required to submit information regarding its finances as well as its current and future projects. Further, CBA and representatives of TIP met to discuss the application information.

It was not known at the time that CBA's management team made numerous misrepresentations to TIP during this meeting related to the PI project, including claiming it had a signed contract and expected to generate $700 million in future revenue, which was included in its backlog.

Based on this false information, CBA obtained two years of professional liability insurance as a result of the initial meeting with TIP. The following year, Cunningham requested an additional year of coverage and again provided bogus financial information to TIP. CBA obtained the additional year of coverage as a result.

A Trickling Cash Flow

Despite Cunningham's new vision, CBA's financial condition continued to deteriorate. The changing market and CBA's poor performance on projects were creating a cash-flow crunch that the company could not manage. CBA was forced to sell assets to generate funds and was operating on a day-to-day basis. In an attempt to salvage its business and stem the losses, CBA entered into a contract with a Cedar Rapids Electric Company (CREC) to close an energy facility in Iowa. The new job provided CBA a very tidy margin.

Despite the new contract and ongoing sale of assets, CBA's cash-flow crisis did not improve and the company fell behind on vendor payments associated with the CREC project. In an attempt to hide the company's financial condition, Nicholas submitted lien waivers to CREC falsely claiming the subcontractors had been paid in full. Ultimately, CREC management discovered the deception and terminated CBA. Shortly thereafter CBA filed for bankruptcy.

In an attempt to recoup losses from the CREC contract, Cunningham and Nicholas submitted a claim to TIP under the errors and omissions coverage afforded under the policy. They were seeking to recover in excess of $50 million.

The TIP agent who reviewed CBA's claim discovered a number of discrepancies in the representations CBA made to the insurance company and the actual documentation management provided. After further review of the paperwork, TIP entered into litigation against CBA for material and false representations in records used to obtain insurance coverage.

During the court proceedings, significant questions arose related to CBA's financial and accounting practices and, more specifically, the PI project. There were allegations of bribery, corruption and a cover-up, and key documents were missing. As a result, our firm was retained by TIP to analyze CBA's financial records, financial and accounting practices and information and documentation related to its project performance.

Comparing Claims to Reality

The first concern we were to investigate was the accuracy of the representations made by CBA's management in obtaining insurance. If management had falsely represented CBA in getting coverage the claim might be void. We focused on the following questions:

- Was all the relevant information disclosed?
- Were the representations made to TIP true?
- Was the provided financial information accurate?

We performed detailed analyses of financial and project records and reviewed correspondence and testimony. We wanted to understand what CBA employees knew, when information became available to them and how it affected the company's performance and overall financial transactions. We then compared our analysis to the numbers CBA provided to TIP.

We compiled documents from a variety of sources, put them in chronological order and analyzed them. It quickly became clear that the PI project was the source of most of CBA's misrepresentations and attempts to deceive TIP.

Imaginary Contract

During initial negotiations with TIP, Cunningham and Nicholas claimed they had a signed contract with PI that would generate $700 million in revenue, but the documentation we gathered indicated otherwise. The PI project negotiations were plagued by problems and a final contract was never executed, nor was the actual scope of the work agreed to by the parties. In fact, there were seven varying iterations of the scope of work discussed, none of which were formalized.

We discovered that at the onset of negotiations with CBA, PI's leader, Todie, demanded that Cunningham provide him with kickbacks by inflating the value of the contract by approximately $150 million. Cunningham was then supposed to send the excess funds to Todie's personal bank account. Our investigation revealed that CBA did in fact inflate cost estimates and its bills to PI but did not remit any money to Todie.

CBA's general counsel tried on multiple occasions to explain to CBA's management team that it could not participate in the scheme, but Cunningham kept looking for ways to reimburse Todie. Obtaining the contract was of paramount importance to Cunningham and to CBA's financial health, so he was willing to do just about anything to keep the transaction alive and to create the appearance of a valid contractual agreement.

The pressure to obtain the $700 million contract was such that CBA began work on the PI project under a letter of intent and then a short-term interim agreement. CBA entered into numerous agreements with subcontractors and suppliers during this time, many of which could not be canceled. Although CBA received a healthy advance payment from PI, the accounting quickly became cash negative and management was projecting significant losses. The failure to execute a final contract would result in devastating consequences. Nicholas began to refer to the mess as the 700-pound gorilla that would kill the company.

Falling Like Dominoes

Our analysis indicated that CBA had improperly reported revenue under the interim agreement. CBA collected more than $140 million in payments from PI Industries, including approximately $15 million of excess billings from the kickback scheme. As the agreement expired, CBA was in a no-win situation. No money was recycled to Todie, who — feeling that he had been cheated — refused to make any additional payments for the project work already completed. CBA's management knew that Todie had no source of funding to cover past-due and future payments. And more damaging still, CBA's contracts with vendors were non-cancelable.

Cunningham and Nicholas were well aware of CBA's dire situation when the PI interim agreement expired. They knew the project was dead and that the client was essentially bankrupt. They were fully aware that past due amounts were not going to be collected and that no future revenue was going to be earned. The two also knew that CBA had ongoing liabilities associated with its vendor commitments. If word leaked out that the PI project was over, CBA would most likely fail because:

- CBA needed a big backlog number to survive. The market, the insurers and the owners of the CREC were looking at backlog and CBA couldn't disappoint.
- CBA specifically needed the CREC project to help fund the deficit from the PI deal.
- The company's own cash projections regarding PI showed hundreds of millions of dollars in exposure. That alone would require recognition under accounting rules.

In a final desperate move, Nicholas oversaw the fraudulent recording of more than $500 million into the projected CBA backlog. Further, CBA continued to record and recognize revenue from PI for more than two years after the project was suspended. Nicholas merely carried and maintained balances in accounts receivable that he knew were uncollectable.

To further conceal the deception, Nicholas presented Tom Sword, the lead auditor, with an initialed engineering, procurement and construction (EPC) contract from PI and claimed its execution was imminent and just a formality. Further, he falsely represented that work being performed was covered by amendments to the expired interim agreement but we found that these had ever been executed. He provided Sword copies of invoices for project billings, many of which were never sent to PI Industries. He also booked revenues for work performed with the knowledge that payment was highly unlikely. Nicholas restated all the prior project billings to adjust amounts collected and billed, ultimately increasing the job's percentage of completion and the company's profits. This accounting maneuvering also made the accounts receivable appear current, not past due. Sword's standard audit tests were not devised to uncover such schemes, and he relied heavily on management representations.

CBA's financial reporting and application of generally accepted accounting practices (GAAP) were inaccurate, false and misleading. Our analysis indicated that significant journal entries would have been required to make the financial information in accordance with GAAP. The adjustments would have presented a significantly different picture of CBA and its ability to continue as a going concern.

Our investigation and analysis confirmed the following about Cunningham and Nicholas in their dealings with TIP:

- They were aware of the damaging information and made the decision to conceal it.
- They made false representations.
- They provided misleading financial information.
- They failed to disclose detrimental information.

Since TIP's decision to insure CBA was not based on full factual information, the insurer continued with litigation based on our findings. After numerous attempts, a settlement was reached between CBA and TIP, and CBA's ability to recover under its policy was limited by its failure to provide accurate representations and information to its insurance carriers. The company closed due to bankruptcy.

Lessons Learned

This case reinforced critical concepts in fraud detection and prevention that are often ignored. Most important, we realized the need for professional skepticism in business. This involves not relying on typical expectations or outcomes and instead approaching a task with a questioning mind and a skeptical attitude. It requires an individual to ask tough questions and not accept ineffective answers. This is a critical business skill.

Many people involved in auditing CBA lacked professional skepticism — the people who should have been asking questions were

(continued)

(continued)

not. When people did ask a question, they accepted answers that didn't make sense, were not factually accurate and were not reasonable. Moreover, Cunningham and Nicholas didn't ask themselves tough questions before starting work for PI:

- What would happen to CBA if the PI project failed?
- Was Soartu Todie, PI's owner, able to pay CBA?
- Did the company want to do business with Todie?
- Was CBA comfortable with Todie's demand for a kickback?
- Did the company have any other options beyond the PI job?

These were tough questions with difficult and painful answers, but professional integrity would have demanded that Cunningham and Nicholas ask them. To make things worse, CBA's auditors didn't question the financial data or the status of work with PI; they simply accepted management's representations. They also failed to make site visits or speak with Todie or PI personnel.

Professional skepticism allows us to look at organizations differently. It requires looking at organizational tone, processes and procedures, relationships, people and controls in a different way. Trusting that controls are functioning properly is insufficient; the actual data must be assessed, evaluated and questioned.

The tone set by top management has a direct correlation to the way employees view ethical situations and their behavior. Cunningham and Nicholas were focused on company performance and personal success above all else. They established an organizational tone that valued profits over communication and complaisance over professional skepticism. Even though many employees knew the PI project was dead, they didn't question the accounting practices related to it. When internal auditors probed into the issue, they were told not to waste time with trivial questions.

We also realized the power that relationships can have on the recognition and reporting of inappropriate behavior. Relationships and trust are common themes in fraud matters. Cunningham and Nicholas were a strong team with tight bonds, but they didn't even question one other. Instead they supported each other's deceptive efforts and were able to manipulate the external auditor based on personal trust. Sword had been CBA's auditor for years and CBA was a top client for his firm. He readily accepted unsupported claims about the financial statements made by Cunningham and Nicholas and he failed to question blatant red flags.

Recommendations to Prevent Future Occurrences

Practice risk mitigation by identifying risk areas and addressing them. The ultimate goal is fraud prevention, but early detection is also a benefit. Identifying risk can be a difficult process and can take you out of your comfort zone. When evaluating risk, focus on assessing the potential for damage. This requires a close critique of people, processes and procedures.

In this case, if CBA's management and auditors had examined the relationships and tone at the top, they would have had difficult questions to ask, and the answers could have revealed the scheme at hand. Instead, they relied on trust and were dominated by two leaders. The end result was a bankrupt company and massive litigation.

About the Authors

Paul Pocalyko, CFE, CPA/CFF, is a partner in the Forensic, Litigation and Valuation Services practice of ParenteBeard. He has provided a variety of financial, consulting and accounting services to attorneys, insurance companies, governmental agencies and corporations since 1982. Mr. Pocalyko has a bachelor of science degree and a master's in business administration from Lehigh University.

Colleen Vallen, CPA/CFF, is a partner in the Forensic, Litigation and Valuation Services practice of ParenteBeard. Ms. Vallen has focused her attention on forensic and fraud investigations and the preparation of financial damage analysis. Ms. Vallen has a bachelor of science degree in accounting from Rutgers University.

CHAPTER 5

The Broken Trust

AARON LAU

Peter Sun was a Malaysian of Chinese origin. An accomplished linguist, he was proficient in the English, Malay and Chinese languages. Peter had been married to his lovely wife, Jane, for ten years and they had two intelligent boys. Peter was extremely proud of his sons' early academic and extracurricular achievements.

Peter's parents both worked as farm laborers, and Peter grew up humbly, deprived of many of the luxuries that youngsters today enjoy. Money was tight in Peter's family, and it was not easy for his parents to support and raise their three sons and three daughters. But Peter was determined to get a good education and succeed in the business world.

Peter started working as an assistant chemist at Hybiscus Manufacturing, a company that manufactured cosmetics, after he obtained his associate's degree in chemistry. His diligence at work was admirable and enviable, according to one long-term employee who said, "He was always the first to arrive and the last to leave the factory."

In spite of his heavy workload during the day, Peter found time to enroll in an evening part-time chemistry program at a local college and worked toward his bachelor's degree in chemistry. After earning his degree, he was promoted to chemist.

He was not satisfied, however, with his position and salary. His strong desire for academic excellence and drive for success propelled him to pursue a doctorate in chemistry, and he sacrificed a year and a half to prepare for his dissertation. Through sheer determination and hard work, Peter earned his Ph.D. and was hired back on at Hybiscus in the position of senior vice president in charge of operations.

The chairman of the company was so impressed with Peter that he quickly promoted him to director and, not long after, managing director of the company. The chairman thought of him as an ideal employee and frequently suggested that other staff try to emulate Peter.

Hybiscus Manufacturing (Hybiscus), with a staff of 30, had been in the cosmetics manufacturing business for more than 25 years. The business was started by two brothers, Hyacinth and Emmanuel Lee. Both brothers worked hard to develop the company and its reputation. They purchased a piece of land about 60 miles south of Kuala Lumpur very cheaply during an economic meltdown in Malaysia. Their fortune took an unexpected upswing when Delta Corp (Delta), a multinational investment holding corporation, purchased their entire operations for $15 million. Thereafter, Hybiscus operated as a fully owned subsidiary of Delta.

An Important Call

I vividly remember the call I received from the chairman of Delta's audit committee early one misty morning.

"Hello, good morning! This is Aaron; can I help you?" I answered.

"Please hold the line. Datin would like to speak to you," said the calm voice at the other end of the line. *Datin* is a title of prestige given to the wife of a *Datuk*, which is an honor bestowed by the sultan of a state.

I interrupted her and inquired, "Can you tell me the surname of Datin?"

"It is Datin Tan," she said.

Over the phone, Datin Tan explained her position as the chairperson of the audit committee of Delta Corp and told me that she was looking for a professional firm to investigate one of the directors of Hybiscus. I could sense the urgency in her voice when she brought up the closure of Hybiscus and Delta's financial year. Datin wanted the investigation completed quickly and the findings incorporated in the year-end financial statements.

The next day, I met Datin Tan and Hita Gonzales, the head of Delta's internal audit department. Hita told me that since Peter became the managing director, he had found it difficult to complete an internal audit. When his team arrived to conduct an audit, Peter would put them in a room next to the boiler room in the manufacturing plant, which made them too uncomfortable to do any work. There were no windows, electrical outlets or air conditioning. In addition, the room was quite far away from the administrative office. Peter and the other employees were also uncooperative.

Hita said that Peter was considered "untouchable" because he was a favorite of Delta Corp's chairman (Hybiscus' former chairman who was promoted after the acquisition). Any complaints about Peter were rejected by the chairman, and the person who complained would get a personal call from the chairman's office to warn him or her about complaining.

The Confirmation

A few days later, after our meeting and submitting our proposal, Datin Tan called to inform me that the board of directors had approved our proposal to undertake the investigation of Hybiscus. The first thing I did was ask Michael Chow, my project manager, to e-mail Hita and Datin Tan to assemble a list of required documents before our investigation team started working.

A week later our team arrived at Hybiscus. The first thing we did was request a factory tour to familiarize ourselves with the area, but we didn't notice anything unusual (like obsolete inventory lying around).

Frances Lee, our IT specialist, managed to download the vendor master file, customer master file, employee master file and general ledger for the past six years from a very old accounting system and started examining them. Michael was reviewing all the employee files, expense claims and related documentations made available by the Human Resources department. We went through the data and documents for more than a week but could not pick out anything to indicate that a financial fraud had been committed.

Very Slow Delivery

When Michael conducted a sales cut-off test for the previous financial year, he found that there was no improper sales recognition and that all the delivery orders were correctly dated. We thought the revenue was properly recognized.

We then moved on to the expenses from the purchases ledger using the data that Frances had reviewed. We tested it using Benford's Law and discovered an unusual skew on the digit 1.

I asked Michael and Frances if the data could have been wrongly compiled, but Frances assured me that it was not possible. We retested the data and confirmed the skewed result, so we went back and pulled out all the documents based on the purchases ledger and found out that they were mostly related to freight and haulage charges.

"Bingo! Here's something significant!" exclaimed Michael, raising his clenched right fist. "It looks like we've got an improper revenue recognition on our hands. The actual delivery dates shown on the haulage documents were at least three months after the dates on delivery orders and invoices."

The delivery orders were issued by the production manager, Keith Ong. It appeared that the orders were printed and issued three months before the delivery dates to prevent the external auditors from suspecting that improper sales were being recognized.

Michael compiled and compared the delivery dates (based on the freight and haulage shipping documents), sales invoice dates and sales delivery dates for the previous financial year end. We checked the company's revenue

recognition policy, which stated that "sales of goods are recognized upon delivery of products and when the risks and rewards of ownership have passed
to the customers." The policy confirmed that we had, in fact, uncovered improper revenue recognition.

Michael and Frances knew that they had to face the enormous task of
going through all the sales invoices, freight and haulage documents and
delivery orders again for each financial year. They went through documents
for the past six years and compiled the over-recognized revenue on a yearly
basis, which is shown in Table 5.1.

We compiled the group and segment turnover to compare against the
net impact of the over-recognition (see Table 5.2).

There was little effect on the group annual revenue, but the revenue
recognition scheme had a major impact on Hybiscus' revenue because the
net revenue had to be adjusted.

**Table 5.1   Comparison of gross over-recognized revenue against the
Hybiscus' annual revenue**

	Year 1	Year 2	Year 3	Year 4	Year 5	Year 6
Revenue over-recognized (in thousands)	$ 160	$ 89	$ 95	$ 149	$ 126	$ 330
Annual revenue (in thousands)	$1,719	$1,596	$1,712	$1,875	$2,312	$2,140
% of annual revenue	9.3%	5.6%	5.5%	7.9%	5.4%	15.4%

**Table 5.2   Comparison of net over-recognized revenue against Group,
Segment and Hybiscus' annual revenue. Dollar amounts are in thousands.**

	Year 1	Year 2	Year 3	Year 4	Year 5	Year 6
Group Revenue (a)	221,000	220,000	256,000	15,627	60,773	19,557
Group Segment Revenue (b)	5,470	5,497	5,205	4,838	5,649	9,248
HMSB Revenue (c)	1,719	1,596	1,712	1,875	2,312	2,140
HMSB's Net Revenue Adj (d)*	160	(71)	6	54	(23)	204
% of Group Revenue ((d)/(a))	0.07%	−0.03%	0.002%	0.35%	−0.04%	1.04%
% of Segment Revenue ((d)/(b))	2.93%	−1.30%	0.12%	1.12%	−0.40%	2.20%
% of HMSB Revenue ((d)/(c))	9.32%	−4.47%	0.37%	2.88%	−0.99%	9.52%

*Positive means over-recognized revenue.

Disappearing Customers

Frances then analyzed the customer master file and found that many of
the new customers Hybiscus had acquired in the past three years made one

transaction with the company and then disappeared from the records. Considering the effort required to get a new customer, we were surprised that Hybiscus would let them slip away so easily.

Dorothy Chen, an accountant at Hybiscus, was the only senior staff member who had access to the accounting system and to the software; after analyzing the log files, we were able to confirm that Dorothy had deleted the new customers' names from the master file. Once we discovered this red flag, I asked Frances and the team to be alert for payment vouchers on different rented locations or other unusual delivery orders that do not match the customers' addresses.

Next up, we scoured the vendor master file and realized that Hybiscus was slowly channeling all of its purchases of raw materials from its standard five vendors to just one supplier, Wong Suppliers.

Frances called Hybiscus' old vendors and asked them why they stopped working with the company. They all had similar explanations that included complaints from Peter that their raw materials were not up to par, inevitably followed by Peter terminating their contracts. She asked the terminated vendors for pricing information for raw materials and determined that Wong Suppliers invariably charged Hybiscus at least 15 percent above the average market price.

On examining the time cards for the past five years, we found that five employees always clocked in at or around the factory start time for the past three years, and they never had overtime requests rejected. Worst of all, these five employees never worked at Hybiscus factory — they were based in a regional office in Johor!

We looked for anomalies in the general journal entries and discovered two suspicious entries that recurred every year for the past three years: (1) one-third of salary expenses were capitalized as part of finished goods, and (2) half of traveling expenses and claims were capitalized as part of finished goods. The total capitalization for the past three years amounted to $2.5 million.

The Straw That Broke the Camel's Back

One evening while walking around the factory, I saw some finished goods being loaded onto a ten-ton truck. I casually asked the driver, Sham Sing, where the goods were heading.

"They are going to Peter's factory in Johor. Don't you know about it? It's been going on for years," he cracked. I pretended that I did not know about the factory and asked Sham exactly where it was in Johor. He told me the directions were too complicated, but if I wanted to follow him on the delivery the next day, he could show me.

The next day, we followed Sham to Johor, which is the southernmost state in Malaysia. It took us almost two hours to reach the factory, which was as big as Hybiscus. We trained our telescopic camera onto the factory from a distance and took shots of people, parked cars, buildings and trucks that were coming in and out of the factory. The name of the company was prominently displayed by the side of the entrance — BeautyTech Industries.

Adjacent to the factory was a huge pile of what looked like obsolete goods. Frances asked Sham, "What are those goods sitting under the hot sun?"

Sham explained, "Those are finished goods that were rejected by Hybiscus customers; I was told to bring them here."

When we got back to Hybiscus, Michael ran a company search and a land title search on BeautyTech. In due time, we learned that the directors and shareholders of BeautyTech were Peter; Keith Ong, Hybiscus' production manager; and Renny Soa, the human resources director at Hybiscus. Peter and Henry Wong owned the land.

Michael extracted BeautyTech's past audited financial statements and learned that the company had been operating for three years, and their total revenue in those three years was $4.5 million. BeautyTech's principal activity was manufacturing cosmetics, the same as Hybiscus.

As required by the Malaysian Companies Act of 1965, all company directors are required to disclose their shareholding interest and directorships in other companies. Peter did not disclose his shareholding interest and directorship in BeautyTech to the board of directors of Hybiscus and, therefore, violated the Act. His offense was akin to a conflict of interest.

We reported our findings to Datin Tan and Hita. Datin Tan, upon hearing the report, exclaimed, "What? How could this have happened? We will definitely seek legal counsel and recourse for what Peter has done. We cannot just let him go!"

Interviewing for Admission

Henry Wong, the owner of Wong Suppliers, sold raw materials to Hybiscus. Our earlier analysis revealed that Henry charged at least 15 percent higher than the market rate and that of previous vendors. Michael interviewed Henry, who quickly spilled the beans. Henry confessed that he charged Hybiscus an inflated price as part of Peter's plan to finance the purchase of the land on which BeautyTech was built.

Later that day, Michael interviewed the sales manager, Carol Rene, who had recently traded in her Nissan Sentra for the latest BMW 3 Series. Carol told Michael, "Peter instructed me not to take new sales as part of Hybiscus' revenue; new customers were channeled to Peter's company. For doing this, Peter offered me 10 percent of all sales orders that I channeled — it was too good to pass up." Michael asked her why she helped Peter even though she knew it was wrong. She broke down in tears and said, "I needed the money to pay for my parents' medical bills."

Next, Michael interviewed Dorothy Chen, the senior accountant at Hybiscus. Like Carol and Henry, she did not hesitate to divulge what had happened. She said that she knew what was going on but complied with Peter's plan out of fear of losing her job. She said her predecessor was fired because he did not follow Peter's instructions. She complained once to the chairman but to no avail.

The interview with Keith Ong, the production manager, was more difficult than the others. Initially, he was defensive and cautious. He denied that he was a director or shareholder of BeautyTech and claimed to have no knowledge of the company despite being shown the BeautyTech's registry. He remarked angrily, "I sign lots of documents every day and I cannot remember everything I signed during the past five years. I do not have a photographic memory!"

We showed him two pictures that were taken at BeautyTech — one showing him walking into the factory and another of his car parked in the directors' parking lot. Keith looked completely devastated. He remained silent for almost 15 minutes before admitting that he was both a director and shareholder of BeautyTech and that he knew it was contrary to the interests of Hybiscus. In a subdued tone, he said, "It was Peter. He made me do it. He threatened to tell my family about an affair I had with Renny years ago. He used the affair to blackmail both of us."

Completing the Jigsaw Puzzle

Improper revenue was recorded as sales on Hybiscus' books in the fourth-quarter of each financial year. Delivery orders were placed three months before deliveries were actually made to give the impression that the sales had been transacted, in the hope that auditors would not apply a sales cut-off test. Inventory from returns and finished goods were kept in a separate ledger, and Peter had inventory secretly transported to BeautyTech without delivery orders. As such, the inventory balance kept increasing and sales were understated by more than $1 million over a period of three years. Datin Tan had to write off the inventory balance because it was nonexistent at the time of our investigation.

Hybiscus had a fixed production capacity and each time Carol received a sale, she would check with Keith to see if the production schedule could accommodate it. If Keith could not fit the new sale into his schedule, Carol channeled the sale to BeautyTech. In three years, $4.5 million in sales was channeled to BeautyTech, which earned a profit of close to $3 million. Carol received $450,000 in sales commissions for the diversion scheme while Hybiscus lost $4.5 million in revenue.

The cost of raw materials increased over three years by an average of 15 percent — or approximately $1.1 million — due to the consolidation of purchases of raw materials from Wong Suppliers. The premium that Wong Suppliers charged was used to purchase the land for BeautyTech's manufacturing operations.

At least five employees on the Hybiscus payroll were working full time at BeautyTech. Renny clocked them in each day and Keith confirmed their attendance and overtime claims to legitimize the operation.

Higher raw material prices coupled with increased salary expenditures caused the production costs to escalate. Dorothy pointed out these figures to Peter monthly, and he told her to charge some of the salary and traveling expenses to the finished goods account. During the three years BeautyTech was operating, the mischarged expenses totaled $2.5 million. As a puppet accountant for Peter, Dorothy followed his instructions and helped him paint a rosy picture of Hybiscus to the board of directors during their meetings and to shareholders during the annual general meeting.

After all the findings were assessed, Hybiscus auditors had to restate their financial statements as follows:

- Adjust $204,000 for over-recognized revenue.
- Write off more than $1 million worth of nonexistent inventory from sales returns.
- Write off $2.5 million in capitalized expenses that were classified as inventory.

We turned all the documents and our report over to Hybiscus' legal counsel for review, who decided to file charges against Peter for manipulating the revenue and inventory, presenting fraudulent financial statements at the annual general meeting and breaching his fiduciary duties as a director. The other employees involved in Peter's scheme were also charged.

- Renny, Carol, Dorothy and Keith were charged with engaging in fraudulent practices and causing substantial losses to the company.
- Peter was sued in civil court for $6 million of lost business, breach of fiduciary duties as a director, engaging in activities that bore a conflict of interest with that of the company and fraudulent manipulation of financial statements (in particular, revenue and inventory balances). He pleaded not guilty.
- All the cases are currently pending hearings.
- Wong Suppliers was permanently removed from Hybiscus' approved-vendor list.

Lessons Learned

Our findings reaffirmed the time-tested adage, "crime does not pay," particularly not for a man like Peter, who struggled so hard to attain success. The truth must have been a great disappointment to his colleagues, family, associates and friends. Peter's fall was devastating.

In fraud investigations, data and information gathering is essential. Employees in the organization must help the investigating team and they should be assured that the company will be more lenient in meting out disciplinary actions to those who cooperate.

Interviews should include all employees, not only the senior-level staff. In this case, if the truck driver Sham had not been approached, Peter's factory in Johor and the conflict of interest violation would not have been so readily uncovered.

While it is a good practice for directors to place their trust in their colleagues, such trust should not be granted profusely. They should place greater importance on implementing internal controls, checks and balances and a stricter internal audit policy.

Frauds do not just happen; they are caused and perpetrated by people who are avaricious and possess a strong desire to strike it rich fast. The case also revealed that corruption or graft is a precursor to fraud perpetration. An organization should discourage its employees from accepting gifts, money and favors from their business associates.

Recommendations to Prevent Future Occurrences

Occupational frauds arise for various reasons, ranging from poor work conditions, low wages, poor management-staff relations and an absence of a reporting mechanism for disgruntled employees. Accordingly, we made the following recommendations to Hybiscus.

Fraud Hotline

The formation of an independent and anonymous fraud hotline is one way to deter, detect and prevent fraud. Anonymity is important because most whistleblowers do not want to be identified, especially if the complaint involves senior personnel. A fraud hotline is easy to implement and inexpensive to maintain. In this case, Carol and Dorothy would have benefited from a hotline.

(continued)

(continued)

Fraud Prevention Policies

The inclusion of fraud prevention policies as part of the employee handbook indicates a zero-tolerance policy. Classifications of minor and serious fraud offenses should be listed in the policy and it should state that violations will be subject to disciplinary actions including, if found guilty, summary dismissal.

Conduct Frequent Internal Audits

The internal audit function is an important control within the company to ensure that there are checks and balances. Frequent internal audits at site locations are important to detect rogues like Peter. In this case, placing the internal audit team next to the boiler room was a display of Peter's intolerance of the internal audit team checking up on him.

Job Rotation and Mandatory Vacation

Peter was successful because he was able to compel Hybiscus personnel to engage in his fraud. If employees were required to rotate job functions, Peter's scheme would have been uncovered and exposed. Similarly, mandatory vacations would have helped deter Peter's scheme. Employees would be cross-trained in each other's positions, putting a fresh set of eyes on each position.

Functional Responsibility

Companies should establish reporting lines that don't require employees to file suspicions directly to their managing director. Dorothy reported her concerns about the financial statements to Peter, but he instructed her to conceal the rising production costs.

Sadly, these deterrence methods were not in place at Hybiscus earlier, but I hope that they will serve the company well in preventing future schemes.

About the Author

Aaron Lau, CFE, CAMS, FCA (Aust.), CA (M), ATII, is the founder and managing partner of AITLAU Management Services, an accounting and business advisory firm specializing in fraud investigation and anti-money laundering compliance in Kuala Lumpur, Malaysia. Other services offered to business owners are accounting services, internal audit, data mining and analytics and human resource consultancy. He has more than 14 years of international experience as an auditor, chartered accountant and a corporate financial investigator. Aaron is also a popular speaker on fraud and anti-money laundering related topics. He is the current secretary general of the Malaysian ACFE chapter.

CHAPTER 6

The Perfect Family Business

ALEJANDRO MORALES

The end of World War II marked the beginning of a rebirth of economic activity in several parts of the world. Europe and the United States particularly benefited from the so-called postwar economy, which created a vast number of enterprises that formed the cornerstone of economic development in many countries.

In Latin America the phenomenon was similarly strong. After the first wave of factories and basic industries, the 1950s and 1960s were advantageous for entrepreneurs with a shortage of funds but plenty of determination to forge new economic relationships. Huge markets opened in postwar Europe, the United States and later Asia that generated a continuous demand for raw materials and semifinished goods as the economies compensated for the restrictions on consumption created by war.

Many enterprises were born, grew and consolidated in this environment of a seemingly endless demand for new goods, as the inhabitants of these new post-conflict economies were anxious to possess new cars, domestic appliances and the future gadgets that technology was about to invent for them.

Advantage Enterprises was in its first and second generations of directors and officers, the founders and their sons — who had stronger academic preparation than their predecessors to manage the businesses. An estimated 50 percent of the companies that made up the Advantage conglomerate were owned entirely by a single family and managed by the heirs of the founders. As children from wealthy families, these heirs enjoyed the best education in schools and universities in Venezuela and, when the time came, the best postgraduate programs abroad to strengthen their capabilities and acquire that distinguished jetsetter status so useful in conducting a global enterprise.

From a very early age, James Castillo was known for his leadership abilities. The only boy in a family with five sisters, James grew up confident in his natural position as a leader. His very proud father never doubted the clear message sent by destiny about the future of his beloved only son as his successor as president of Advantage. As the only male in an affluent family, James had no problems with that. After graduating from university he went abroad to learn two other languages. His parents were meticulous about all the aspects of James' upbringing — except spending time with him and developing a relationship with him. Their extended business and leisure trips and their total commitment to the company left the Castillos with little time to provide their children with ethical values and a sense of social responsibility. In reality, the six children grew up without parents; surrounded by material things but with no clear guidance about how to behave among themselves and with the rest of the world. His youth in the custody of maids and tutors left James ethically impaired and increased his distance from the real world; he felt conflicted about his vocation to be the ruler over everybody around him, and the lack of affection that he would later try to fulfill in a wrong way.

On rare occasions when the family gathered together, the adult Castillos beamed about how lucky they were in their wealth and discussed the importance of hard work as a way to become even richer and more important. "Someday you will manage Advantage Enterprises. Someday all this will be yours — it will be under your command and responsibility," James' father repeated to him, in a kind of ritual and a reminder of the necessity of sacrificing everything to the supreme objective of creating an empire.

Inevitably, James' pleasant time in college and abroad came to an end, and he had to return home to confront his well-planned future. James returned, eventually met a woman from a wealthy family and similar upbringing and got married during a very impressive ceremony and reception that announced not only his social status but also his entry to the local business community.

A Sense of Entitlement

Advantage Enterprises was founded by Carlos, Manuel and Angelo Castillo, three brothers. Manuel and Angelo semi-retired early and left Carlos — James' father — in charge. Manuel and Angelo were devoted to their families and only participated once or twice a year in the board of directors' meetings. During meetings, members discussed the key issues facing Advantage, but over time they seemed to lose interest in the company's activities until the meetings devolved into annual, five-minute get-togethers over coffee, during which directors rubber-stamped pending acts that Carlos presented. The meetings were held simply to comply with statutory regulations. This arrangement allowed James' father to present financial statements to the board without worrying that members would actually review the documents. The potential to hide expenses not related to the business and disguise a massive fraud was clearly present in Advantage Enterprises.

In the beginning it was only cash expenditures. Then Carlos started to buy luxurious estates abroad, using the international division of the company as an alibi to hide the transactions. His fortune skyrocketed as the company's declined year after year. Using his unchecked powers, he bought a large company overseas, named himself president, set huge salaries for himself and James and kept the shares for himself and his family.

The table was set for James, who joined the company to assume a post created for him — with the enigmatic and incoherent title of Junior Advisor for the President. His arrival to the company was welcomed by his uncles and cousins, owners of some shares who lived out of the country and were accustomed to receiving a yearly check with substantial dividends. His extended family couldn't be bothered with the daily chores of the business, and were glad James would be there to oversee things and help Carlos. James quickly proved capable of contributing almost no value to the company, but demonstrated magnificent skills in golf, polo and partying. Soon he took the reins of the companies, assuming his father's role in the board meetings and acting as CEO in most of them. The only apparent "benefit" James contributed was to add a section in the shareholders' annual reports requiring everyone at the meeting to praise his accomplishments and, in effect, devote three of the meeting's five minutes took to applauding him. This seemingly harmless and egotistical detail later proved to be the strongest nail in James' coffin, prepared by the partners themselves.

Welcome Home

After living abroad for ten years, Marco, one of James' cousins, decided to return to Venezuela to settle down. It was not his intention to get a job, of course; he was used to the fat check he received regularly from the company as payment for his dividends. He wasn't surprised at all when he received a letter announcing that Carlos resigned as the company's president and passed the torch on to his beloved son. The real and nasty surprise came in March, when Marco received the company's financial statements in the mail, asking him to sign documents and return them to Advantage. There was not a single word about his dividends! He grabbed the phone and made a call to James and, after a series of recordings and small talk with staff, his call was diverted to a secretary. Sourly, she explained that James was too busy at the moment to be interrupted, even by a shareholder and relative. And no, she did not know when he would be available to speak, let alone to have a personal meeting.

This left Marco astounded, not knowing why James refused to talk with him and why his dividend earnings had ceased without any notification or explanation. To his limited knowledge, the company's affairs had been strong and profitable all his life and the flow of cash constant. There were no indicators of failure or losses. Unless . . .

Having returned so recently to the country, he had no local contacts to ask for help. He called an old friend from school and she mentioned the name of a legal firm that might be helpful. "Lawyers? I don't think you understand me. We're talking about my cousin and my business. What I need is an accountant or something." Reluctantly, he called the law firm and explained the situation. During the first of what became countless meetings, he explained the situation to the lawyers, who advised Marco how to proceed. First, they needed to have access to the books and records of the companies, not an easy task even for full-right shareholders. Access to the books was necessary to perform a complete and detailed audit — to check and test every account, movement, investiture, reclassification and note to the financial statements, for the past ten years. There was only one way to do this: gather a group of forensic experts under the direction of a fraud examiner, take a deep breath and start from the very beginning.

Ungrateful Relatives

To gain access to the books and papers, the law firm sent several letters to James on behalf of Marco. Angry, he finally agreed to meet the lawyers in his office. He greeted them with fake smiles and false politeness. As the fraud examiner selected for the case, I was present in the first meeting as well.

During the meeting, he seemed truly amazed by the nature of the inquiries, interrupting us every five minutes to mention his family ties and extol the virtues of understanding and sympathy among relatives; he even shed a few tears when he talked about ungrateful relatives. He said, "All we've done is work hard so they can keep getting a fat check every year. How do they dare to question us now?"

When we asked to see the books, his tone changed abruptly; he said he was the guardian of trade secrets protected by the law. The lawyer replied that the same law granted access to such information to the shareholders. After a sullen pause he said, "Okay. Then come back the second week of March, next year, 15 days before the board meeting, and I will allow you access. Have a good day." His total lack of knowledge regarding commercial and administrative matters seemed incongruent with his proficiency in the labyrinths of the law.

We left the office and walked into the bright August sun, considering our options. James was right. Under the Venezuelan legal system, there were only two ways to review a company's books: (1) 15 days before the annual shareholders meeting, the books are open to the shareholders, or (2) a judge can mandate the release of books based on necessity. March was seven months away and a judge would not hear us unless we presented a solid case with irrefutable evidence, which could only be found in the books. Or maybe not?

While I briefed the investigation team, the lawyers contacted the rest of the shareholders who were excluded from the company's administration (and were therefore not earning dividends). We slowly amassed shareholders who represented more than 50 percent of the total shares. None of them had a clue as to how the company was managed, but some kept old financial statements and official communications from Advantage, which they were happy to provide to the team. It was great news — we had something to work with!

We began arranging the documents and information in a way that would allow comparison, a difficult task because it quickly became evident that the financial statements changed from one year to the next, and the figures were presented in a different way without any kind of sense or explanation.

After several weeks of exasperating work, the team managed to decipher details in the vast web of companies, subsidiaries, subordinates and investments management had made during the past 20 years. One thing was evident: Advantage's value dropped steadily, while the directors' wealth skyrocketed. Hidden in the absurd rows and columns of the financial statements, the investigators managed to find more than one hundred possible violations of the law and the duties of a manager, including conflicts of interest.

We found one contract that James made to hire *himself* as a consultant, at a substantial fee. We also found evidence that James made moves to acquire shares on his behalf to increase his interests in the company, bought a company car and paid for membership in a country club with company funds and took leisure trips abroad with his entire family. These and other personal expenses were hidden in Advantage's financial statements as company expenses. In addition, every new business venture he entered into ended in total failure but he somehow maintained an exasperating Zen-like attitude throughout our investigation.

If we were able to obtain such evidence from a poor and unreliable source — shareholders' financial statements and unofficial communications — what could we find in the real books and papers James was dutifully guarding? Surely it was worth the wait until next March to have a look at them, but instead of twirling our thumbs and waiting, the lawyers visited the regulatory authorities and informally presented the case. They received some sympathy but also were advised of the biggest flaw in the case: year after year, the shareholders unanimously approved a motion of congratulations to the president for his excellent work in guarding the corporation's wealth. Whether those expressions of joy and satisfaction were insincere, they were nonetheless signed by the same people who now intended to remove James from the presidency to regain not only the direction of the companies but the stolen assets as well. Our lawyers knew this was a large hurdle if we were going to win a case for the shareholders.

Discouraged but not defeated, the shareholders issued powers for the lawyers to represent them in the board meetings, which were about to begin. We were finally given access to the books but we weren't allowed to review the source documents, which confirmed our suspicions. Convinced that we were dealing with a real crook, we readied ourselves for the annual board meetings season.

There were dozens of annual meetings to attend, some of them on the same day and a few far from the city. We divided our investigative team into small subgroups and tried to include in each of them at least one lawyer, accountant and fraud investigator. The week before the meetings commenced, the subgroups prepared the documents and considered the possible outcomes of the meetings, in an effort to anticipate James' movements.

It was a blast. Not a single meeting concluded in a civilized manner and everyone argued angrily and demanded rights evidently in conflict with those of their counterpart. James' lawyers came and went, attempting to halt our progress and eventually the season ended with no discernable advantage earned by anyone.

Into the Spotlight

The investigation team gathered after the conclusion of the board meetings. It was evident that our position was a little stronger than six months earlier because we managed to obtain new incriminating evidence and uncover other infractions committed by James and his managerial staff, but the senior lawyers weren't optimistic about our chances in a trial. The best-case scenario suggested a long process, meaning at least 20 years in court, during which time James would surely keep his post and our clients would not receive dividends.

It was exasperating! All those hours poring over books and records, all that time spent acquiring and assembling small pieces of information, like tiny parts of a big puzzle, only to find that James had a carefully planned strategy, devised over the decades by himself and his father, to take over not only the presidency but all of Advantage's property as well. His lawyers and pocket auditors worked for him, threading a vast web of corruption, legalized in part with the laudatory letters signed by our clients every year at the board meeting. As the commanders of a siege, we knew we needed to find a weak spot in the well-defended walls of James' fortress.

It was clear to us that he had broken the law. Our problem was proving it with the documents we had. We had to proceed with caution to avoid being sued by James for libel or slander. First, we filed a complaint against the external auditors for the severe inconsistencies in the financial statements. Some of them were sanctioned by the college of auditors and had their credentials suspended. Following that, we asked for the dissolution and liquidation of Advantage Enterprises and its subsidiaries, acting in the name of the majority of the shareholders. This was a long shot, but it prevented James from selling the companies without authorization or causing further damage to the few remaining assets.

None of this seemed to faze James, so we decided to use our last resort — go public. As a true jetsetter and a prominent member of the local society, we knew nothing would scare James more than a public scandal. As we expected, there were dozens of journalists eager to hear our side of the story, so we selected the most suitable forum for our purposes: a respectable TV news program, with a respectable anchorman ready to interview us and, of course, to give James the opportunity to express himself, for the sake of impartiality.

I went to the TV station with the lead lawyer and our best accountant. Carefully, professionally, minding every word we said (and limiting ourselves to things we could irrefutably prove), we told our version. As soon as the interview aired, the public was abuzz. Everyone knew Advantage Enterprises and the Castillo family, but no one suspected James' crime. For an entire week after the TV station aired our interview, I would hear people in the streets debating the issue. Every country club and social event was filled with the tale of a very wealthy family fighting for the control of their business.

Not an Ideal Deal

The public scandal was too much for James. After a week of torment, he raised a white flag; he sent a messenger to tell us he wanted to negotiate. We took the news cautiously, knowing that breaking his stubbornness was only the first step to ending the case. He still needed to be convinced that the vast fortune he managed was not entirely his, and that shareholders had a legitimate claim on some of the funds, too.

After three months of struggling with James' legal team, we managed to sign a deal; it was not ideal, but it was a deal at last! James bought our clients' shares of Advantage at an agreed upon rate, in cash, and became sole owner of Advantage. Our clients took this deal because they got real cash, an end to the fighting and a lesson they never will forget. The option of a long trial for a larger sum was rejected by our clients, in part because of its uncertain outcome and because of the amount of time needed under our legal system to complete such an action. Some of our clients were well over 75 years old and might not have lived to see a trial end, and that no dividends would be distributed while the trial was ongoing was not an option.

As expected, the few shareholders who chose James' side during the fight were rewarded in true James style: They were told that no dividends would be paid during the next few years because of the financial stress Advantage was under to fulfill payments to the other shareholders.

Lessons Learned

There is a lot to learn from a case like this. For the stockholders or owners of a company, if you do not take an active interest in your investment, sooner or later you could receive a nasty surprise. If you own shares in a company, the least you should do is pay close attention to the financial information periodically received; you cannot expect to have a seat on the board of directors of a big oil company if you have 100 shares, but you can always have a look at the newspapers when they mention "your" company.

If you own a significant part of the shares of any given company, you should not blindly trust the administration; that is the road to poverty and destitution. If you don't have the time or knowledge to monitor the business, you can ask somebody else to do it for you. But you should never, under any circumstance, give this surveillance task to the same person in charge of managing the company.

For auditors, there is another message to be gleaned from this case. Rogue managers can ask you to perform tasks outside of your duty, your ethical comfort zone and often the law, but you are not obliged to do so. Remember that this kind of action may save your job for a moment, but when the time comes to answer for your actions, you will be left alone. In this case, James offered his loyal auditors to us, blaming them for everything bad we found in the financial statements.

For fraud examiners, it is important to realize one case is seldom similar to another. This particular experience taught me that in extreme circumstances, for example, when I cannot force the crook to deliver the documents and the law is not doing me any favors, I should sit and rethink the whole case, without giving up hope. The outcome won't always be satisfactory (James was forced to pay for the shares, but it was a very small price), but it's always worth trying to catch the bad guys.

Lateral thinking is a useful way to get another perspective of the facts and it can give you fresh and innovative ideas.

Recommendations to Prevent Future Occurrences

When fraud comes from the top, there are few people who can deter it, except for the owners and the auditors. Both have a duty of utmost good faith, and in some countries they are vested with legal powers,

(*continued*)

similar to public notaries. When an auditor fails to honor the public trust granted to him, the total economic system could easily collapse, as recent scandals have proved.

Never leave management alone. If you suspect something is wrong, demand an explanation. Blind trust is not good in businesses.

A good fraud examiner is always prepared for the unexpected. Dare to be creative, and you will find ways of solving even the most difficult cases.

About the Author

Alejandro Morales is a CFE, CPA and M.B.A. with more than 30 years of experience in fraud risk analysis and fraud investigations for private and public companies and institutions. He is a lecturer for a number of universities in matters related to fraud issues, ranging from vulnerability identification to the execution of improvement plans. He writes a column about fraud issues for local newspapers.

Auditor's Loyalty

JYOTI KHETARPAL

Adler Clooney was a bright student who excelled academically. His friends saw him as someone with an eagle eye and iron will. He was close to his family, particularly his younger brother Jim. They were from a well-off family that was known for never compromising on integrity for the purpose of prosperity. While Adler was sharp, Jim was an average student who let his brother choose his career path for him.

Both brothers went for the highest degree in accountancy — Adler exceeded everyone's expectations in school, and Jim managed to scrape by to earn his professional degree. However, their differences never affected their bond, which became stronger as they grew older. They eventually started their own accounting and auditing practice under the name Clooney Brothers. With their family connections, clout and money, their business flourished. They also became tax advisors to many famous individuals and entities. Their exposure to big entities and their favorable resolution to tax issues made Clooney Brothers experts in identifying loopholes in tax law.

After a few years of practice they did not find consultancy as lucrative as they wanted, so they decided to start a new business venture. The kind of business exposure they had received over the years made them confident about starting their own business, and they decided to enter as partners into a very capital-intensive business with limited competition.

Blissful Ventures

Bliss Carriers was a transportation operator formed by Adler and Jim Clooney. Initially the brothers focused on tourist excursions during summer and winter vacations. They started with a fleet of a few vehicles; gradually they diversified and forayed into the transportation of food and other items from customers' factories to warehouses, distributors and retail outlets. Later they moved out from the tourist excursions and focused on goods transportation.

Eight years after Bliss was formed, the company was lauded as a renowned goods carrier by local media. Bliss had become the largest local carrier of all kinds of goods and employed 1,800 people in five regional offices and twelve branches across the country.

The Clooney brothers were also honored twice with entrepreneur of the year awards by different business circles and associations. Bliss Carriers became a hot topic of discussion among private equity and venture capitalists as an investee company.

Revealing Comparisons

I was associated with a risk mitigation company providing strategic investment opinions to private equities and venture capitals. My job usually started once these entities completed their legal and financial due diligence, but I always preferred my job to start before these steps because reputational due diligence requires a maximum amount of time, being qualitative in nature.

A private equity firm was considering an investment in Bliss Carrier when they hired my company to carry out a quick investigation to gather information about the company. I was not sure whether I would be able to do justice to the assignment in such a short span of time; however, on the client's request, I accepted the project.

At first glance there was nothing wrong with Bliss Carriers. My initial notes on the company were positive — the financials were strong, and it had good profitability, leverage and liquidity ratios. But I was not comfortable with the smooth sailing of Bliss Carriers over the years because I knew that it was difficult to have steady growth in the transportation industry. I wanted to compare Bliss to industry trends, which were not readily available. Since my time was limited, I had to opt for selective parameters that, based on my discretion, were extremely important to clear my doubts.

The comparison of standard ratios was available in the presentation submitted by Bliss Carriers to my client. They had, in fact, given a comparative analysis with their close competitor, but it was not as exhaustive as I needed. Considering the time constraint, I asked my team to get me a comparison of Bliss' operating expenses and profits compared to its close competitors. My team, knowing my eye for details, provided me with a comparative chart.

Bliss Carriers was spending huge amounts on operating expenses, and when I compared the employee cost to revenue ratio of a few close competitors of Bliss Carriers, I was taken aback. Bliss Carriers did not appear as clean as I originally thought.

Trouble in Paradise

The comparative analysis of employee cost to revenue indicated that Bliss Carriers' employee cost was 50 percent of the industry average, while its employee retention rate was 95 percent. These contradictory ratios hinted toward something suspicious.

I explained my suspicions to my client, but the managers took my concerns lightly, saying they were not convinced by my reasoning. They argued that it could be the brand name, company atmosphere or perks that caused employees to stick around. However, I was not convinced by their arguments because I know money plays a big role in someone's career choice, especially for employees in the transportation industry.

I had a detailed plan in mind to investigate further, but the client was not willing to let me continue just to clarify a small doubt. What I needed was a complete profile of the management team, employees and ex-employees of Bliss Carriers. I took the initiative and gathered a small list of current and past staff, and decided to follow up with one ex-employee, Adam Right. After many conversations, Adam reluctantly divulged to me that sometimes he was paid a portion of his salary in cash. Everything else he told me about Bliss Carriers was positive, but I now knew where to dig further.

Cash dealings are seen as part of the transportation industry, as collections are largely in cash considering the business-to-customer (B2C) revenue model. This model is often for the betterment of the company; however, if applied for personal benefit, management can take it far beyond anyone's imagination.

In the meantime, a report based on the scrutiny of corporate records in the past five years was prepared by my team. There was relatively no change in the board of directors, key employees and even auditors' reports during these five years.

I asked my team to give me complete details on the employees, senior management and the auditors of Bliss Carriers and their possible connection with the company or the Clooney brothers, knowing that they were from the auditor community. After we profiled all the employees, the management team and the auditors of Bliss, we found another angle to investigate.

Of Bliss Carriers' employees, a full 80 percent could not be identified. There was no trace of them on the Internet, and our few attempts to connect to them over the phone were in vain. We started to think they were possibly ghost employees. Of the other 20 percent, the majority had accounting backgrounds. A few had transportation experience, but the accounting employees by far outnumbered all other employees. When profiles of the senior management teams were ready, we saw that they all had accounting and auditing backgrounds and qualifications. This raised our suspicion that the Clooney brothers were still carrying out accounting and auditing practices.

Bliss Carriers' internal and external auditors were from two different and independent firms, each headed by professional accountants with no past association with Bliss Carriers. However, I was not satisfied with the auditors' role as our investigation was pointing toward the possibility of ghost employees and questionable accounting practices by the Clooney brothers, but the auditor's reports were not raising even a single query about these matters.

When I discussed my doubts with one of my team members, she conducted some online research and found an old annual report of a listed company, written by Adler with one of his partners when he was working as an auditor. Adler's partner at the time was now a partner at the audit firm employed by Bliss.

The auditors' office was on my way home, so one fine evening I decided to swing by. While I was looking for a parking place, I noticed an unfamiliar face smiling at me from the sidewalk in front of the office. When I got out of the car, the man approached me and asked me what I was doing. A little taken aback, I uttered that I was looking for an auditor's office. He told me he worked as an auditor in the building, but that most of the other auditors had left for the day. When I did not react to his overly pleasant demeanor, he asked if I remembered him; he said his name was Andrew and that we attended college together, although he was a couple years behind me. Now I understood the odd smiling from the sidewalk as I was parking.

I casually asked him about his employer; it was Bliss Carriers' auditor. This gave me all the reason I needed to invite him for coffee, which he readily accepted. After pleasantly catching up with each other's personal highlights since college, we started discussing our professional lives and the assignments we handled. Since most of our investigations were confidential, I did not reveal much about my cases but told him I worked as a consultant. When I asked him what sort of cases he had researched recently, he happily started sharing all sorts of information, much of it related to Bliss. His chattiness bridged gaps in some of my findings and gave authentication to other hypotheses I was developing.

When I asked who ran his firm, he said the managers came from the prestigious former Clooney Brothers auditing firm. He explained that long ago, after earning his chartered accountancy certification, Adler Clooney started an auditing practice with his brother and they began receiving prestigious auditing assignments. Once Bliss started generating unexpected revenues, the brothers withdrew their names from the auditing firm, divided the company in two and made their trusted employees partners of the divided firm. These two auditing firms were now Bliss Carriers' internal and external auditors. However, the two firms were registered to Clooney Brothers' former employees, so they could not be connected to the brothers themselves. Andrew also explained that Adler Clooney enjoyed accounting so much, he continued to manage a few clients for the external audit firm.

My inquiries made it clear there were so many more avenues of investigation in the case, but it was my client's decision whether to pursue them, not mine. I could only provide the leads. I reported the following to my client.

Bliss Carriers was maintaining two sets of financial records with the help of their audit firms — which were none other than the Clooney brothers' own entities. The concept of an arm's-length relationship with auditors was completely abandoned at Bliss.

The Clooney brothers were the masterminds behind the scheme. They did not record all the cash receipts in their books, and sometimes used unrecorded cash to pay employees. Both employer and employees were happy to avoid taxes through this arrangement, especially because Bliss Carriers was located in a highly taxed state. These arrangements were approved by their internal and statutory auditors. Adler Clooney, off the record, was still enjoying a consulting role at his old auditing firm. In addition, the possibility of ghost employees at Bliss was blatant.

Passing the Torch

After reviewing our report, my client immediately halted negotiations with Bliss Carriers. They appreciated the fact that, although we weren't asked to, my team and I investigated further and submitted a comprehensive report. While we were discussing the findings with our client, the tax and revenue department conducted raids of Bliss Carriers and its two auditors. As more details emerged, we realized the fraud was much bigger than we anticipated.

During his initial tax consultancy days, Adler Clooney had identified his clients' desires to avoid paying their taxes. They didn't want to break the law; they just wanted to take full advantage of all the loopholes.

Adler, with his sharp mind, came up with an idea of floating a sham entity — Bliss Carriers — with the purpose of providing fake, but very high-priced, services to Adler's consultancy clients. He started by providing tourist excursions, knowing that the high-cost services would increase the marketing budgets of his clients; some clients even started including these costs on their financial statements without providing the service. However, these costs to Adler's clients were too small to cover their tax avoidance needs, so he gradually switched to goods transportation.

Adler purchased a fleet of 50 vehicles to give legitimacy to Bliss' supposed business, and even began to provide services to independent clients for their genuine transportation needs. However, Adler and Bliss Carriers mainly showed movements of goods from factories to storage places or consumers, when in fact there were no actual movements. Occasionally they would help clients transport their goods from a factory or warehouse without paying taxes or duties, which saved them significant money.

To secure a reputation in the market, Adler exaggerated Bliss Carriers' volumes, which precipitated a need for more vehicles and employees. After all, a company can't keep growing like Bliss without having to hire more staff. Adler's solution was to create ghost employees to handle the fictitious workload.

Adler himself prepared Bliss Carriers' financial statements every year. He mapped out the costs based on industry benchmarks. His own audit firms, run by his trusted employees, served as the internal and statutory auditors, and were responsible for carrying out stock audits, employee counts and audits of other operational aspects.

The tax raid on Bliss was prompted when a truck driver was found transporting goods at hours that conflicted with his transportation documentation. This discrepancy raised doubts in the minds of tax and revenue officers, who decided to conduct a search of Bliss' parking lot. Although the officers were not expecting all the delivery trucks to be present, they were somewhat surprised at how few were accounted for. Also, the employee in charge of tracking the delivery trucks' movements and assignments was unable to explain where all the missing vehicles were. This doubt resulted in the raid on the Bliss Carriers and its auditors' offices.

This case was a classic example of white-collar crime in which auditors' loyalties were to their clients, not the law. Not only did the auditors support and facilitate the fraudulent transactions, but they also steered their clients to indulge in such practices.

Just after the tax raid, the Clooney brothers' professional certifications were revoked by the granting organizations, and Bliss Carriers was immediately dissolved. Adler was arrested, released on bail and charged heavy fines. He and his brother were interrogated for months to divulge the names of all the entities they were supporting or associated with. The internal and external audit firms were also dissolved.

Considering the reputation of the Clooney family, no one expected the brothers to ever compromise their integrity for money. Frank Clooney, the patriarch, publicly condemned the actions of his sons. Adler and Jim admitted to their fraud and asked for public forgiveness.

Lessons Learned

This was a complicated fraud investigation in which the culprits were not employees or external parties, but the owners themselves. It was not a stand-alone case of financial statement fraud showing exaggerated operations or sham employees; rather, it was an individual masterminding the nexus between two industries.

This case gave me and my colleagues a new perspective for viewing fraud investigations. We started an assignment of reputational due diligence, but it eventually turned into an investigation. We learned that investigation is not all about what is presented on paper but must go far beyond that. Thinking creatively and connecting links are essential to complete investigations.

This assignment also changed my opinion of antecedent checks. Previously I held the notion that if I ran an antecedent check for past offenses, but found no negative information on an entity or management, I could rely on them. Not so, as Adler Clooney and his spotless background taught me. I learned the relevance of present scenario and circumstances. Certainly, the past helps us understand the background of an individual and entity, but we have to rely on the present. An investigation is not just collection of historical data presented skillfully; it involves analysis of circumstantial evidence and relevant factors.

The things that helped us the most in this investigation were rounds of discussions about our findings among the team members, understanding of possible implications and interviews with employees at Bliss Carriers and the auditor firms.

Also, as anti-fraud professionals, we cannot ignore rumors or gossip. It is rightly said there is no smoke without fire. When a rumor is confirmed by more than two individuals, it is especially important to look for an explanation.

In this investigation we also went back to basics to clear our doubts. We knew that fraud is not necessarily perpetrated out of need. It may be greed for money or fame or a restless personality. An organization is not just an entity but a consortium of the people running it. An investigator needs to lift the corporate veil to see the background of employees and management, their interests, their reputation and their desires. Human behavior is difficult to map but possible to understand.

Recommendations to Prevent Future Occurrences

After this investigation, we prepared a checklist for the research team to highlight certain issues they found during their research process. We listed the following focus areas:

- Profile key people in an organization.
- Map employment histories of key people to understand their associations beyond the subject entity.
- Map the qualifications of key people to understand their common academic interests.
- Map memberships of key people with industry forums and social or professional clubs to understand their social interests.

(continued)

(*continued*)
- Determine the industry standing of the subject entity.
- Establish the auditors' independence.
- Develop certain critical ratios that are not normally considered for financial rating purposes, for example, employee cost to turnover ratio and management's relevant experience to total experience.
- Study the people managing an entity in detail.
- Be aware that information available on open sources is limited and presented in a manner that might support the investigation but rarely helps in reaching a conclusion.
- Be open to serendipitous, independent inquiries or interactions, as these can provide new leads and substantiate or deny existing findings, as well as give you a new perspective on an investigation.
- Investigators should maintain skepticism toward the subject entity or individual even if it is proved unnecessary.

Remember, you can restrict fraud; you only need to follow the correct path and have the right intentions.

About the Author

Jyoti Khetarpal is a qualified chartered accountant in India with more than 12 years of corporate experience with organizations that include Dun & Bradstreet and American Express. She has been instrumental in outlining risk management methodology, analytics and assessment. Jyoti is currently working with Alea Consulting to provide reputational due diligence, corporate (fraud) investigations, intellectual property protection, KYC and other related services.

CHAPTER 8

Easy Come, Easy Go

BRAD MROSKI

Mike Morris and Tony Vincenti had been good friends for years, with a friendship dating back decades when the two had worked together at global telecommunications giant Aster in Dallas, Texas. With a bond formed through sharing various projects, it was not uncommon to find the two men over drinks after hours while discussing the numerous opportunities that existed for entrepreneurial minds in their rapidly evolving industry. Mike, an engineer by trade, was never short on ideas for dynamic new products while Tony, who worked in Aster's finance group, was very aware of the riches that could be made by start-up companies in the telecommunications arena. Therefore, it was no surprise that when Mike left Aster to start his own company, WireTech, he reached out to Tony to be his chief financial officer.

Tony was a charismatic individual who fancied himself as Mike's right-hand man. He thrived in the fast-paced environment of a startup company and found enjoyment in negotiating financing agreements with lenders and investors. In fact, Tony would be the first to tell you that he never viewed himself as an "accounting guy," but as a deal maker who was responsible for facilitating WireTech's growth. Tony understood the importance of accurate accounting and a robust control environment, especially in a fast-paced and dynamic environment such as WireTech's, but he needed to focus on big picture issues. He could always rely on the people he hired to do the nuts and bolts accounting and control work; after all, isn't that what good leaders do?

In the beginning, Tony and Mike met constantly to evaluate WireTech's performance, set operating goals and discuss the infrastructure that needed to be put in place to ensure that the company stayed on track. WireTech was growing fast and it was necessary for the company to be agile. It wasn't long before Mike decided that they need to bring in some top sales talent to take WireTech to the next level, which led to the hiring of Bob Larsen. Bob was a veteran sales leader with a stellar background and proven international contacts. His addition to the company changed the dynamic of the management

75

meetings and it was evident that a more sales-centric organization was taking shape. The focus with each passing meeting became more and more on how to increase sales and production capacity and Tony, appreciating the priorities of the company, wanted to do everything that he could to help.

Picture-Perfect Start

From the beginning, WireTech experienced dramatic growth. It was a high-tech company in business-friendly Dallas, and Mike and Tony were plugged in to the telecommunications scene by virtue of the contacts that they had made at Aster. WireTech's business model was simple; they primarily produced innovative wireless components that were sold to manufacturers for installation into their products. As a result, most of WireTech's customers would enter long-term product purchase agreements that specified the quantity, price and delivery dates of a fixed amount of orders. Sometimes WireTech's customers would experience unforeseen increases in demand, which would lead them to request additional product from WireTech beyond the quantities specified in their purchase agreements. When these situations arose, WireTech was all too happy to accommodate them.

The addition of Bob had been a great move for the company. Since joining WireTech, Bob had significantly expanded the company's international presence, bringing in customers from Europe, Asia and South America. WireTech was truly becoming a global organization.

Over time, WireTech's overwhelming success drew the interest of private equity investors and investment bankers. WireTech was growing at breakneck speed and Mike and Tony's desire to facilitate additional growth made them eager to agree to meetings with potential investors. Throughout the process, and due in no small part to the salesmanship of the private equity investors and investment bankers, Mike and Tony became keenly aware of the fortunes that awaited them once WireTech became a public company. They also came to know that any investment from an outside firm would be accompanied by demanding expectations for continued growth coupled with a decrease in their overall control of the company. As they discussed the trade-offs that would come with such a big step, it was apparent to the two of them that this was the only way to realize the vision that they had. Furthermore, they were confident that it would not take long for the company to be in a position to pursue an initial public offering (IPO). The market had been particularly receptive to IPOs of technology companies as of late and WireTech's consistently outstanding performance had everyone in a positive frame of mind.

When WireTech ultimately accepted private equity funding, things kicked into high gear. Within a year of receiving the private equity money, the investment bankers began to "groom" the company for an IPO — the market was hot and the time was right. One of the first orders of business was to engage a well-known and reputable auditing firm for name-recognition purposes. It saddened Tony to fire the small local firm that WireTech had been using, but the investment bankers were right; nobody would want to invest their money in a small, unknown company without a large audit firm attached to it.

Alarming Sales Tactic or Ideal Growth Strategy?

The introduction of the investment bankers added a whole new level of pressure as their demands for top-line growth were nothing short of astonishing. Tony, as the primary point of contact for the investment bankers, felt the weight of their unyielding demands more than most and he was becoming increasingly frustrated with them. WireTech's salesmen were pushing as hard as they could and the company was locked into long-term purchase contracts with their existing customers. Historical growth had been amazing, and he understood the need to show the same, if not better, results prior to an IPO, but he just didn't see how the company could deliver on what the investment bankers were looking for.

Due to the immaturity of their market and the penetration strategy of the company, increasing product pricing as an option was out. Therefore, the only solution to increase revenues was to gain additional customers or get the current customers to increase their existing orders. One of WireTech's salespeople, Sofia Emilia, was having amazing success in Latin America. Mike, Tony and Bob thought that it would be a good idea to get Sofia's thoughts on what the rest of the sales team could do to mimic her success.

When the three men met with Sofia, they discussed a myriad of strategies for how to win customers over. One thing that caught Tony's attention was when Sofia mentioned that her customers often felt more comfortable when she gave them a guarantee that if they ordered items from WireTech and subsequently discovered that they didn't need them, then she would take them back and give the customer a credit toward future purchases. Tony was shocked by this admission — how could Sofia not realize the accounting implications of these types of arrangements? How was he going to deal with this? As Tony looked over at Mike and Bob, he realized that he was the only one in the meeting who understood what such arrangements could do to the bottom line.

Tony would be the first to tell you that he wasn't the sharpest guy when it came to accounting rules, but this was pretty basic stuff. He pressed Sofia on the issue, "So tell me Sofia, is it often that you make these arrangements with your customers?" "Oh, yeah," replied Sofia, "all the time. And the great thing is, my customers never actually return the items. They always find a way to use what we send them." This encouraged Tony, at least. If customers hadn't historically returned items, then there was no reason to believe that they would start doing so now. By the end of the meeting Tony's fear had turned to excitement. This might just be the answer he'd been looking for to get the investment bankers off of his back! Armed with this new mindset, Tony set off to dazzle the investment bankers and get that IPO done.

At the end of the year, WireTech's new auditors arrived to begin their initial audit. Based on their knowledge that WireTech had experienced dramatic growth and was on the verge of completing an IPO, the auditors had a heightened level of skepticism. In their experience, fast-growth companies had a tendency to be aggressive, choosing to focus their efforts on finding additional ways to grow the company rather than on ensuring the sufficiency of processes, controls and other risk-mitigating activities. With this in mind, the audit team decided to increase their testing of revenues, as this was typically a higher than normal risk area, ripe for fraud.

During their testing, the auditors came upon a series of suspicious purchase orders from Sofia's customers that contained handwritten notes such as "right to return if unable to sell" and "additional 5 percent discount." Upon learning that the revenue related to these purchase orders had been recognized when WireTech shipped the products that could be returned, the auditors immediately took the purchase orders to Tony for an explanation. Tony, not knowing how to respond to the auditors, tried to downplay the issue. "This is nothing guys! I'm sure that this is a mistake; let me speak with Sofia to see if I can figure out what it means. I'm positive that none of our salespeople would be giving these types of terms to their customers; we just don't do that!"

The auditors were not convinced with Tony's explanation, and they had concerns that there were potentially other sales being made with similar terms. With that, the auditors met with WireTech's board of directors and requested that they initiate an investigation to determine if revenue was being recognized prematurely and if so, if the conduct was intentional. Upon this request, WireTech's board of directors immediately formed a special committee to investigate the matter, and reached out to attorney Matthew Washburn to lead the investigative efforts. Matthew and I had worked on numerous cases together, and he wasted no time in hiring me to assist in the investigation and lead the forensic accounting/fraud examination work.

A Story Told Through E-Mails

At the onset of the investigation, Matthew and I met to discuss our strategy. It was important to the special committee that our efforts be as efficient as possible while maintaining the appropriate amount of diligence. Based on these instructions, we decided that the appropriate course of action was to immediately issue a data preservation order to the entire staff of WireTech. The cost of processing and analyzing electronic data was significant and we both felt that it was unjustified based on the information that we had at this point in the investigation, but we wanted to ensure that we had it preserved, just in case.

One of my first steps was to review the purchase orders in question and try to identify any common characteristics. It quickly became apparent that all of the purchase orders came from Glow Star, a customer under the responsibility of Sofia Emilia.

Armed with this information, we decided that a good starting point would be to look at all the purchase orders for each of Sofia's customers over the past year and, sure enough, we found numerous instances of purchase orders with notations signifying a right to return the product at the customer's discretion. After completing our initial review, we felt that it was necessary to bring Sofia in for an interview to further clarify the notations on the purchase orders. Sofia was based in Miami so it took a couple of days for her to arrange travel to Dallas to meet with us. As it turns out, the timing played to our advantage. Upon learning of our request to interview her, Sofia became nervous and made a point of going back through all of her old e-mails and documents that were responsive to the preservation notice that we had sent out when we commenced the investigation. When Sofia arrived for our interview, she gave us a series of e-mails detailing communications with her customers. In the e-mails, Sofia offered various types of incentives, such as the right to return along with purchase price discounts if customers agreed to accelerate their prescheduled orders. As Matthew and I reviewed the e-mails, we immediately understood that the content of the communications had significant revenue recognition implications. We also understood that the discovery of relevant e-mail communications related to the subject of our investigation meant that we needed to expand our procedures to encompass e-mail and other electronic document review.

In her interview, Sofia disclosed to us that she routinely provided these types of incentives to her customers. She described a culture at the company that valued sales at all costs, but stopped short of saying that anyone at the company directed her to offer these types of incentives to her customers. She was certain that Mike and Tony knew what she was doing; after all, they had discussed it months before at a meeting. She assumed that if she was doing something wrong, Tony would have let her know.

When we shared the e-mails that Sofia had given to us with Tony, we were surprised at his nonchalant response. As we continued to impress upon Tony the gravity of the situation, he appeared to gain an understanding of the implications of our findings. Upon this realization, Tony was quick to paint Sofia as a rogue salesperson who was not following company policies. "She's off the reservation; I don't know how she could have possibly had the impression that such behavior would be tolerated here!" said Tony. He promised us that he would deal with Sofia and thanked us for bringing these transactions to his attention. As far as Tony was concerned the investigation was complete, and the problem was limited to Sofia.

Unfortunately for Tony, Matthew and I shared a different view. Upon learning of Sofia's e-mails, I notified one of my forensic technology specialists and they came to image Sofia's hard drive while we were interviewing her. The data that they had collected had just been processed and was ready for our review.

Once our team began reviewing the e-mails, we realized that WireTech's problem extended well beyond Sofia. In the e-mails, we found communications from Tony to Sofia aggressively pushing her to increase sales.

From: tvincenti@wiretech.com

To: semilia@wiretech.com

Subject: crunch time

Sofia,
I need another 20k units of sales before quarter end. Reach out to all of your customers and offer whatever is needed to get them to take more product. Two days left in the quarter; get it done!
Tony

What was Tony doing sending e-mails like this? Wasn't he supposed to be a steward of the company, the one who understood the rules and made sure that everyone was playing by them? This concerned Matthew and me and we immediately made the decision to image Tony's hard drive as well as all of his information on WireTech's servers.

Once we started reviewing Tony's e-mails, we found a bevy of disturbing information. Tony, it seems, was functioning more as a sales manager than as the company's CFO. He was directly negotiating product discounts and return agreements with customers in an effort to drive sales. In addition to these fairly standard means of "pushing" sales on customers, Tony had some more creative methods. For many of WireTech's overseas customers we found Tony instructing the shipping department to send product via the slowest method possible, even when this contradicted the specified shipping method in the customers' purchase order. This method, which Tony referred to in his e-mails as "slow boating," was clever in its simplicity. If, for example, a company requested an order be sent via two-day air to be delivered on July 6, Tony would instruct the shipping department to send the order on June 30 via a slower delivery method and record the sales before the June month-end. Often, customers would receive orders early and complain, but Tony had learned that he could appease these customers by offering them a discount on future purchases. After all, it wouldn't affect the revenues that had already been booked.

In addition to pushing sales on existing customers, Matthew and I found evidence that Tony was circumventing his own credit approval policies to approve new customer orders. In his e-mails, he brazenly told potential customers that although their credit check had failed, he would be willing to approve their application for credit if they would agree to a certain level of purchases within a specified timeframe.

When we confronted Tony with these e-mails, he seemed agitated that we would waste his time with what he considered banal communications. "I don't understand what it is you're concerned about. This is what executives do. I drive the performance of the company!" Tony seemed in denial of the fact that his actions had significant implications on revenue recognition, and when asked directly about his understanding of the accounting impact, he claimed that he didn't think there was any.

Ultimately, we expanded our procedures to include a review of all customer purchase orders for the preceding five years, an examination of all customer credit files, and all of Tony's, Mike's and Bob's e-mails and other electronic files to ascertain the extent of the scheme.

Forsaking Responsibility for Growth

Once we had accumulated all of the information from our forensic accounting procedures, interviews and e-mail review, Matthew and I sat down to piece it together and communicate our findings to the special committee. Ultimately, we had found that a total of 422 transactions during the course of four years had been inappropriately accounted for, and the financial statements for those years would need to be restated.

As for Tony, while we were troubled by the fact that he claimed to not understand the accounting impact of his actions, we were more troubled that he had not been completely forthright with us at the onset of the investigation. Tony had forsaken his role as the financial guardian of the company, instead adopting a "make the numbers at all costs" attitude. His actions not only resulted in erroneous accounting, but increased Wire-Tech's risk by virtue of taking on marginal customers that a prudent CFO would have turned away. It was therefore up to the special committee to decide, based on our findings, what actions they should take.

The special committee acted swiftly in their response, terminating Tony and installing an interim CFO to oversee WireTech's financial statement restatement and process remediation procedures.

Lessons Learned

Thankfully for the directors and officers of WireTech, Tony included, the discovery was made prior to filing an IPO. One can only imagine the mess that WireTech, Mike and Tony would have had to deal with if they had filed materially misstated financials with regulators. Ironically, in

(continued)

(*continued*)

Tony's haste to appease the investment bankers and get an IPO done, he facilitated a large-scale scheme that delayed WireTech's IPO indefinitely.

This case reinforced the fact that investigations don't have a map; each one requires a certain degree of navigational judgment. With WireTech, we had a classic example of an investigation that appeared fairly straightforward at the onset but became more complex as we obtained additional information. When performing investigative work it is necessary to continually evaluate the "what if" with the "what do I know." More often than not, you will find that the "what if" changes as the "what do I know" increases.

Recommendations to Prevent Future Occurrences

This was a classic example of a company that had grown up fast and management who got caught up in their perceived need to show continued success. With the potential riches from an initial public offering of the company's stock and the pressure from the investment bankers, the executive team created a culture of "show growth at all costs" that permeated throughout the organization. Tony, in his position as CFO, was meant to be the one who ensured that the company was playing by the rules with respect to financial reporting. Unfortunately, he bowed to the pressure from outside interests and instead used his position to serve those interests.

Tone at the top is an oft-used example of fraud risk but it fits this case to a tee. When the company started, WireTech's tone was strong, with a focus on infrastructure, processes and controls. Unfortunately, as the pressures and incentives for successful performance grew, the tone from Tony deteriorated from a "do the right thing" attitude to a "win at all costs" mentality.

About the Author

Brad Mroski is an Assistant Chief Accountant with the Enforcement Division of the U.S. Securities and Exchange Commission. Prior to joining the SEC, Mr. Mroski worked for an international audit and consulting firm where his practice focused on accounting investigations and litigation consulting expert services. He is a Certified Public Accountant and a Certified Fraud Examiner.

The Securities and Exchange Commission disclaims responsibility for any private publication or statement of any SEC employee or Commissioner. This case study expresses the author's views and does not necessarily reflect those of the Commission, the Commissioners or members of the staff.

Organized Crime Is Not Just for the Usual Suspects

DAVID SHAPIRO

Felix Forme was not a big man. However, he dreamed large and desired fine wines, first-class international travel and a house by the beach. A plumber's son, he didn't start out as a master of the universe, though he could fit pipes better than the highest-paid investment bankers of his day. He worked his way through public schools and earned a bachelor's degree at a state school in central Pennsylvania, where he did the practical thing — he studied accounting and business. Academia prepared him for debits and credits but not for the addictive allures of Bordeaux, Brooks Brothers and Asian call girls.

"Honey, I don't want to be a glorified clerk forever," he complained to his wife and former childhood sweetheart, Margaret. "I want to create things," he said, "and get paid lots of money." But their second child was on the way and it was no time for castles in the sky.

"But you're not a clerk; you're a CPA," corrected Maggie.

"Right," concluded Felix without satisfaction or a smile. "How do you suppose investment bankers get rich?" asked Felix, not waiting for an answer from Maggie as he opened the door and headed to the train station.

The years accumulated, exceeding a decade. Felix did his time, plugging holes in financial statements for a while but losing enthusiasm — if he ever had it — for public accounting. After another five years as a CPA, he was done with adjusting journal entries and reviewing past transactions. It was time to create future transactions, his own deals.

So he gravitated to where the money was — that is, other people's money — becoming a private banker for a financial institution based in Europe. But he was eager to earn fees and collect interest from anywhere and anyone in the world. Anyone, that is, who could afford a multimillion-dollar deal; anyone who had so much money they could assume the risk of losing a few million, on- or offshore. So Felix decided to structure loans and investments for the highly affluent.

"What do you say we put a bid in on that house we saw at the beach last weekend?" Felix asked Maggie.

"Do you think it's big enough, Felix? Three bedrooms will cover us and the girls, but they're at that stage where they won't go anywhere without a friend . . . or three," advised Maggie.

"Well, we could always add on," concluded Felix, and the issue was solved for the moment.

Sitting on the hardened, cracked leather coach of the commuter train from the shore to the city, Felix wondered about many things. He liked his job — heading the financial engineering department of his company. It offered him five staff members he could move like pawns, a couple of whom were quite pretty, even by his own demanding standards, and six-plus figures in monetary remuneration. But the department didn't get the respect it should from corporate headquarters. It was as if they didn't appreciate or understand exactly what he did for a living, although, in their defense, he wasn't really sure of that himself.

"Daddy, what do you do for a living? I have to interview you for a school project," said Alice, the baby of the family by two years and already overflowing with the desire for more knowledge — but mostly for more stuff like the latest apps and designer clothing.

"I work in the Department of Financial Engineering," replied Felix almost proudly, "we create loans and investments for our clients."

"But why would they go to you and not a real bank like Chase?" asked Alice. "My deals are special," answered Felix, "we are a relationship bank and not a bureaucracy like other banks. I get to know my customers, and I create exceptional opportunities for them to make more money more quickly than they could elsewhere."

"How?" was Alice's deadpan follow up. She looked into her father's dark brown, cavernous eyes. Felix was speechless.

It was August, and the sun beat down on the residents and tourists alike. The windblown sand scratched Felix's face, but he didn't feel a thing there. Only the ache of unmet ambition somewhere deep inside persisted.

Growth and Ego

Banking and Investing Inc. (BII) was a large bank headquartered in Sweden and concentrated in northern Europe. More accurately, it was a group of different banks operating in disparate cultures. Though BII formally had tens of thousands of employees, it could hardly be said to control these individuals, as smaller institutions were rolled up into the group during the go-go 1980s.

The lack of centralized control was good for Felix, allowing his creative juices to go with the flow. BII even sponsored a legally separate subsidiary,

Financial Innovations Inc. (FII), in luxurious midtown Manhattan. Through FII Felix, the subsidiary's managing director, created and marketed financial engineering products and services. The FII offerings were made available to wealthy individuals who required a bit of professional ingenuity to limit the income tax effects of living large in developed economies.

BII's 24 credit committee members convened weekly by telephone. It was a diverse but old-fashioned group, each member different from the others where it didn't matter. No one could imagine the bank would do anything other than loan money. They especially disliked having to review FII applications, a legal entity that, under the leadership of Felix, seemed more interested in form than substance. However, no one would admit this; FII was way too profitable.

"This is the modern world," reminded Felix as he glanced at the committee's questions on the cover sheet for his set of new clients. "Innovate or die." Felix was frustrated; the credit committee just didn't get it.

"Maybe we should get clarification from the management committee," suggested Felix. "I want to be sure we take advantage of these special opportunities without delay," he desperately urged the credit committee chair in a special face-to-face lunch meeting at a tavern in Manhattan in mid-June.

"I haven't hurried in 35 years," declared the credit committee chair as he caressed his gray-bearded chin. Unfortunately, Felix believed him. I guess he hadn't heard that quip about how time is money, thought Felix as he flashed his corporate smile — the one that didn't crinkle his eyes.

BII's management committee comprised 12 individuals, all of whom resided in upper-class bastions in Europe. Many lived in quasi-castles. They were smart enough to know that the enterprise could not stand still — especially as so much of its business was dependent on cultivating relationships with financial partners — but not smart enough to understand that management at a distance entailed significant risks. In theory these risks were mitigated through video conference calls and e-mails to distribution lists. In practice — who knew?

Felix touched down at the Stockholm-Bromma Airport on a Wednesday morning in early July, three hours before a scheduled meeting with the management committee. He wished he were home at the beach. It wasn't just that the air in Stockholm smelled old, as if the battles and wars over the past centuries caused the European atmosphere in general to become weary and passive. Felix breathed deeply and briefly saw his long deceased grandfather smoking a pipe.

"Your offices are so elegant and beautiful," complimented Felix, forcing the corporate smile, which merged into his tired eye muscles, making detection of his false play of sincerity nearly impossible.

"It's so good to have you," declared Dr. Hans Nyberg, management committee chair. "Please, sit down."

Felix nearly drowned in the leather chair. He must have listened to Dr. Nyberg for what seemed like ten minutes without breathing.

"Are you OK?" inquired Nyberg, staring at the beads of sweat forming on Felix's brow.

"Just jet lag," responded Felix without allowing a pause of polite consideration after the doctor's expression of concern. "There's really no problem here at all," began Felix with the speech specially designed for the management committee that he had practiced before heading for Sweden. "We are already behind the curve," continued Felix. "However, it's not too late to make good money out of these deals, unless, of course, you'd rather let our competition make the easy money."

"If I understand you correctly," summarized Dr. Nyberg, who seemed to possess the only mouthpiece among the 24 ears and eyes, "we have insubstantial risk on these transactions, but we earn fees without actually having to set aside any capital whatsoever, right?"

Staring at each other, the two men nodded in apparent agreement. Felix thought about adding a wing to his beach house; the doctor thought about the brilliance of his oversight. Nobody thought about the U.S. Internal Revenue Service (IRS).

Mr. Forme Goes to Washington

Three years had passed since Felix and Nyberg faced each other like bobble heads in reverie, and the world didn't stand still. Businesses were formed; businesses died. The cycles of growth and decay progressed, but there was one constant: Nobody wanted to pay more taxes.

Across the Atlantic Ocean, a man walked into Theodore Walters' office on a mission. The receptionist looked up and smiled as he walked into the lobby. She asked for his name and checked it against her appointment book. "He's expecting you. Go right in."

"I have a big problem," declared William Vance to tax attorney Ted Walters, in a voice heavy and raspy from not enough sleep, his eyes sharp and white. "And I hope you can help me with it."

"Please, have a seat," advised Ted, "and tell me what I can do for you."

William began to explain. He seemed hesitant to go into details of the investment he had entered with FII and Felix Forme, especially regarding the effect it had on William's personal income taxes, but was eager to talk about how FII now seemed to be misusing his funds. Ted took notes and asked follow-up questions that he hoped wouldn't scare off William. He knew there was a case here, and that it was much bigger than one man trying to avoid paying his taxes with shady investment vehicles.

Later that evening, after Ted had concluded his meeting with William and contacted the internal audit department at BII — FII's parent company — Ted was flipping through the TV news channels when one story caught his eye.

The sight of Felix on TV was initially prepossessing. Brooks Brothers would have been proud to have the vision of Felix's pinstriped suit and bold silk tie beaming around the earth. Like a well-oiled politician, Felix carried himself with dignity.

"There's nothing untoward about the program," counseled Felix, hoping that the U.S. congressional subcommittee members would think about the word *untoward* and not the program.

"So you're telling this subcommittee that the program as you described it was properly approved by your bank," countered the only congressman up for reelection next November, who was hoping to impress voters and viewers who do not think too much. "And the responsible individuals at the bank were fully informed about the program?"

Habit is a useful device. It has been one of the primary means and methods by which individuals believe their own words. Say it once — maybe it's a slip of the tongue. Say it over and over — it begins to sound like the truth, especially where appearances are the currency of public opinion.

"So help me God," declared Felix.

As he carefully strolled out of the large room occupied by America's legislative leaders, Felix tried to think about the big picture. He understood his motives to develop the program and why he had been able to convince BII's senior management to adopt it, but he could not understand why he had been called to appear in front of Congress. He was just another player in the game — maximizing after-tax profits and minimizing real liabilities. What was wrong with that?

Facing the Truth

"Who the hell are you?" asked Felix in the tone that he habitually reserved for subordinates and people unlikely to be potential clients, adding a smile like an afterthought — perfume on poop.

"I'm with the team hired by corporate in Stockholm to assist the internal auditors," I responded with forced calmness. My experience with investment bankers was that they tended to overvalue themselves and undervalue anyone appearing to make less money per day than they did in their personal dealings. However, when it came to business, hype was the norm. "I'm here to ask you to please come to the executive conference room. Dr. Nyberg wants to see you."

Felix stared at me. I didn't think that he really saw me then. He seemed to be imagining a future that had a change of forecast — from sunny to rain. We waited together for the elevator. Time ticked by slowly.

"Good morning, Felix," greeted Dr. Nyberg, appearing to have left his smile in Stockholm. "It seems that things have not taken a turn for the better with the Financial Engineering Unit. Your program is beginning to smell a bit."

Felix drifted in and out of awareness of the words and worries that were circulating in the conference room. He had gotten stuck on Nyberg's verbal stress on the words *your program.* It didn't seem fair or accurate as he couldn't remember ever having an original thought in the whole process. He was a clerical facilitator, not a tax-evading mastermind.

There were 25 of us on the external team who were hired to assist with the internal audit. For two months we searched through Felix's and his unit's offices, gathering, copying and itemizing hard documentation such as rolodexes, calendars, vendor and consultant files, client files, account statements and promotional and marketing materials that provided too few valuable hints of clearly suspicious activities but an abundance of red herrings of seemingly legitimate activities during the past seven years. The red herrings seemed to bring in hundreds of millions of dollars of loans and related deals. The boxes of paper filled an entire room in the secure office space that Dr. Nyberg had provided to us for the audit.

Documentation can be a fragile thing. A slice of paper can be easily ignited or shredded. Even people's memories become unreliable with the passage of time. Imagination replaces memories, and past events are not so much remembered as they are created.

We spoke with Felix on numerous occasions, most often with his lawyer present. "You can see for yourself who was involved in the tax minimization programs," Felix unnecessarily reminded us as his attorney became distracted by his PDA. "You don't need me. It's self-explanatory, and the programs were approved all the way up. Everybody knew the risks."

Perhaps, but one thing was certain: The financial performance of BII benefited significantly from FII's business activities. FII originated loans — to scores of U.S. and European borrowers for hundreds of millions of U.S. dollars and other currencies — that were converted to Swedish krona. The funds were then aggregated in other loans receivable among the assets disclosed on the BII balance sheets. In addition, the origination and related fees, as well as interest income, were counted in BII's income statements. There was not one default or one loan that required any increase in capital by BII to cover an increase in risk of loss. Felix seemed like a genius on paper.

Felix long insisted that he was clean. Everybody's always innocent. Of course, white-collar crimes, including financial statement frauds, don't exactly leave blood or gunshot residue on the perpetrators' hands. Instead, they often leave electronic bits of data in storage media, silently waiting to be read, interpreted and used by investigators like me.

Our computer forensics team was busy. They imaged hard drives, taking every electronic device from every office and individual who had ever walked by, communicated with and — it seemed — thought about Felix or the Financial Engineering Unit. We would need another room, I thought, if we were going to print out all of the electronic evidence. However, thanks to data analysis software, we were able to diagram connections among hundreds of people, real and fictitious, domestic and international. Our diagram grew like the roots of a tree that seemed to be seeded by the individuals' desire to borrow money from FII. However, the borrowers never appeared to use their funds for purposes other than internal transfers among FII-controlled accounts. That is, except for one individual.

"What's this about a borrower named William Vance?" I asked with my best poker face. I was never that good at poker, but I was okay with cash receipts and cash disbursements. "How come a Santa Monica borrower's account was charged for a payment to a local contractor here in the city for what seems to be the development of a beach house outside the city — in your town, in fact? And why did some guy in the Philippines — whom William never heard of — authorize it?"

I remembered the face Felix made at that moment. I had seen it at the elevator a few weeks back when we were on our way to see Dr. Nyberg in the conference room. I felt a sudden urge to blurt out "Gotcha!" But I reminded myself I was a professional and just said it in my head.

Form over Substance

From the glare that the federal district judge was shooting at Felix, most observers in the courtroom would not have guessed that Felix was cooperating with the government's wide-ranging criminal prosecution. "Mr. Forme," began the judge in a deep voice, "I understand that you have agreed to plead guilty to charges of tax, mail, wire and bank fraud, waiving your rights to an indictment by grand jury and trial by petit jury. Now tell this court what you did," demanded the judge.

"We — I mean I — made deals with people outside the bank to get wealthy clients who wanted tax breaks to open loan and deposit accounts with BII. FII — I mean I — created paper trades under what I called *collateral accounts* to mimic real investment activities, such as swaps of foreign currency, so no one would suspect the loans and deposit accounts were not legit," replied Felix. After a few minutes he touched all of the jurisdictional bases: interstate commerce, using wires, faxes and the mail. . . . It seemed so pedestrian.

His voice faltered a bit here and there. I had the impression that he accepted responsibility under the law for facilitating with others to carry out schemes to help taxpayers evade taxes, but he seemed to be a true believer at heart. As far as I could tell he didn't think what he did was wrong.

"However," continued Felix, "at the end of the day, no money ever left BII."

"Your honor," interrupted Felix's attorney. I could see the vibrations of his PDA creating ripples in his suit jacket. "May I have a word with my client, please?"

One of the things trial attorneys learn in the field is how to whisper in court rooms so that only the intended audience hears the secrets. I could tell by the slackness in Felix's face that he was quietly, firmly being read the riot act. He cleared his voice.

"Your honor," stuttered Felix. "I might have accidentally left a few things out. . . . "

Finally, the set of actions initiated by Felix that triggered our deep examination of the loan programs, accounts and financial performance of FII became evident to all. Felix created fictitious loans on FII's books and used them to create on-paper tax losses for the debtors (or, more appropriately, counterparties), generating hugely overstated management and performance fees for FII, covering these activities with roundtrip foreign currency transactions. Plus, he took a few hundred thousand dollars on the side.

"I took money from the FII accounts," he declared. "I used straw men in the Philippines whom I controlled to pay for improvements to my beach house." His story was embezzlement with international class — electronic debits and credits pinging into and out of accounts under esoteric names through exotic places only to ultimately pay for Felix's groceries and home improvements. It was pedestrian, again.

In the end, Felix pleaded guilty to two counts of criminal conspiracy, one count of criminal tax fraud and one count of criminal wire fraud; he received a few years in jail, and BII got a deferred prosecution agreement. My employer got well over seven figures. I got a story.

Lessons Learned

I learned more from Nyberg's and Felix's mistakes than they would probably have wanted. This case demonstrated the danger of a decentralized subsidiary without sufficient oversight by the parent company. BII executives blindly trusted Felix and his assertions about programs at FII. If Nyberg and the management team had been more active in their oversight, they could have spotted red flags in Felix's plan. The reviews and approval process for subsidiary activity were woefully inadequate. BII also presented a poor ethical example for subsidiaries. Felix saw the lax ethical standards at work in Nyberg and the oversight committee, and figured he could follow suit to turn a personal profit. Turns out he was correct.

In some ways our client, BII, could understand the tax evasion, the conspiracy, the mail and wire frauds, the bogus BII loans and FII trades. These misrepresentation schemes hurt mainly other institutions. It was Forme's embezzlement that really got to them, as if they recognized that the game was customarily played on a field with blurred lines, except for the line separating the employer's property

(continued)

from the employees' property. Sometimes, profit-making and profit-taking served to compromise employee loyalty.

BII learned some unpleasant truths about commercial and investment banking, notwithstanding their decades of experience in these endeavors. Felix was highly compensated for earning the company money and he had no reservations about fictitiously making it appear that he generated even more wealth for BII than he actually did. Creating assets, such as loans, and making roundtrip trades of foreign currencies to juice up FII's assets with extra management fees and interest income didn't pose an ethical problem for him. The income from these trades created false profits on FII's books and records, and, under the terms of his employment agreement, Felix earned "incentive income" on such accounting profits. Therefore, what made FII look good made Felix rich.

Analyzing so much data — from e-mails and instant messages to investment committee meeting minutes and loan applications — taught me this caveat: There is a difference between genuine complexity and a complicated audit trail. Don't let an abundance of data get in the way of transparency.

All told, between the churning of the faux debtors' investment accounts and the creation of the faux debtors' commercial loan accounts, FII (and BII by consolidation) and Felix did quite well for a while. As did the debtors who used the fictitious loans to generate artificially high tax bases to create artificially large tax losses to shelter other taxable income and gains. Financial accounting and reporting as practiced by the likes of Felix is a sham — an enterprise of false accounting entries supported by misleading paperwork.

The outcome for BII was significantly overstated assets and income from FII for several years, amounting to millions upon millions of dollars. Not only was BII senior management fooled into overcompensating the duplicitous Felix Forme, but purchasing shareholders and other stakeholders, including the honest but unwitting colleagues of Felix, suffered damages. Who really knows which was worse — the economic losses resulting from overpaying for the exaggerated financial performance of BII or the emotional damages of trusting too much in FII's business model? Worse yet, these damages could have been prevented.

Recently, on a whim, I spoke with Felix from prison. I wanted to know how he got away with it for nearly a decade. How were so many talented and honest individuals at BII and FII fooled?

"It wasn't as hard as you think," he began, the old confidence restored. "I had documentation for everything, and nobody really

(*continued*)

(*continued*)

wants to question audit trails. I mean, the reams of tedious and technical jargon layered over months and months of account statements supplemented by dozens of attorneys' and tax advisors' opinions. I overwhelmed them with apparent compliance."

Recommendations to Prevent Future Occurrences

My team and I had a post-investigation meeting with Dr. Nyberg and his oversight committee with the goal of offering suggestions for preventive measures. Internal controls programs, which are designed to detect and prevent threats, are inherently imperfect. Systems are implemented by flawed individuals. However, BII representatives and my team brainstormed to develop enhanced controls.

The key to effective compliance is an information and communication system that involves competent individuals at different levels through the organization. Allowing the subsidiary FII to maintain excessive control over both the information in its client files (e.g., account opening documentation at FII) and its flow to other departments within BII (e.g., the tax department at BII headquarters) caused an increased risk of management override at FII. This risk was addressed as follows.

Internal Audit Function

The internal audit team at BII was increased both in number of employees and its annual budget. Internal audit began to be allocated resources based on a formula involving the assets controlled, revenues generated and expenses incurred at each unit under the BII umbrella. The sweep of BII's internal audit department was extended across all of BII.

The management committee created a subcommittee — the audit committee — that comprised financially sophisticated staff members trained in fraud risk assessment. Internal audit became strong and centralized at the highest level of BII to allow the corporate veil to be pierced.

Interdepartment Reviews

BII strengthened interdepartmental reviews between subsidiaries and parent. Separation of departments no longer excused or justified a cursory review.

(*continued*)

The tax department began strictly scrutinizing all new financial services, and department reviews occurred independent of the cost-benefit analysis of the originating department (review of costs and benefits were assessed under internal audit). Profit centers like FII would not be allowed to bully or cajole cost centers by appeal to the opportunity cost of lost prospective business.

Independent Checks

The intent of BII's management committee charged with improving corporate governance was not merely to centralize and empower oversight. They recognized that independent supervision from a distance was important. However, they realized that the attention of individuals in the field near the locus of business activities was essential.

Segregation of Duties

BII's primary concern was the responsible custody of its clients' funds. Assertions by senior managers of special relationships would not be allowed to trump safe and sound banking practices. Control over account openings would be strictly isolated from control over account funds, and client relationship managers would have read-only access to client account data and funds.

Multiple Reviews

Client orders would be subject to multiple levels of review within applicable departments: Speed of execution would not be elevated above authenticity of client instructions. Client relationship managers would not participate in communicating client instructions.

These enhancements were implemented too late to uncover Felix's embezzlement and expose the weaknesses of his FII tax-shelter product, but they should prevent similar schemes in the future.

About the Author

David Shapiro is presently an Assistant Professor in the Department of Economics at John Jay College of Criminal Justice, New York, NY. Formerly, he worked as a corporate fraud investigator and management consultant in the private sector and held the following public-sector jobs: Assistant Prosecutor for the County of Essex, NJ, and Special Agent — Assistant Legal Advisor for the FBI, Albany, NY. He is an inactive CPA and retired attorney.

CHAPTER

10

The Spinster and the Investment

ERIC SUMNERS

As you will see in the following story, all financial statement frauds are not in the billions of dollars. They only need to be big enough to be material to the financial statements.

Francine Gordon was considered a model employee of Small Town Federal Credit Union (STFCU). She had been STFCU's controller for more than 15 years and knew not only the accounting systems but also the data-processing systems extremely well. In fact, when the data-processing clerk was sick or on vacation, Francine would step into the position to make sure that the processes ran efficiently and as intended. Many employees at the credit union — including Francine — believed she knew more about the IT systems than the data-processing clerk. This reputation was built up over a number of years and few employees ever challenged Francine concerning credit union issues.

As with many small financial institutions, the separation of duties was not always practical due to finite resources and extremely tight budgets. Francine was highly intelligent and was an asset to STFCU in that she was able to function in an array of roles (accounting, data processing, member services, etc.) and was not the typical "that's not my job" employee. For years she helped out in many departments and took a leadership role in various projects. These experiences added to her skills and in-depth knowledge of the credit union's internal control systems. As time went on she became something of a dictator in her duties and projects; however, this was tolerated because she was able to resolve issues. Her disheveled appearance and moody temper were hated by some of her coworkers but tolerated by the CEO, Susan Wren, because Francine was a longtime and capable employee who took care of projects and issues; this was a rarity at the credit union.

Although complete separation of duties was impossible, Francine had some unthinkable duties and responsibilities. Her primary responsibility was as the controller; this had her creating financial statements, preparing budgets and forecasts and reconciling STFCU's lengthy and, to some degree, complicated bank statement. She also oversaw and was the backup for the data-processing department. Often an employee would volunteer to cross-train in the data-processing department, but Francine preferred to keep the duties within her control. In addition, and most critically, she was responsible for not only the accounting — but also the management — of STFCU's investment portfolio. This gave her the ability to make purchase and sales decisions concerning investments, although intelligent investment analysis was not a strength that Francine possessed. Because of this, Francine relied on the advice provided by one of the credit union's three approved brokers. This created a "witch's brew" for bad decisions and lax internal controls.

Because STFCU was located on the East Coast and all of Francine's family was from the South, she frequently worked long hours and weekends. Her compensation was good but not in the upper tier of compensation for credit unions of similar size. STFCU's CEO, Susan Wren, appreciated her work ethic and, probably to some degree unconsciously, granted Francine more authority and autonomy throughout the years. Although she was not close to any employee and did not complain about loneliness, it was not hard to imagine that being away from her family, especially during the holidays, took its toll. With no husband, children or significant other, Francine gravitated toward one of the credit union's investment brokers, Steven Edwards. Edwards was an older distinguished gentleman with a silver tongue and a memory that always included Francine's birthday. Edwards was one of the credit union's three approved brokers but was consistently awarded approximately 90 percent of the investment business. In addition it was clear that Edwards' skills were more social than financial. Being a small financial institution, STFCU relied on its brokers to analyze investments and detail how individual investments and the portfolio in total fit into the credit union's balance sheet and future goals. Edwards did not provide these analytics and did not appear to have a solid understanding of how to manage an investment portfolio for a financial institution. In fact, he did not seem to understand financial institutions very well.

Not Sly Enough

Small Town Federal Credit Union, located in a northeastern state, had 22 employees, two locations (a branch and main location), approximately 30,000 members (customers) and $110 million in assets. As with most small financial institutions, taking in deposits and granting loans was STFCU's primary business. However, due to spare loan capacity, the credit union's investment portfolio was vital to earning a reasonable return on excess funds. Typically credit unions and small financial institutions follow the SLY principle of investing — safety, liquidity and yield. However, to implement all aspects of the SLY principle, knowledge of what you are investing in is vitally important.

Not unusual for small companies, particularly financial institutions, STFCU had a somewhat weak internal control environment due to a lack of consistent separation of duties in general; Francine's constantly floating job duties were an especially significant breach of control.

Within the Matrix

When I started working at STFCU I had a wide range of duties, including internal audit and financial accounting. As a CPA, I was concerned about the overlaps in duties but pleased to be working at a credit union. My grandfather had founded a small credit union; I grew up in the industry and was happy to be out of public accounting and back in the industry I had been a part of from a very young age. A regular schedule, not often found in public accounting, and the ability to focus on moving one organization forward was truly appealing to me.

Approximately six months into my tenure I was asked to start reviewing and preparing the bank reconciliation. I was surprised by the volume and the relative complexity of the transactions. I jumped into the project but it took some time to learn the nuances of the transactions flowing through the cash account. After a couple of months I became relatively comfortable with the transactions and did not need Francine's direction and explanation of the reconciling items.

While I was conducting the third-quarter reconciliation of the bank statement, preparing the financial statements and preparing the quarterly 5300 Call Report (a regulatory financial and statistical report), I noticed a significant reconciling item that affected both cash and member shares (deposits at a credit union). Time was of the essence as the credit union's regulators were also on-site conducting their annual review. I was concerned about submitting the Call Report and financial statements without understanding the $130,000 entry, so I decided to question Francine about it. The transaction had her employee ID attached to it, meaning she recorded the entry. In a fluster, she gave me a circular explanation that did not make sense and said we had to quickly prepare financial statements for the regulators. Unsatisfied with Francine's explanation, I met with Susan Wren. Susan was the closest to a friend that Francine had in town; Susan was also concerned about submitting the Call Report and financial statements to the regulators in a timely manner.

The credit union and Wren had a cordial but often tense relationship with the regulators. Sue, an STFCU employee for the past 25 years, had worked her way from teller to CEO and often treated the credit union as her personal, privately held business. This attitude was clear to regulators and made them uneasy. In addition, Sue often met recommendations from the regulators about issues such as internal controls with resistance that bordered on hostility.

With Francine's "explanation" and Wren's direction, I prepared the financial statements and call report so the regulators could move forward with their examination. Surprisingly Francine's explanation concerning the reconciling item was accepted by the regulators; I figured if it passed their review, it must have been valid. I moved forward with my other duties and did not give it much additional thought. The regulators left the credit union in early November and presented their findings — none were significant, and none related to the $130,000 reconciling item.

In mid-December, I began the closing process for November. I was surprised to find the same reconciling item from the September quarter-end. It seemed to me that the reconciling item should have cleared and become a non-issue by now. I again took the reconciling item and entry to Francine for clarification, and she became flustered again. She told me she was extremely busy and would get back to me by the end of the week. I did not realize that would be the last time I would ever see Francine.

Change in Plans

The next morning Susan came into my office and handed me a piece of paper. It was Francine's resignation. Considering she had a 15-year career at STFCU, Francine's letter was short and to the point: "As of December 16, I resign. Thank you, Francine Gordon." I quickly thought but did not say aloud, "Well, happy holidays." Knowing that Susan was shocked and worried about losing Francine, I asked how long she would be around to train and help with the transition. Susan noted that she called Francine but the phone had been disconnected and her office had been cleared of the few personal items she had. It was fairly clear her years of experience and knowledge of the credit union's systems would not be available to help with the transition. After reflecting on the series of events, I made the logical conclusion that Francine's abrupt departure was related to the reconciling item and relayed this to Susan. Susan was even more shocked but could not argue with the strong circumstantial evidence. We agreed that analysis of the reconciling item was a priority.

Approximately a week later, Susan promoted me to CFO and tasked me with quickly determining the source of the reconciling item. With little solid information I set out to piece the puzzle together and prepare accurate year-end financial and regulatory reports. I was curious to review the regulator's work papers related to cash. However, due to our lack of knowledge about the situation and the tenuous working relationship with the regulators, I determined that the investigation should move forward "in house."

Holiday Presents for One and All

With snow falling and temperatures dropping, I began reconciling and often reconstructing various accounting records related to the $130,000. Unfortunately the level of detail and explanation typically related to adjusting entries did not exist with the transaction. However, I quickly noticed the accounts related to the item were cash, investments and customer deposits. Cash, investments and deposits were all accounts with significant balances and voluminous and occasionally complicated transactions. A $130,000 change in any of these accounts was not unusually large. After about a week of reviewing online and hardcopy records, my eyes hurt and I determined that the entry originated approximately three years earlier and pertained directly to investments.

Four and a half years ago, Francine had purchased a mortgage-backed investment from, not surprisingly, Steven Edwards. The investment was purchased at a significant premium and paid principal and interest on a monthly basis. The principal payments were based on the principal repayments of the underlying mortgages associated with the security. Because of this, the premium would have to be amortized on a monthly basis based on the principal repayments. Francine, although highly intelligent, did not appear to clearly understand the investment and she was only amortizing the premium on a consistent basis over the projected life of the mortgage security. The projected life of the security and the actual life were not the same and when interest rates on mortgages dropped, consumers refinanced their mortgages and large amounts of the principal were paid back to the credit union. This should have resulted in increased amortization or expensing of the premium; however, it appeared that Francine realized that proper amortization of the premium would have resulted in a net loss for the year. Instead of amortizing the premium correctly, Francine continued to amortize it on a straight-line basis and then created a "reconciling item" for the remainder and used accounts such as cash, investments and deposits to record the entry. This had the effect of inflating net income for the initial year, and equity for the subsequent years. The reconciling amount remained consistent but the accounts used changed monthly. For three years, the $130,000 oscillated among accounts and passed CPA and regulator audits. It was not possible to determine but it would have been interesting to know if Francine's explanation of the item remained constant or changed with time.

Although we were never able to contact Francine, the picture of what happened and how it was concealed slowly became clear. This was not the holiday present I originally wanted but it brought closure to the issue.

It was also clear that Francine had an overly close relationship with the credit union's broker, Steven Edwards. I learned from other employees that Edwards, always impeccably dressed and manicured, would send flowers to

Francine on her birthday and visit her on a regular basis. This relationship allowed Edwards to sell Francine and the credit union inappropriate investments that were barely understood by management. After further analysis and discussion with other brokers, I realized that Edwards' commission was highest on these types of investments. Not only were they purchased for the wrong reasons, but I now found it difficult to find buyers for them. Therefore, many of the investments were held to maturity even though they were not a good fit for the credit union's balance sheet.

In my new position as CFO I attempted to understand how the investments fit into the credit union's balance sheet, but Edwards was never able to clearly explain their benefit. Much like Francine's explanation of the reconciling item, Steve's explanation of investments was circular and did not logically fit. I decided to embrace my limited understanding of exotic investments and ensure that all future purchases made sense to me and fell under the SLY principle.

Decisions and Consequences

The clear solution was to adjust for the reconciling item by reducing equity. Although STFCU had adequate equity on the balance sheet, the adjustment was nevertheless painful. Equity was a valuable tool in keeping regulators content with the credit union's often stagnant financial and market position. It was also necessary for Susan to contact the regulators and notify them of the situation. They were not pleased, obviously, but treated us fairly, most likely because they realized they had also missed the error during many audits.

Francine did not financially benefit from her fraud. Her motivation was in saving face by not admitting an imprudent investment choice. Susan noted that she would have ranted and yelled at Francine but would not have terminated her for the string of errors. Because of the nature of the fraud, disclosure to law enforcement officials — other than STFCU's regulators — did not seem necessary or beneficial for STFCU. However, due to the significant nature of the crime it was necessary to notify the credit union's bonding and insurance company. This arduous process of filing forms and meeting with bonding investigators fell to Mandy Santoro, the credit union's human resources manager. Mandy and Francine had worked together for a number of years and Francine's bullying and condescending style had not gone unnoticed. Although Mandy was professional, she viewed the process of removing Francine's bond as a late holiday gift. The removal of her bond would effectively prevent Francine from ever working in another financial institution — the only industry she ever knew. With no formal education beyond high school and a tainted work history, Francine's options for future employment were slim and few. The details Mandy provided resulted in Francine's bond being quickly removed. Part of the process grants the accused the opportunity to respond to allegations and provide contradictory evidence. Kurt Marshall, the insurance and bonding company's investigator, told us that Francine never replied to notices.

No one at the credit union has heard from Francine since. There were rumors that she moved out of state and attempted to gain employment at a new credit union and when that failed, it was rumored she took an entry-level retail position. Although her bullying made her an unsympathetic figure, Francine's career ended unfortunately and her motivation was not the typical American greed story.

Lessons Learned

Having well-trained, versatile and intelligent employees is important; however, the segregation of duties is not an abstract theory only applicable in textbooks. Segregation of duties needs to be continually evaluated and understood in organizations of all sizes. Since the Sarbanes-Oxley (SOX) Act, this has been done in larger organizations, but small organizations are not subject to SOX requirements. Also, this case demonstrates that fraud does not always occur for financial reasons. Although Francine may have been concerned about losing her job and her income, it appears that her primary motivation was to not appear incompetent and to continue being viewed as the alpha employee of the organization. Not admitting her error was a significant motivator for Francine.

It was also interesting that Francine left the total amount of the reconciling item throughout the years. My assumption would have been that she would try to chip away at it over the years with the hope of eventually eliminating the item and moving forward. However, she didn't do so, and I wondered if she thought it was easier and simpler to continue moving around one large reconciling item rather than breaking it into many small, monthly, unsubstantiated entries, which might have increased the likelihood of being caught because there would have been more transactions for someone to question. It was also possible that after passing the first couple of audits, she believed it would be easy to continue the fraud into perpetuity, removing her need to eliminate the item.

Because of this on-the-job training, I learned my limitations regarding exotic investments and, after I took over the CFO position, I was guided by conservative investment principles. Although my investment strategy resulted in reduced investment income to the credit union, I was able to sleep at night. Plus it allowed for proper balancing of risk for the credit union.

(continued)

(*continued*)

It is also interesting and important to note that this fraud was not caught by an internal control system or audit. It was uncovered because of the vacuum created by the fraudster's permanent absence. The situation could have continued for some time due to Francine's intelligence, the credit union's less than optimal internal controls and Francine's ability to socially engineer conversations about reconciling item.

Recommendations to Prevent Future Occurrences

Francine rarely went on vacation and when she did it was usually for less than a week. All employees should be required to take an annual vacation of a least a week. In addition, another employee should be trained to process their work. This can be difficult in small organizations, but some degree of familiarity with the work of a supervisor by another employee is vital. Although this might not have prevented Francine's fraud, it would have decreased the likelihood of it continuing.

All organizations should provide resources for the detection of fraud. In tough financial times it is often difficult to allocate funds away from revenue generation; however, such an approach is shortsighted and can be extremely costly in both dollars and reputation. The analysis of fraud risk and segregation of duties should be continual — not a one-time activity. It is also important to remember that fraud can be perpetrated for a number of reasons and they don't always include direct financial reward to the fraudster.

There are significant risks associated with cash, investments and the reconciliation process, and firms should separate them. A lack of separation will probably result in an intolerable level of risk.

All reconciling items — material or not — should have a cogent explanation and be verified by an employee who is independent of the one initiating the entry. It is easy to take a person's explanation of a situation at face value, but reconciling items should be well founded and balanced or cleared in a reasonable amount of time. A recurring reconciling item for the same amount is a concern and presents a high risk to the institution.

About the Author

Eric Sumners, CFE, CPA, is a graduate of Michigan State University and the University of Michigan-Dearborn. He has approximately 20 years of professional audit experience in an array of industries, including financial services, manufacturing, not-for-profit and governmental. Mr. Sumners has also published a number of articles concerning auditing issues.

11

This Might Sound Familiar . . .

JAMES M. BROWN

"As you go forward in life you will be confronted with questions every day that test your morals. The questions will get tougher, and the consequences will become more severe. Think carefully, and for your sake, do the right thing, not the easy thing."
— L. Dennis Kozlowski (Commencement address at St. Anselm College, Manchester, N.H., May 2002)

Four men entered a business situation, each motivated by money, power or simply a firm belief that he was just doing his job. One decade later they parted ways, their professional and personal lives dramatically altered. During that time they raised families and profited handsomely from their business arrangement, but in the end each man was accused of financial malfeasance. One paid a $100,000 civil penalty for his role, but otherwise walked away acquitted. Another was prohibited from practicing as an accountant by the SEC. The other two collectively paid restitution and fines in excess of $200 million, were barred from serving as officers or directors of a public company and were sentenced to prison terms of 8 1/3 to 25 years. When their stories were ultimately revealed, the world's view of the financial markets and the professionals involved in those markets was changed forever. A fifth player, with a peripheral role, was forced to pay $20 million in restitution and more than $2 million in fines and was permanently barred from acting as an officer or director of a publicly held company.

L. Dennis Kozlowski rose from a tough neighborhood in Newark, New Jersey, to lead one of the world's largest corporate conglomerates. Tyco's revenues were about $3 billion and its market cap about $1.5 billion when Kozlowski took over as CEO in July 1992. By fiscal 2001, Tyco's revenues were $36.4 billion and the company's market capitalization was $113.9 billion, making it one of the highest-valued public companies listed on the New York Stock Exchange. As his power in the corporate arena grew, so did the extravagance of his lifestyle. Kozlowski blatantly disregarded the principles of accounting and corporate governance as his leadership style became a symbol of personal and corporate greed in the late twentieth and early twenty-first centuries.

Kozlowski, son of Leo Kelly (an investigator) and Agnes (a school crossing guard), adopted his father's reputed ability to deceive and publicly persuade. Shortly after earning a degree in accounting from Seton Hall University in 1968, Kozlowski began his professional career at SCM Corporation as an auditor in mergers and acquisitions. After a few stints with other firms, Kozlowski joined Tyco in 1976 and began his aggressive ascent up the company's corporate ladder. Kozlowski served as a Tyco divisional CFO and president before he earned the position of chief executive officer in 1993.

Around the time Kozlowski reached the executive apex at Tyco, he and his wife, Angeles Suarez, separated and Kozlowski became involved with his future wife, Karen Lee Mayo, a waitress who was also married at the time. Kozlowski divorced Suarez and married Karen in 2000.

Forming a Team

Though Tyco International began as a research lab that produced high-tech materials and energy conversion products in the early 1960s, Kozlowski transformed the company into a conglomerate that rivaled former Wall Street sweetheart General Electric in scope.

Tyco senior management, led by Kozlowski, orchestrated one of the largest and most egregious financial statement and corporate governance fraud schemes in U.S. history. The consequential accounting misstatements resulted in a $5.8 billion overstatement of income involving improper acquisition accounting; earnings management; improperly matching income and expenses; and a failure to disclose certain related-party transactions, executive indebtedness and executive compensation. The largest accounting misstatement involved Tyco's failure to timely write down its goodwill for which a $4.5 billion charge was ultimately recorded and disclosed. In addition, Tyco improperly recorded approximately $600 million of income regarding ADT connection fees. However, the scandal was not limited to accounting misstatements. The scope of the perpetrators' outrageous scheme included, but was not limited to, $900 million in insider trading, abuse of the company's Key Employee Loan Program, tax evasion, a $20 million investment banking fee to a former Tyco director and illicit payments to foreign officials.

To conceal his material financial statement fraud, along with the corporate governance fraud, Kozlowski enlisted help from within and without the Tyco empire. His go-to guy on the inside was Mark H. Swartz, Tyco's chief financial officer. When Swartz met Kozlowski in 1991, he was working as an assistant controller earning $45,000 a year. After meeting Kozlowski, Swartz began enjoying some of the best years of his life and eventually became the executive vice president and chief financial officer, reporting directly to Kozlowski. His income, net worth and status all increased exponentially as he rode Kozlowski's coattails, but ultimately at a great cost.

Kozlowski was also allegedly assisted by general counsel, Mark Belnick, a blue-chip attorney who Kozlowski recruited. Prior to joining Tyco, Belnick was a highly successful and respected litigation partner at Paul, Weiss, Rifkind, Garrison & Wharton (Paul Weiss), where he earned approximately $600,000 to $1 million annually. Although his earnings were significant by most standards, he reportedly still felt undercompensated at the firm. Belnick later admitted he was attracted to the significant earnings potential Kozlowski offered him. However, while Belnick financially excelled at Tyco, he didn't fit in with the corporate culture; it wasn't the collegial environment he had become accustomed to at Paul Weiss.

During the SEC's initial investigation, Belnick hired the law firm Wilmer, Cutler & Pickering to represent Tyco in connection with the SEC's document requests. Kozlowski and Swartz quickly complied with all the requests except for one, calling for a single-page memo. Swartz told Belnick that the memo listed operations that he and Kozlowski were thinking about discontinuing and — although he was amenable to producing the document for the SEC — he and Kozlowski believed it could be troublesome with company insiders.

When Belnick and the outside counsel finally saw the memo, they learned it did not concern the potential termination of certain operations, but rather the potential termination of a Tyco officer. The memo simply said "Belnick termination" and $5 million, indicating Belnick's proposed severance. Belnick apparently reconciled his differences with Kozlowski and Swartz, but he first warned, "You would never get rid of me that cheaply."

Kozlowski encouraged his senior managers to run their business units in a largely autonomous fashion. His executive style was completely decentralized. As long as his managers met their profit goals, they were permitted to run their divisions as entrepreneurs. Indeed, Kozlowski welcomed Belnick during his first day on the job at Tyco with an abrupt indoctrination.

Kozlowski pulled an index card from his pocket. "Let me show you how I manage this company," he said. The card had six phone numbers on it [the numbers of his senior managers]. He added Belnick's number. "If I need something," he said, "I'll call you. Other than that, you run your show and you do it right."[1]

Out of Control

Although publicly traded companies like Tyco typically establish internal accounting controls to prevent and detect financial fraud, even the best controls are ineffective when they are overridden by senior management. Tyco's CFO, Mark Swartz, assisted Kozlowski in the execution of the Tyco fraud by overriding accounting records and reporting controls (overstating assets, understating expenses and failing to report senior officer compensation), authorization controls (approving bonuses and loan forgiveness without requisite board approval) and asset stewardship controls (misuse of corporate assets).

Responsibility for preparing GAAP-compliant financial statements ultimately resided with Kozlowski and senior management, but the investing public also relied on the independent auditor's opinion of Tyco's financial statements. Indeed, auditor independence is often referred to as the cornerstone of the auditing profession, since it is the foundation for the public's trust in the attest function.

Pricewaterhouse Coopers (PwC) was Tyco's audit firm while Kozlowski was perpetrating his financial statement fraud and PwC helped conceal the fraud by issuing unqualified (clean) audit opinions on Tyco's financial statements. Even though numerous red flags were present, PwC's engagement partner, Richard P. Scalzo, CPA, did not reassess risk for the Tyco audits or perform additional audit procedures.

Fool Me Once . . .

From 1992 to 2002, Kozlowski transformed Tyco from an industrial manufacturer into a multinational corporation and increased revenue more than tenfold with his aggressive acquisition strategy. Between 1994 and 2001, Tyco acquired 1,000 companies for $63 billion, earning Kozlowski nicknames like "Deal-a-month Dennis" and "CEO on Steroids." Kozlowski's acquisition criteria were reasonable and prudent in the early to mid-1990s, when he focused on acquiring companies that were underperforming yet offered immediate earnings accretion for Tyco. Between 1996 and 1999 Kozlowski spent $30 billion on acquisitions (all but $3 billion paid for with Tyco stock), including $850 million for AT&T's undersea fiber-optic cable division in 1997, $3.3 billion for U.S. Surgical in 1998 and $11.3 billion for AMP in 1999.

Although Tyco's debt tripled between 1997 and 1999, its profits continued to rise. During fiscal year 1999, Tyco earned $2.6 billion on sales of $22.5 billion. Investors acquired Tyco shares as aggressively as Kozlowski acquired takeover targets, progressively driving Tyco's share price to new highs. While Tyco's stock price climbed and Kozlowski and Swartz touted the company's financial strength, the two corporate officers systematically cashed out with handsome profits. Senior management treated Tyco as their personal bank, fleecing the company and misleading shareholders for their own personal gain with blatant disregard for their fiduciary corporate duties, accounting standards and the securities laws.

Kozlowski's accounting improprieties at Tyco were not formally investigated by the SEC until 1999. The initial SEC investigation took place from 1999 to 2000 and centered on accounting practices, including spring loading, for the company's many acquisitions. In spring loading, the pre-acquisition earnings of an acquired company are underreported, giving the merged company the appearance of an earnings boost afterward. After an exhaustive yet narrowly focused probe, the SEC sent a letter informing Tyco that it was not taking action.

After achieving this victory, brought about with the help of Belnick and Swartz, Kozlowski began to commit some of the most egregious fiduciary, corporate governance and accounting violations since the SEC was established. In addition, the three Tyco executives orchestrated one of the largest money grabs in the history of corporate America. Within months of the SEC's no-action decision, Kozlowski had forgiven some $100 million in outstanding relocation loans and began publicly touting Tyco as the second coming of GE.

Tyco director Frank E. Walsh, Jr., added fuel to the fire of the company's acquisition frenzy with a recommendation that Tyco acquire CIT, a financial services company. The CIT deal went through in 2001 for $9.5 billion and was structured by Kozlowski with an interesting stipulation. Kozlowski agreed to pay Walsh a $20 million finder's fee for the recommendation, yet the fee was not disclosed to the other board members or the shareholders, nor was it properly authorized.

In 2002, Walsh pleaded guilty to charges of securities fraud after receiving the $20 million fee. Although Walsh's plea deal did not include jail time, he consented to a judgment permanently barring him from acting as an officer or director of a publicly held company and ordering him to pay restitution of $20 million to Tyco. In addition, he agreed to pay $2.25 million to New York State and New York City in lieu of fines and $250,000 to the Manhattan District Attorney's office for prosecution costs.

Perhaps Kozlowski's most extravagant and outrageous act as the CEO of Tyco was the $2.2 million birthday party he threw for his wife on Sardinia in June 2001, half of which was paid for by Tyco. The party included toga-clad waiters and a few indecent displays involving a life-size cake and an ice sculpture of Michelangelo's David.

Fool Me Twice . . .

Though Kozlowski successfully shook the SEC off his trail once, a day of reckoning was looming on the horizon. His scheme began to unravel in 2002 as investigative pressure progressively intensified. In January 2002,

Tyco's stock price began to significantly decline. Concurrent with the drop in stock prices was news that: (1) Tyco was being investigated for tax evasion and money laundering by the U.S. Treasury Department, (2) Tyco's accounting was called into question in connection with the $20 million payment to Frank Walsh and (3) the Manhattan district attorney was tipped off by New York State banking regulators regarding a $4 million wire transfer from a Tyco account to a New York art dealer, which was then transferred to an account in the Bahamas.

In a period of less than two months, all three of Tyco's senior executives either resigned or were fired. The exodus began on June 3, 2002, when Kozlowski resigned "for personal reasons" on the eve of being charged with evading more than $1 million in sales taxes on artwork. Kozlowski was replaced by John Fort, a former Tyco CEO. Next, Belnick was fired on June 10 and sued by Tyco for breach of fiduciary duty and fraud. On August 1, Mark Swartz resigned.

On September 12, 2002, the SEC filed charges against Kozlowski, Swartz and Belnick for failure to disclose information to shareholders regarding the multimillion-dollar low-interest and interest-free loans that the officers borrowed from Tyco.

Restating and Sentencing

I was one of four forensic accountants employed by Milberg LLP who was assigned to the Tyco case over the course of the litigation. I assisted attorneys with filing the consolidated amended complaint in January 2003 and throughout the litigation until the case was settled in 2007.

Along with analyzing more than a dozen categorical class period restatements, including a $4.5 billion goodwill impairment restatement and several other restatements in the range of $100–$400 million, I assisted attorneys with preparation for depositions, oral arguments and briefs. Our investigation included a review of SEC filings, analyst reports and other pertinent documents.

Belnick was accused of aiding and abetting Kozlowski's violations of federal securities laws and eventually settled with the SEC. He agreed to pay a $100,000 fine to settle without admitting or denying the allegations against him and was prohibited from serving as an officer or director of a public company for five years. He was acquitted on all criminal charges by a Manhattan jury.

For those interested in courtroom drama, the trial of L. Dennis Kozlowski did not disappoint. Video clips of the fortieth birthday party of Kozlowski's wife on Sardinia were presented to the jury and a mistrial was declared after one juror, Ruth Jordan, purportedly made an OK signal to the defense. But in the end, Kozlowski and Swartz were not as lucky as Belnick. They were charged with looting Tyco of hundreds of millions of dollars and were convicted on 22 counts of grand larceny, falsifying business records, securities fraud and conspiracy. In September 2005, Kozlowski and Swartz were sentenced to 8 1/3 to 25 years in prison.

In addition, Kozlowski and Swartz were fined $70 million and $35 million respectively and ordered to pay $134 million in restitution. Tyco sought disgorgement of more than $500 million in benefits and compensation from Kozlowski as a result of his breaching fiduciary duties to Tyco. On December 1, 2010, U.S. District Judge Thomas P. Griesa granted Tyco's wish. Judge Griesa ordered that Kozlowski forfeit all compensation and benefits earned from September 1995 through his termination in June 2002.

Liability and guilt were not limited to Tyco executives. The SEC found that Richard Scalzo, Tyco's external auditor, was reckless in not knowing that the Tyco audits were not in accordance with generally accepted auditing standards (GAAS) and recklessly allowed PwC to issue false audit reports. The SEC ruled that he committed and caused violations of Section 10(b) of the Securities Exchange Act and engaged in improper professional conduct pursuant to Rule 102(e)(1)(ii) of the commission's Rules of Practice. In addition, Scalzo was denied the privilege of appearing or practicing before the SEC as an accountant.

The civil case against Tyco and PwC was ultimately settled for $3.2 billion, with the companies paying $2.975 billion and $225 million respectively. The Tyco settlement payment was the largest cash payment ever made by a corporate defendant in the history of securities litigation. In addition, the PwC settlement was one of the largest recoveries from an independent auditor.

Lessons Learned

There are numerous lessons to be learned by investors, accountants, attorneys and aspiring executives in connection with the Tyco scandal.

Developing strong functional leadership and mentoring grounded in both integrity and competence is essential for corporations. Absolute power tends to corrupt, so executives need to be kept in check by ethical leaders who can push back. Ethical conduct training as well as lines of communication to report wrongdoing should be made available to employees.

Additionally, leaders should be subject to a system of accountability. At Tyco, Kozlowski took the company from $300 million to $36 billion with essentially the same leadership team. According to Erin Pillmore, senior vice president of corporate governance at Tyco, Kozlowski "designed a structure of loyalty around him with little accountability."[2]

(continued)

(*continued*)

Corporations should devise ways to prevent, detect and report fraud at all levels throughout the organization. Kozlowski succeeded in part by limiting the number of employees he interacted with. Few were aware of his wrongdoings and he restricted the amount and type of information each key person knew.

An inappropriate business plan can steer a company in the wrong direction and growth by acquisition can be very risky when a significant debt burden is taken on to facilitate the acquisitions. An acquiring company that overpays for acquisitions inherits goodwill whose fair value might be overstated, and the company's future earnings might be negatively affected by goodwill impairment charges. The actual earnings could be unfavorable compared to projected earnings and cash flows estimated at the time of the acquisition.

Recommendations to Prevent Future Occurrences

To prevent misuse and unauthorized use of corporate assets, focus on setting an ethical tone at the top grounded in integrity and competence. Executives are typically evaluated (and rewarded) based on their ability to hit projected numbers, but there usually isn't much assessment of their character. Tyco now evaluates ten character traits in top managers annually, including qualities such as "managerial courage."

Improving employee communications and clearly defining values, expectations and policies throughout the organization is another critical objective. At Tyco, employees now receive copies of "Passport for Ethical Leadership," a handout that outlines prevention techniques, how to recognize risk factors and how to handle issues when they arise. The passport helps employees recognize and prevent bribery; discrimination and harassment; conflicts of interest; and environment, health and safety issues.

In the aftermath of financial statement fraud, strengthening leadership and corporate governance is common. Tyco changed leadership, policies and communications. The company established a guide to ethical conduct for every employee around the world, proactive responses to shareholder concerns and a new compensation plan.

Management also established a hotline and receives about 4,000 calls annually, of which 400 are investigated. This has resulted in more than 200 terminations each year. Tyco now increases the perception of

(*continued*)

detection within its organization by publicizing the incidents to all 250,000 employees.

In the end, perhaps the greatest lesson was delivered from L. Dennis Kozlowski, prisoner 05A4820, when he made the following statement to *60 Minutes* reporter Morley Safer during an interview in 2007 at Mid-State Correctional Facility in upstate New York:

> In my wildest imagination, when I would project myself into my late 50s and early 60s, where I would be or what I would be doing [*sic*]. If I make a list of a hundred different places, or a hundred different things, here would never make that list[3]

About the Author

James M. Brown is a forensic accountant for Milberg LLP, a firm specializing in securities class actions. He collaborates with attorneys and investigators on all phases of Milberg's litigation practice, including the development of case theories, drafting accounting sections of complaints, streamlining intensive document reviews and assisting with depositions. The securities fraud cases that Jim worked on at Milberg resulted in total settlements in excess of $5.4 billion.

Notes

1. http://nymag.com/nymag/features/9572/index1.html.
2. http://executiveeducation.wharton.upenn.edu/ebuzz/0609/seniormanagement.html.
3. http://www.cbsnews.com/stories/2007/03/22/60minutes/main2596123.shtml.

CHAPTER

12

Pulling the Strings

JAY DAWDY

Bill "Papa" Thomas was the warehouse manager for Jenkins Manufacturing in Lubbock, Texas. He was a native Texan and a straight shooter who had worked at Jenkins for more than 30 years. Everyone at the firm knew him and they all just called him Papa. He was friendly, but Papa called them like he saw them. He wasn't afraid to speak his mind in that big Texas drawl he had. Jenkins Manufacturing had recently been acquired by a large multinational conglomerate, Yellowstar Industries, and Papa was being asked to perform write-downs of inventory that far exceeded anything he'd done in the past. He didn't understand why these write-downs were necessary. Papa was pissed, exclaiming to one of his colleagues, "Why in the Sam Hill do these pencil neck geeks from Yellowstar want to write down this perfectly good inventory?" But ultimately Papa didn't want to disappoint his new bosses. He and other Jenkins execs were being granted stock options in Yellowstar as part of the acquisition and he wanted to cash out and retire. Papa did what they asked him to do. Papa was a puppet.

Karen Jillwater, better known as "Jill" to all of her colleagues, was under a lot of pressure. She was a senior accounting manager at Hope Electronics in Annapolis, Maryland, where she'd been working for about 10 years. She was stressed out that her new bosses at Yellowstar Industries, which had just acquired Hope, had a different way of doing things. Jill was a good accountant — she knew the right and wrong entries to make — so Yellowstar's requests didn't sit well with her. But she was also young and ambitious and wanted very much to please her new bosses. Yellowstar's accountants and their outside auditors were specifically directing Jill to defer revenue on some recent shipments, which she didn't understand. The shipments had gone out and had already been received by the customer. The revenue should have been recognized according to GAAP. But in the end Jill didn't want to raise a ruckus with Yellowstar's managers.

She reasoned that Yellowstar was a public company, with big firm auditors, so they must know what they're doing. Jill was a puppet.

The puppet master's name was Maxwell Cruz, the CFO of Yellowstar. He was more commonly known as "Crucut" given his legendary prowess in cutting costs. Crucut was an intense number cruncher and a difficult man. He berated his staff when they failed to do what he asked or questioned his commands. Cruz expected total loyalty. He didn't tolerate any disagreement. And usually employees came around to Cruz's way of thinking or they weren't around for long. Cruz was small in stature, bald and wore thick black-rimmed glasses. He was rat-like in appearance and demeanor. What he lacked in size and looks, he made up for with a fierce intellect, a sharp temper and a prodigious work ethic. Although he was comical looking, you didn't want to mess with Crucut Cruz. He'd take your head off.

A former external auditor, Cruz was now the right-hand man to Shelby McGinnis, the larger-than-life CEO at Yellowstar. McGinnis was obsessed with growth and keeping Yellowstar's stock price high. McGinnis wasn't a details guy when it came to financial statements or cutting costs, but he damn well expected performance and he knew that Cruz delivered results. When Yellowstar's earnings flattened and its stock price sagged a few years earlier, McGinnis brought in Cruz to fix it, exclaiming "you make these damn earnings forecasts, Crucut, and I'll make your ass rich!" Together they cooked up an aggressive expansion plan that relied on acquisitions to rapidly grow Yellowstar and boost earnings. The acquisitions were initially scouted out by McGinnis, who left the accounting, integration and other details to Cruz, who never let him down. For his part, Cruz had learned how to squeeze every last bit of earnings from the acquired companies. He cut costs like crazy, earning him that infamous nickname, and he pushed to maximize revenues. But he also implemented some new and creative accounting techniques that made all the difference for Yellowstar.

Hostile Takeovers

Shelby McGinnis was a mover and a shaker. He was tall and gangly, but physically imposing. He wore cowboy boots with his suits, was clean cut with wavy dark brown hair and had a deep, demanding voice. He grew up in Shaker Heights, Ohio, just outside of Cleveland where Yellowstar was based. Shelby spent most of his childhood trying to please his father, the founder of Yellowstar. But he never quite accomplished that objective. After toiling away in various mundane departments of Yellowstar for the first 15 years of his career, Shelby finally moved into an executive role working directly for his father. And then after the old man's untimely demise, Shelby took over as the CEO. He immediately wanted to grow the company bigger, better and more profitable than his father had ever dreamed. He really didn't care how he got there. McGinnis was obsessed with beating his old man and showing the "pretty boys" and "crackheads" on Wall Street, as he often called them, that a good old boy from Ohio could be wildly successful in corporate America.

Shortly after becoming CEO, McGinnis took Yellowstar public and embarked on his crusade to expand the firm. But he found out in short order that Wall Street brutally punished those who did not meet earnings expectations. After some up and down quarters and a very volatile stock price in his first few years of running the company, McGinnis searched for a way to expand more rapidly while also delivering the steady earnings growth that Wall Street craved. McGinnis called the stock analysts "those crack heads on Wall Street" because they were addicted to earnings growth. Of course McGinnis had his own addictions and selfish reasons for pleasing Wall Street — he was Yellowstar's biggest individual shareholder and he stood to make a fortune if he could keep driving up the stock price.

McGinnis pushed his first CFO, Jane Simmons, to make acquisitions and squeeze out more profits. But Jane was old school. She'd worked for Shelby's father for several years and preferred his slow and steady hand to Shelby's volatile demeanor and demands for growth. During a meeting with the outside auditors one day, when McGinnis was bellowing for more earnings, saying "come on Jane, get your ass in gear and close more damn deals." Simmons responded by telling him they just couldn't do any more. That's when an outside auditor named Maxwell Cruz made his first big impression on McGinnis. Cruz approached McGinnis after the meeting and described a strategy to acquire more aggressively and squeeze out more profits. Cruz said he could make this happen if McGinnis made him CFO. And that was all Shelby McGinnis needed to hear. Simmons was fired the very next day and Crucut Cruz took over as the new CFO. More important, Cruz became the point person for heading up and integrating all new acquisitions at Yellowstar.

Acquisitions, Whistleblowers and Qui Tams

Five years later, McGinnis and Yellowstar were on a roll. Wall Street was praising McGinnis for delivering results, which he thoroughly enjoyed, and the stock was soaring. Cruz, meanwhile, had become the full-fledged puppet master. Both men were sitting on a pile of money generated from their Yellowstar stock holdings. Crucut had been leading the charge on all new acquisitions and he had helped McGinnis grow the company exponentially. In each new acquisition, Cruz led a team of accountants and auditors from his old accounting firm in performing surgery on the books of the acquired companies and heading up the integrations. They cut costs savagely. They also changed the way the accounting was handled at the acquired firms in some creative ways. Sure, they got some resistance along the way, but as Cruz reasoned and McGinnis supported, these people worked for him and they better damn well do as he directed. And one way or another, they usually did.

Then something troubling happened. A whistleblower emerged from one of Yellowstar's acquired subsidiaries that was engaged in government work. There were the usual allegations of overbilling to the government, which was the main focus of the qui tam lawsuit, but there were also allegations of improper acquisition accounting at Yellowstar. Shortly thereafter, the press got a hold of this information and began to peel back the onion on the firm's questionable accounting practices. In fact, Jane Simmons, Yellowstar's former CFO, was quoted in one of the articles, which pissed off McGinnis to no end. From there, things started to unravel quickly. As questions were raised in the press about manufactured earnings through improper accounting, Yellowstar's stock price got hammered. Now the precious commodity that Yellowstar relied on for buying companies was devalued and their acquisition pace began to slow. As acquisitions slowed, earnings declined for the first time in 20 consecutive quarters, and the stock fell even further. The game was unraveling. The house of cards was crumbling. And Shelby McGinnis was hitting the roof. "Crucut, you freaking idiot, how in the hell could you let this happen?" He screamed at Cruz in their weekly Monday morning meeting.

A National Investigation

It was August in New York and things were a little slow as they sometimes are during the dog days of summer. I was looking for the next big case to jump into and keep my staff busy. The weather was a little cooler than normal and I was really enjoying it. I left work early for a meeting and I was driving down the highway — windows down, music up. That's when I felt the familiar vibration of my BlackBerry and saw that one of my clients, Toby Sid from a major law firm, was calling. After rolling the windows up and turning the music down I eagerly took Toby's call. He was a good client, with serious cases, so I always wanted to speak with him.

Toby was a no-nonsense, hard-nosed former prosecutor and he got straight to the point of his call. He explained that his firm was representing investors in a case against Yellowstar. The lawsuit specifically alleged that improper acquisition accounting had been employed to boost earnings and artificially inflate the stock price. When news of the scheme started to leak, the stock price declined and the investors Toby represented got clobbered. Toby wanted my firm to investigate the accounting for multiple acquisitions that Yellowstar had engaged in. I remember thinking, "Hot damn, here's that next big case I've been looking for." Toby and I set up a time to chat with cocounsel the next day and put together a game plan for the investigation.

From the start, we suspected that the accounting for the acquisitions might involve various financial statement fraud schemes, principally premature recognition of expenses, delays in revenue recognition and re-serve/inventory manipulation. These schemes, it was believed, were employed by Yellowstar to cook the books of the acquired company during the acquisition period, making them look unprofitable. Then, after the acquisition was completed, the same entries would be reversed in order to *spring load* (improve) the financial results of Yellowstar in the consolidated financial statements.

The investigation initially included financial statement analysis and docu-ment reviews, but extensive interviews and in-person meetings with witnesses became our primary focus as the case progressed. We were hoping to flesh out details with witnesses as to how the schemes worked, who was calling the shots and how high up the chain of command the fraud extended. We de-cided to first focus on the highest-dollar, U.S.-based acquisitions where some initial evidence already existed regarding the spring-loading allegations. After a review of the financial statements and documents that had been obtained, we developed a top-20 list for interviews. On this list were Jenkins Manufacturing in Lubbock, Texas, and Hope Electronics in Annapolis, Maryland.

We then embarked on a process of identifying and interviewing witnesses from these 20 companies to develop details on the suspected scheme. Given the number of witnesses and their widespread geographic distribution, we began with phone interviews to identify the best witnesses for later, more in-depth, in-person interviews. We hit pay dirt with a number of witnesses in short order and deployed investigative teams to various parts of the country to interview them in person and obtain signed statements where possible.

When I got off the plane in Lubbock, I was as hot as I've ever been. I was sweating profusely, my shirt was sticking to my back and the sun was beating down intensely. I'd never been to Lubbock and didn't know much about it. I seemed to recall that a guy I knew years ago went to Texas Tech, which I thought was located in Lubbock. We called him "Tex." Not a very creative nickname in hindsight, but I remember that Tex was always bitching about the heat in Lubbock. With that pleasant memory seared into my brain, I walked into the airport terminal to meet up with one of the attorneys on the case, thinking "this is going to be a lot of fun, that is, if I don't die of heatstroke first."

The attorney I was meeting had come along for the interview of Papa Thomas, formerly the warehouse manager for Jenkins Manufacturing. Since Papa was a warehouse guy, I dressed down a bit — I didn't want to look like a "suit" from the East Coast coming into Lubbock to interrogate him. I'd learned long ago that the most important initial step in any infor-mation-gathering interview is to make a good first impression and a solid connection with the witness, which helps build rapport. Unfortunately for the attorney along for the interview, he didn't have the same approach.

He was wearing a dark wool suit and looked like he was heading to the courtroom. I remember laughing to myself and thinking, "if I'm hot, this guy must really be burning up."

Despite our difference in appearance, we made a nice team. We met Papa at Wild Bill's Fried Chicken House in Idalou, Texas, where he lived, just northeast of Lubbock, off highway 82. Wild Bill's was Papa's choice, not ours; it was a destination of his choosing so he'd be comfortable in familiar surroundings. On a side note, that was some of the best damn fried chicken I've ever had.

We started the interview and Papa walked us back through the information he provided in his initial interview. He described how Crucut Cruz and his minions had dictated various inventory write-offs that seemed nonsensical. "It didn't make a damn lick of sense to me at the time," he explained, "but I figured those new cats from Yellowstar are calling the shots now, so I better do what they say." But when Yellowstar's accountants later reversed those same write-offs, after the financial statements were fully consolidated, Papa was livid and wanted some answers. "At that point, I just figured they were either dipshits or couldn't make up their damn minds. I never figured it was part of a grand plan . . . that is, till I started poking around some more," said Papa.

After Papa started asking some questions, one of the accountants at Jenkins told him exactly what was going on — by reversing the inventory write-off, Yellowstar was making their income statement look better in the current quarter. The Jenkins' accountant told Papa that it was all just a big earnings game and that was how Crucut Cruz wanted it done. He also shared with Papa that he heard through the grapevine that Yellowstar did this sort of thing with all of their acquisitions. That's when it really dawned on Papa that Cruz was cooking the books. He explained, "I thought, holy shit, these guys aren't dipshits, they're crooks." Papa stuck around for a few months to get his severance, and then he "got the hell out of Dodge." He told us he hadn't thought about the inventory issue again until we called him a few weeks earlier asking about accounting abnormalities at Yellowstar. Papa said it felt good to get this information off his chest. He also wasn't too sad to see "Yellowstar and that idiot Crucut Cruz get what was coming to them." Papa didn't like being a puppet.

A few weeks later I found myself sitting in a Denny's in Highland Beach, Maryland, just south of Annapolis. The Grand Slam breakfast was good, but I couldn't wait to move on to some good old Maryland crab cakes later in the day. Over eggs and bacon, Karen Jillwater described the details of her experiences at Hope Electronics — both before and after the company was acquired by Yellowstar Industries. It was clear from our conversation that Karen, who insisted we call her "Jill," was a top-notch accountant. She really knew her stuff. Before working at Hope, Jill was a Big Four accountant, so she'd been an external auditor and she knew what the auditors should be doing. Jill was a reluctant interviewee. She had moved on in her life and had three young children; she didn't really want to get mixed up in the litigation against Yellowstar. But she was also appalled by what she saw at Yellowstar and it was important for her to set the record straight. "I knew something wasn't right with what Cruz and those Yellowstar accountants were telling me to do," she said.

After some encouragement, Jill described in detail a number of entries that Yellowstar and its external auditors (Crucut's old firm) pushed through at Hope during the acquisition period. In addition to holding back on revenue recognition when shipments were already made, Jill said that Crucut and his team prepaid a number of expenses and ran them right through the current period's income statement. She thought this was crazy at the time, explaining, "When I went to Cruz and told him those expenses should be booked as a prepaid asset, not a current period expense, he told me to shut the hell up and do as I was told. What a nasty man he was." But when she saw how good the financial statements looked after the acquisition, it dawned on her what the method to Cruz's madness was. Post consolidation, the revenue figures were up (because the revenue held back on shipments was now recorded) and the expense figures were down (because many expenses had been prepaid and recognized), so the earnings figures for Yellowstar were fantastic.

We heard countless stories like Papa's and Jill's from other witnesses across the country, which really helped build the case. What Jill, Papa and the others didn't realize at the time was that there was a much larger financial statement fraud being perpetrated by Yellowstar. Once McGinnis and Cruz came to terms with all of the acquired companies, they quickly took over the accounting and starting cooking the books in every acquisition. They'd been doing this for years, in hundreds of acquisitions, and they knew just how to go about it. But it was only a matter of time until the truth came to light.

The Final Cut

Our investigation in this case consisted of a number of steps, including document reviews, financial statement analysis, as well as extensive research and, most important, detailed interviews of witnesses across the country. Overall we identified and interviewed several key witnesses who provided detailed information and documents supporting the spring-loading allegations in several acquisitions. In-person meetings were accomplished with a number of the interviewees and we obtained signed statements from the most significant witnesses, which proved invaluable to the case.

The litigation carried on for quite some time, but ultimately the witness statements were crucial in establishing that financial statement fraud had in fact taken place. Our interviews also helped Toby Sid in negotiating a settlement for Yellowstar's investors. More than $1 billion in damages was ultimately awarded in the resolution of the investor suit. Meanwhile Shelby McGinnis and Crucut Cruz were unceremoniously dumped from the company and began fending off SEC and DOJ probes into their actions at Yellowstar. Ultimately both were convicted of fraud and served prison time for their actions.

Lessons Learned

Proper Incentives

I'm a firm believer that incentives are a great motivator for executives, but it's important to structure incentives in a way in which they don't incent the wrong behavior. For the most part, executives will do what they're incented to do and what's in their own best interest, often times at the expense of the company and the shareholders. It was clear in this case that McGinnis and Cruz were driven exclusively by short-term earnings growth, at any cost, to drive Yellowstar's stock price higher because they were heavily compensated through stock options versus other compensation metrics. Stock options are great, but they shouldn't be the only measure of performance. Stock rewards have to be offset with other long-term bonus incentives and must include claw-back provisions that allow the company to recover damages in the case of criminal activity, earnings restatements or other improper actions.

Co-Opting of Auditors

This fraud was made possible, in part, because the internal and external auditors, who were supposed to serve as the gatekeepers, were actually co-opted by crooked company executives. Cruz knew that he didn't need to deceive the internal and external auditors; rather, he just needed to get them onboard with his scheme. So he gave them a powerful incentive to do what he wanted. For the internal auditors, that incentive was large stock option awards. The internal auditors wanted the stock to keep going up as much as McGinnis and Cruz did so they would be rewarded through the increase in Yellowstar's stock price. As for the external auditors, McGinnis and Cruz's strategy didn't raise any red flags with them because Yellowstar's prodigious acquisitions created a huge amount of work for the external audit firm. Additionally, Cruz was previously employed by the same firm doing Yellowstar's audits, so he knew which partners to employ and what buttons to push. The external

(continued)

auditors knew where their bread was buttered so they went along with the scheme.

Collusion and Control Frauds

When senior management is in collusion with internal and external auditors, it's known as a *control fraud.* Control frauds are huge in their scope and magnitude, because there is little to stand in the way of the scheme given collusion at high levels. Thank goodness for whistle-blowers and in this case for the qui tam lawsuit that brought the accounting issues to light. Had that not happened, this control fraud could have gone on much longer and been even bigger than it was.

Recommendations to Prevent Future Occurrences

Whistleblowers must be encouraged. As I've seen in numerous other frauds, the most effective detective and investigative tool is an insider who blows the whistle. Without an insider filing the qui tam lawsuit against Yellowstar, this financial statement fraud likely would have gone on longer and been larger in scope. The witnesses we spoke with in the case also illustrate the value of a witness or whistleblower in any fraud investigation — they will often provide the details and leads that you won't find anywhere else in your case. Recently there have been some increased protections and encouragements for whistleblowers, which is terrific and long overdue. Companies should also encourage whistleblowers internally, which they can do through anonymous fraud hotlines, another powerful deterrent and fraud detection tool. Witness interviews should always be pursued as part of any serious fraud investigation.

Incentives must be well thought out and properly structured. Incentives must take long-term performance and company value into account as opposed to simply rewarding short-term targets such as stock price, revenue and earnings. Additionally, there should be downside risk for executives who cook the books or drive companies into financial ruin as a result of poor decision making. As we've seen in the recent financial crisis, too many executives take excessive risks because there is no downside risk to them personally. If they bet big and win, they reap enormous compensation, but if they bet big and lose, they keep their salaries and live to fight another day. Even if they're chased out of the company, they often receive substantial golden parachutes. Through
(continued)

(*continued*)

claw-backs and other mechanisms, executives have to be accountable and compensated based on long-term performance — both good and bad. McGinnis and Cruz ultimately paid the price through their criminal convictions, but criminal cases against corporate officers don't happen nearly enough.

Pay attention to red flags. Auditors, investors, shareholders and other parties relying on corporate financial statements have to pay more vigilant attention to red flags. Too often these parties are happy to "go along for the ride" when a company is putting up spectacular numbers. We all need to be more skeptical, ask the tough questions, pay attention and investigate any apparent red flags more aggressively.

About the Author

Jay Dawdy, CFE, CMA, is the president of Gryphon Investigations. He has more than 20 years of finance, accounting and investigative experience and concentrates on complex financial, litigation support, due diligence and fraud investigative cases. Jay served as an instructor in investigating financial fraud at Baruch College and presents and writes frequently on fraud investigation and prevention.

CHAPTER 13

A Tale of Two Books

JOHN BEARD

It was shortly before lunch time in late January when the phone rang. I answered and it was the boss, Steve. "Can you check to see if we have any bank accounts with Peach Bank in New York?" he asked. "Sure," I said. "When do you need the information?" "ASAP," he answered. I took the elevator up two floors to the Treasury Department and spotted Frank, the lanky assistant treasurer from West Texas who was responsible for all bank accounts for the company. "Frank, do you have a minute to look up something for me?" I asked. Frank said that he had a lunch appointment but the lookup wouldn't take long. "Do we have an account with a New York bank called Peach?" I asked. He pulled out this three-ring binder and turned to the first tab, the table of contents. "If we do it will be right here. We only have about 223 bank accounts. You said Peach, right?" Frank asked. "That's right." Frank scanned down the table of contents and said, "Well, I don't see one here, but maybe it's an old account that's been closed. Let me check that binder." He pulled down a red binder similarly organized and scanned the table of contents there as well. "Nope, I can't seem to find it here either," he said. "Maybe you should check with accounting. You know, with the merger and all, maybe everything hasn't gotten sorted out and sent to me yet. Let me know what you find out." So off I went to the 35th floor where the Accounting Department was located.

I was hoping that Charles, the manager of general ledger accounting, hadn't gone to lunch yet. I was in luck; Charles was just leaving his office when I stopped him. "Hey, Charles, you got a minute to check something for me?" "Sure," he said, and I repeated my request. Charles pulled out his copy of the current assets subledger detail and began to scan. "Do you know which business unit the account is supposed to be for?" he asked. I said that I was told it was for the New York trading group we gained as a result of the merger. Charles continued scanning; ten minutes went by. I was getting that sinking feeling in my stomach that we would come up empty. And we did. Charles said, "I don't see anything that even comes close." I told him Frank in Treasury also came up empty handed. I thanked him and prepared to break the bad news to the boss. Back down the stairs I went.

"Steve, I have some information on that Peach Bank account for you," I said. "Neither Frank nor Charles could find any record of our having that account on the company's books. Do you have any other information about the account that I could use to check it out?" Steve said he had the mailing address and the names of the signers on the account, if that would be helpful. "It sure would," I said. "I could check with Fred, the auditor we picked up in the merger who was responsible for auditing that operation. Fred now reports to me." Armed with the new information, I went to Fred's office and closed the door.

"Fred, I sure hope that you can help me with this situation." I said. "Do you know the address 704 South Tarrytown Road?" Fred said without hesitation "I do, that's Tim Morrison's house in White Plains." "Are you sure?" I asked. "Absolutely, I've had dinner there many times over the years, nice place but Tim has lots of cats. Why do you ask?" "Oh I was just asked to check out this address. It showed up on some documents that Steve had. Thanks again," I said in leaving. It was looking funny to me, but it wasn't my call. I went back to Steve's office with the news that the bank statement had the business unit's controller's home address on it. Strange! And so the mystery started to take on a life. I was wondering what other oddities we were going to find while searching for the truth.

After I told Steve that the company had no record of the Peach Bank account but Tim's home address was associated with it, he immediately notified Gary, the general counsel. Gary instructed Steve to conduct an investigation under his direction. Steve then called Peach Bank to request copies of all the transaction activity from inception to date and arranged for us to travel to New York to meet with bank officials. We were set for a Monday departure.

The Investigation Takes Off

There was a lot of discussion on the flight about why this particular account would be set up — and with Leon, the president, and Tim, the controller, as the signers. Steve was convinced that there had to be a sound business reason, and I was hopeful for the same. Unknown to us, Gary had requested that the trading division's management be prepared to discuss and defend the establishment of the bank account. A meeting was scheduled for Thursday of the week we were in New York. This was made known to us when we arrived at Peach Bank on Monday; there was a message for Steve from Gary waiting for us. After introductions, Vince, a VP with Peach, handed Steve the records and offered to walk us through them. Vince had gathered all the records related to the bank account's opening, including copies of the resolution and signature cards. Sure enough, the account was opened by Tim Morrison, Treasurer of International Trading (IT), and the authorized signatories included Tim and Leon Breaux, President of IT. Steve asked Vince, "What prompted you to call the company about this account? All of the paperwork appears to be in order." Vince replied, "We're a fairly small retail bank and, as you can see from the bank statements, our statements are not set up to handle transactions larger than $1 million. Also, we thought that it was strange to have overseas wire transfers in and out that exceed these amounts. We were looking at this as money laundering, hence the call." Steve thanked Vince. We then called Gary and told him that we had the records and would start scrutinizing them. Gary told Steve to go out to International Trading's offices and get Tim and Leon's reason for the account, but not to let them know what records we had. Off we went to White Plains.

Upon arriving at the IT offices, we had a general "get acquainted" meeting with Leon and Tim. Steve was masterful in this meeting, alluding to how inconvenient it was for us to be there, since he had to cancel a ski trip to come, but nonetheless he thought that we could get our work done and be gone the next evening. We just needed to have some time alone with Tim and the records that he had for the account. Leon agreed and we broke to meet with Tim. Steve got right into the subject, asking Tim, "Why was the account set up and why was it not on IT's books?" Tim's reply was not what we expected. He said, "You all know that since the merger, we are the only division that is consistently profitable, right? Management in Houston had requested that we 'manage' our profits in the trading division so that the earnings reported will be smoother. Our business has spikes of highs and lows. Leon and I thought that this would be a good way to do that; we could simply defer some of the activity from one period to another by using this bank account to handle the settlements. In addition, I guess someone dropped the ball in not putting the account on the books. Before the merger, we knew what to do for these things, but since then it's gotten complicated and I guess it was an oversight." Steve said, "Tim, you realize that there are ways to account for the timing of transactions using accruals that could accomplish the same thing without having a bank account?" Tim said, "Steve, I'm the treasurer; we don't have a controller up here, and I was simply doing my best to comply with what Houston wanted to do. Let me assure you that there's nothing going on here!" Steve responded with, "Okay, I understand; it's getting late in the day. Here's a list of items that we would like to review for tomorrow: bank statements and resolution. We'll sit down with you tomorrow morning first thing, to get your input on whatever transactions have been executed. Can you have that for us in the morning?" Tim agreed and we headed back to our hotel for the evening to ponder Tim's explanation. Tomorrow we would dig into his story.

The next morning when Steve and I arrived at the IT offices at 8:30, Tim greeted us looking like he had been there all night long. Steve and I made no reference to his appearance and went to work looking at the stacks of documents he had gathered for us. Steve told me to review the contracts for the "usual stuff" — counterparties, banking instructions and general terms and conditions. Tim had provided examples of contracts with three different counterparties: Eastern Oil, Island Petroleum and Petro Trading. I thought to myself, "I've never heard of any of these companies before." In the library where we were working, I noticed a set of Stalsby's trading directories, collections of known trading partners by commodity. The information is critical for any company seeking partners to trade commodities. I took the volume called *Oil & Gas* and began to look for Eastern, Island and Petro. After a thorough search, I determined that they were not in the Stalsby.

I looked at the banking instructions on the contracts, which were Telex documents, the standard for international trading. I noticed that all three companies used a private bank called Standard Bank in the Channel Islands. Next, I examined the Telex contracts by comparing each to a contract with a known company, one of the major oil companies. I noticed something unusual about the Telex number stamped on the documents for all three companies — it began with a letter prefix *IT* then the number. None of the Telex numbers for the contracts with the majors had this marking. I picked up the telephone, called Telex and asked about the numbering scheme. The person at Telex told me that the letter prefix indicated that the document was sent collect by the sender to the receiver. This was quite odd since it is customary for each party to bear its own administrative costs. My mind was racing now. I had to let Steve know what I was thinking.

I found Steve talking with Leon, poked my head in and said, "Excuse me, Steve, but I need to have a word with you." Steve and I went outside to have a conversation about my findings. I told him, "It looks to me like the counterparties to the trades with Island, Eastern and Petro are bogus because I could not locate any of them in Stalsby, the Telexes were sent collect and they all banked with the same offshore private bank." Steve cautioned me not to jump to any conclusions based upon that information. Leon had been giving him very good business explanations for the transactions. Leon had explained in much more detail what Tim had told us the day before about the account being used to smooth the profits from one period to the next. Steve said he was going to call our external auditors to see if they could come up with the identity of the counterparties. In the meantime, Steve contacted Gary, our general counsel, to tell him what we had found. Gary instructed Steve to secure our records and return to Houston for a meeting with top management. The meeting was scheduled for Monday in the office of the chairman, Ned; Leon and Tim were to present their case.

On our way back to our offices, Steve and I talked about what our next steps in the investigation would be. We both agreed that if our suspicions were true — that Tim and Leon created fictitious trading partners to conduct off-book transactions using an unauthorized bank account — we had a pure form of fraud on our hands. However, we didn't know the real reason behind IT's charade. Steve told me that Gary had called in the external auditors to be ready to conduct a deeper investigation. They had many clients in the same business and could access "unofficial" information through their firm. This was important because Ned didn't want the market to know that we might have a problem.

Full Disclosure?

Monday arrived and the meeting began. Leon explained that the Peach Bank account was set up to help IT manage its profits from period to period for the benefit of the company and nothing else. Leon went on to say that there had been a lot of confusion since the merger regarding the proper protocols for adding not only bank accounts but also new customers, trading partners and general ledger accounts. He further stated that everyone knew that Tim was not an accountant but a banker type who was invaluable as treasurer of the organization. With that, Leon turned the meeting over to Tim. Tim started in with a presentation on the banking information in detail, transaction by transaction. Steve noticed that Tim had omitted some transactions; he was not aware that we had *all* of the banking information straight from Peach Bank. Steve abruptly interrupted Tim's explanation to ask, "What about the checks made payable to certain individuals, including you?" Tim, obviously caught off guard, said, "I didn't want to divert attention or confuse anyone from the real purpose of the account. We did use it on a couple of occasions to handle some personnel matters."

It was time for a break. Steve approached Ned and Gary and said, "Can you believe that these guys doctored the documents for their presentation that was supposed to be a full explanation? They should be fired on the spot." Gary said that the company would take that into consideration in deciding how to move forward. Gary told Steve that the external auditors were going to do an in-depth investigation into the matter and that internal audit would not be involved after the meeting concluded. Gary left to have a discussion with Ned regarding what process changes needed to be made in addition to any personnel changes that would be prudent. I found out later that Ned told Gary, "You know that profits have been hard to come by since the merger. We all made promises to 'the street' regarding how the combined companies would be more dynamic than the two companies managed separately. Leon and his team are the *only* group that has delivered on what we told the investors."

After the break, Ned spoke to the group. "You all know that the combined companies haven't delivered the profits that we had expected, except for Leon and his people. There is no way I can pull the plug on the only part of the new business that is delivering as promised. What I will do is beef up the controls over the treasury function at IT. We will also be watching everyone in the IT group closely over the months to come. You are instructed to cease being creative when it comes to the accounts." The meeting was then adjourned.

Ned called Steve aside after the meeting and told him that our group was going to be replaced with a group of external auditors. "Steve," Ned said. "I believe that Gary has indicated to you our preferred strategy for getting to the bottom of this. The firm can keep the lid on the investigation. We don't want to unnecessarily alarm the markets." Steve acknowledged the order by saying, "I understand perfectly." He told me as we were leaving that he couldn't believe Ned was making this call. Internal audit would have to be a good company citizen until called upon again.

Four months had passed since the meeting when Leon made an unannounced trip to Houston to meet with Ned. After a brief exchange of pleasantries, Leon told Ned that IT was in trouble. "We exceeded our trading authority and ended up on the wrong side of the market. The entire equity of the company is at stake." Ned was in shock — he seemed to think his admonishment regarding IT's creative accounting four months ago should have solved the company's financial troubles. He immediately called Mickey Capel, the head of products trading, into his office. Mickey was a long-time trusted colleague of Ned's. Since the initial discovery of the Peach Bank account, Mickey had been cautioning Ned and other senior managers about the riskiness of having this type of trading activity occur without extensive controls in place. Leon explained the situation to Mickey, and Ned asked him to go to White Plans in the hopes of salvaging the company.

Too Little Too Late

Once he arrived in White Plains, Mickey began his investigation by changing the locks in a supposed attempt to secure the office. He then started interviewing staff, beginning with Tim, which proved to be quite revealing. Mickey told Tim that he knew Tim had to have a second set of books to keep up with all of the off-book trades that were being backed by IT. Tim said, "How do you know that?" Mickey responded, "We've had to fund nearly $90 million in margin calls this week. I know something wild is going on here. You're betting the farm on a significant price drop, but the market is going up. That's how I know. It would be in your best interest to come clean and to show me now." Tim told Mickey that he had the records at his house, so they went to retrieve them together.

Armed with the trade details, Mickey was able to set up additional trading positions to reduce the potential exposure and resulting losses. The trick was to do it without alarming the market, so Mickey set about his business with trusted legitimate trading partners. Over the course of the next four days, Mickey made trades to mitigate the damages — IT had been in danger of losing $1 billion, but Mickey's trades reduced the losses to $180 million.

One year after we received the first call from Peach Bank, IT's external auditors conducted an investigation that was eventually referred to the Department of Justice. Leon and Tim were both fired and they pleaded guilty to filing false government documents and conspiracy to defraud. Leon was sentenced to one year in prison. Tim received a suspended sentence. Leon was fined $5 million and Tim $250,000. The investigation revealed exactly what we at internal audit suspected a year earlier — the transactions through Peach Bank were shams. However, we discovered they were executed not primarily to manipulate profits (which they did), but to manage earnings to increase the employee bonus pool. Employees were incentivized with a formula that included revenue; the sham trades with the fictional oil and gas companies increased revenues and the resulting bonus pools.

As a result of these fictitious revenues, IT had to restate its earnings for three years and file amended income tax returns as well. IT also had to revise the financial statements to show the real and legitimate losses of nearly $180 million that resulted from Mickey's countertrades. Mickey's swift action allowed the company to lose only $180 million instead of the $1 billion loss it was facing.

The office in White Plains was closed and most of the staff members were terminated. As a result of the investigation, we learned that nearly everyone in the office had played some part in the deception — not surprising given that the main motivation was to increase employee bonuses. The other employees in the office who participated in the scheme to earn their bonuses were ordered to pay restitution as well.

Lesson Learned

The essential lesson I learned from this case is that senior management should pay attention to red flags when they arise and thoroughly investigate them. After the case was resolved, various staff members told me that they had suspected monkey business in White Plains but chalked it up to adjustments resulting from the merger.

Recommendations to Prevent Future Occurrences

Because of the inherent risk associated with trading operations, certain basic controls and functions should be in place to deter fraud, such as the following:

- Create an independent control or oversight function that reports directly to the audit committee of the board of directors. Such a hierarchy helps maintain the control's independence.
- Impose strict trading controls and limits on individual traders and the business group as a whole. These limits should be monitored by the independent control function and violators should be dealt with surely and swiftly.
- Establish a policy of job rotation to prevent key personnel, such as the treasurer or controller, from circumventing controls to commit fraud.
- Conduct independent and thorough background checks on employees with approval or commitment authority. Had a comprehensive background check been done on Leon, we would have found out that he had had a similar problem at a previous employer.
- Enforce a policy stating that employees who perpetrate fraud against the company will be prosecuted to the fullest extent of the law.

I have to wonder whether the outcome of this case would have been different if IT had a robust corporate culture supported by a tone at the top that told its employees it was okay to contact people outside their direct reporting chain if they suspected wrongdoing. However, I can only look back at what happened in the absence of such a culture.

About the Author

John C. Beard, CFE, CPA, has nearly 40 years of experience in internal auditing and corporate investigations in the energy sector. He is a graduate of Louisiana State University, has been a member of the Advisory Board to the Center for Internal Auditing at LSU for over 30 years and makes frequent talks to the students regarding real business experiences. John has been a member of the AFCE since 1993.

The Family Man Behind Bars

ANTONIO IVAN AGUIRRE

Eddie Bentz was a senior bookkeeper in the Accounting Department of Nasdall Bank's West Coast Central branch. He prided himself on being a self-made man who earned his college degree through hard work and diligent study. He came from a poor family in a rural Midwest area and he strived to finish his education by working part-time at a fast-food restaurant. He was determined to earn his degree because he knew it was his passport to success. His work ethic was incomparable and earned the approval of his supervisors — he became the role model for what a Nasdall Bank employee should be. His knack for understanding the accounting and clearing operations of the bank earned him the trust and confidence of his immediate supervisors, accounting personnel and bank tellers.

Remembering the difficult times he experienced in his youth, Eddie vowed that he would never go back to a life of poverty and pushed himself to the limit by working almost 12 hours a day. He mastered the accounting entries in the branch's operations, including the intricacies of check clearing and settlements. As a result, the branch accountant entrusted him with the task of posting journal entries in the daily financial statement — which was known as the daily statement of condition — without reviewing the accuracy of the entries.

Eddie's life after work was simple — almost dull — and without any telltale sign of high-finance living. He had a good reputation and those who knew him praised him for sending hard-earned money to his siblings for their education. He stood almost blameless in the public eye, and no one seemed to realize that Eddie's habit of helping his family and providing money for his siblings' educations had become too expensive for him to maintain.

For Eddie, bookkeeping was routine work that lacked challenge. However, consolidating the entries to prepare the daily statement of condition ignited Eddie's curiosity. The branch accountant seemed to think it was foolproof, so Eddie decided to test the system and see how he could manipulate the entries. At first it was just a game for him but he quickly spotted a weakness in the system — in the branch's income and sundry debits accounts. The sundry debit was being used to temporarily post nominal charges and expenses, which were reversed the following day in a real account. Considering the small amount of charges these transactions involved, nobody took notice except Eddie — who would do just about anything to help his family back home.

Nasdall Bank had been engaged in commercial banking for more than 50 years and was highly reputed, particularly in the Midwest, for its efficient service and trustworthy employees. Furthermore, Nasdall emphasized a hands-on management style and invested sizeable sums of money for technological development. It had 900 branches and employed 12,000 people.

Eddie Bentz came out squeaky clean during Nasdall's routine, prehiring reference check. He had a decent academic record and his work ethic was praised by previous employers. However, his dedication to his family developed a dark side that went undetected for several years.

An Anonymous Caller

As the head of the Special Audit Department of Nasdall Bank, I conducted a regular investigation of the bank's fraud cases and red flags. In my more-than-a-decade tenure with Nasdall, most of the cases involved petty and white-collar crimes with fairly small losses. However, I was about to uncover a case seven years after it began affecting the bank's financial statement that was serious enough to prompt us to revamp the entire Accounting Department.

The case was brought to my attention by an anonymous caller who informed me that the recording of charges on cleared checks at the West Coast Central branch looked suspicious. The caller did not provide details except to say that the charges looked manipulated and income had been posted without supporting documents. He suspected people in accounting were engaged in unsound financial practice.

Too Much Trust

I discussed the call with my special audit staff and we reviewed the branch's daily statement of condition. Indeed, we saw income coming from charges on checks that were not reflected in the books and various entries in the sundry debit account with no corresponding transactions. I decided to accompany an investigation team to West Coast Central to investigate the anonymous caller's claim. When we got to the branch, Eddie Bentz suddenly filed an emergency leave request and did not return.

On the day we made our surprise audit, we were able to intercept a check deposit slip for Eddie's savings account. The processing teller had credited Eddie's account without the accompanying check. When we asked the teller about the transaction, she told us that it was a regular practice to accept deposits from Eddie without the actual checks because he assured everyone that the checks were already included in the outward clearing check items.

Eddie Bentz turned out to be an excellent financial statement cook. He was able to spot loopholes in the system that allowed him to siphon income from clearing checks for seven long years. He manipulated various entries in the statement of accounts, clearing proof sheet and tellers' journal, all of which affected the branch's financial statement. We discovered the following modus operandi:

1. Eddie Bentz opened a savings account at Nasdall's West Coast Central branch, which he used to conduct his unscrupulous transactions.
2. He made various check deposits in this savings account and indicated these were drawn from different banks in the West Coast area on each deposit slip.
3. He presented the deposit slip without the corresponding check to a teller for processing.
4. When the teller asked for the supporting checks, he informed them that the checks had already been sent out for clearing and assured them that they were included in a batch of outward clearing checks.
5. Unwittingly, the processing tellers accepted his word and made credit entries to his savings account. The tellers later told us they trusted him because he was a senior staff member of the branch and they thought of him like a big brother.
6. Being in charge of the clearing statements and the daily statement of condition, Eddie Bentz manipulated the corresponding accounting entry on the amount credited by the teller to his savings account.
7. To ensure that the amounts credited in his savings account tallied with the daily statement of condition, he used the following accounting entries:
   • Debiting the income account of the branch
   • Underposting the branch's daily income on service charges or fees
   • Debiting "sundry debit account — others"

Illustration:

Debit:	Income	XXX.XX
	Sundry Debit	XXX.XX
	(nonbooking of service charges)	XXX.XX
Credit:	Savings Account	XXX.XX

Example of entries made in a week for Eddie's account:

| Credit to Savings Account | Contra-Account | | Nonbooking to income |
| | Debit | | |
	Income	Sundry	
$6,000.00	$ 2,000.00		$ 4,000.00
5,000.00	3,800.23		1,199.77
6,000.00	2,400.00	3,000.00	600.00
6,000.00	1,200.00	3,000.00	1,800.00
6,000.00	2,105.00	3,000.00	895.00
6,300.00	1,900.10	2,000.00	2,399.90
6,000.00	1,300.00	2,000.00	2,700.00
9,000.00	2,100.00	3,900.00	3,000.00
50,300.00	$16,805.33	$16,900.00	$16,594.67

8. To avoid an audit trail, he altered the amounts posted in the proof sheets for entries under sundry debit, income and savings deposit account.
9. He then withdrew each fictitious check deposited to his account.
10. Eddie's scam went undetected for seven years. During that time, he was able to deposit 1,405 fictitious checks totaling $1.38 million.

Digging up an Audit Trail

My team was able to trace and document Eddie's fraud in its entirety. We submitted our report to our chief legal counsel and coordinated with the police and legal authorities.

Nasdall terminated Eddie as a result of his abstraction of cash through fictitious check deposits to his savings account while manipulating entries to the branch's income and sundry debit accounts. Eddie was able to beat the accounting system by preparing a financial statement (statement of daily condition) with false and fictitious information. He recorded a false debit against the income account or posted a lesser amount of the branch's daily income on service charges and fees or did not record the service charges at all. As a result, the expense account on the branch's financial statement increased while income decreased due to nonrecording and underrecording. Also, he understated the income account and siphoned the difference to his conduit savings account. Because the maintenance of financial records involved a double-entry system, fraudulent accounting entries affected two categories on the financial statements. In this case the understatement of income and overstatement of expenses resulted in decreased earnings per share, although the amount was not substantial enough for the bank to notice.

Eddie deliberately misrepresented the statement of financial condition through the intentional misstatement of revenue and expense accounts. He was successful because of weak or nonexistent internal controls over recording income and expense accounts. Eddie's supervisor, Timothy Scheer, failed to properly review his posted entries and did not compare or require supporting documents for the entries. Eddie was entirely unhampered by supervision. Furthermore, the person in charge of verifying transactions posted to the statement of financial condition, Brian Ezekwe, failed to conduct the mandatory check of the original documents.

The tellers of the branch, recognizing his seniority and friendliness, allowed Eddie to post deposits he claimed were personal checks. However, there was no physical verification by the tellers that the checks existed. There were around ten tellers who processed such entries during his seven-year scam. We also learned that Eddie and the tellers frequently went to happy hour together after work. They said they never questioned Eddie's integrity because he was so amiable with them.

During the seven years, the branch's financial statements were misrepresented, which created doubt about Nasdall's integrity when the public found out. Nasdall assured its depositors and stakeholders that it was an isolated incident that did not affect the substance of the financial statement presented to the public. Nonetheless, the bank's reputation suffered as a result of Eddie's fraud.

Eddie Bentz was able to amass a total amount of $1.38 million during a seven-year period. Warrants for his arrest were issued with charges of qualified theft through manipulation of the bank's financial statement, but Eddie remained at large for two years. Nasdall coordinated with the police in a nationwide search. Eddie was on the run through various states but eventually surrendered after his family convinced him to face the consequence of his crime. He was recently sentenced to a five-year jail term.

Furthermore, Nasdall Bank suspended and terminated the tellers who processed Eddie's false deposits. The branch accountant, supervising bookkeeper, branch operating officer and branch manager also received severe sanctions, including suspension and even termination.

Eddie was able to manipulate Nasdall's financial statements due to the following contributory negligence and internal control weaknesses:

1. Lack of reconciliation of sundry entries: The branch failed to conduct reviews of income and expense items by comparing the entries against original documents.

2. Ineffective records management: Many supporting documents — such as tellers' journals, clearing statements, deposit slips and debit and credit memos — could not be located or were damaged. My team members worried that missing documents would hinder the investigation and case against Eddie, but we were eventually able to prove connections between transactions that showed how Eddie manipulated the financials.

3. The following were the existing and available documents we used to prove our case:

Documents	Relevance
Check deposits to Eddie's savings account for the past seven years	Used as evidence that Eddie deposited various fictitious checks to his savings account. However, some of the corresponding deposit slips — totaling $160,850 — were not available.
Tellers' journals	Used as evidence in lieu of unavailable check deposits posted/credited to Eddie's account. The total check deposits covered by the retrieved tellers' journals amounted to $30,550.
Withdrawal slips on Eddie's savings account for the past seven years	Used as evidence that Eddie benefited from his crime by withdrawing the amounts deposited to his savings account.
Statements of deposit account for the past seven years	Used as evidence that the said fictitious check deposits were posted/credited to Eddie's savings account and immediately withdrawn for his personal gain.
Clearing proof sheets	Used as evidence of Eddie's manipulation of the bank's income and sundry debit accounts. He disguised his fictitious transactions in the books to prevent detection. However, only a few of these proof sheets were retrieved during the investigation, in the amount of $145,800.
General ledger/subsidiary ledger for the seven-year period	Used as evidence to show that fictitious check deposits credited to Eddie's savings account were reconciled to the income reversal and sundry debit booking.

Accountable Individuals

Eddie Bentz was the sole perpetrator of this crime. However, there were contributory negligent actions that made his fraudulent scheme more successful.

Tellers

Ten bank tellers accepted Eddie's deposits without proper documentation for seven years. They relied on Eddie's assurances that the checks were already included in the outward clearing. The tellers repeatedly stated that they trusted him because he was a long-serving employee and they looked up to him as a big brother. We also learned that Eddie regularly treated the tellers to dinners, happy hours and even a few karaoke sessions. They believed that Eddie was a good person who was just friendly to everyone. However, they failed to realize that they were letting their friendship override the bank policy that required all deposit slips to be physically accompanied by cash and/or checks.

As a result of the investigation, five of the tellers were terminated for cause due to willfully posting deposits to Eddie's account without the accompanying checks. The remaining tellers, who were new to the job, were given a one-month suspension without pay and no promotions for a period of two years. Subsequently, most of them were rotated to other nearby branches. As a result of this management decision, most of them voluntarily resigned.

Assistant Accountant

Brian Ezekwe, the assistant account, also came under fire for his negligence. He failed to perform the mandatory review of daily transactions by comparing the source documents against the entries posted in the statement of financial condition. He did not perform this essential internal control for almost seven years. The bank terminated Brian for cause for gross negligence in the performance of duty and his benefits were forfeited. He made an appeal regarding the forfeiture of benefits but a final decision came from the labor court upholding management's decision.

Supervising Bookkeeper

For failure to review the entries and supporting documents posted in the statement of financial condition, Timothy Scheer, the supervising bookkeeper, faced repercussions. He failed to consistently notice that the suspense entries, income and expense accounts were posted without contra-accounts consistent with the bank's policy on dual entries. The bank terminated his services due to gross negligence in the performance of basic duties.

Branch Operating Officer

Joel Rousso, the branch operating officer, was reprimanded for failure to supervise the tellers under his direct command. He could have identified the nonexistent checks that were credited for deposit to Eddie's account if he properly performed the midday balancing, whereby deposit and withdrawal transactions are compared against the original checks, cash and other clearing items. For failing to properly perform his job duties and oversee his staff, Joel was suspended without pay for three months and required to undergo retraining on the branch operations.

Clearing Clerk

Colin van Dyke, the clearing clerk, did not account for the number of checks actually sent out for clearing by comparing the deposit slips and physical number of checks against the clearing statement. Instead, he entrusted this function to Eddie, who manipulated the number of checks sent for outward clearing. This was repeatedly done in a period of seven years and created a huge internal control weakness on the clearing of outward checks. Colin Van Dyke was suspended for three months without pay, but his sentence was reduced to one month when he acted as one of the vital witnesses for Nasdall.

Branch Manager

The branch manager, Scott Stewart, was responsible in ensuring efficient and effective branch operations and for the general supervision of all activities at the branch. He failed to implement Nasdall's directive on mandatory job rotation as part of the minimum internal control system. As a result, he was suspended for two weeks.

Lesson Learned

Considering the duration of the fraud, my team had a surprising amount of difficulty retrieving the source documents, such as statements of accounts, clearing proof sheets and tellers' journals, to establish an audit trail and evidence. It was a painstaking effort on our part to reconstruct all the accounting entries and link together the manipulated accounts.

My team learned the importance of ensuring the audit trail in all transactions that affect financial statements. It was difficult to prove Eddie's manipulation of the income and sundry accounts mainly due to a lack of direct links to the perpetrator, and the court considered those entries as circumstantial evidence. We underwent difficulty in linking the income against the amount deposited in his savings account.

My investigation team had a challenging mission in retrieving the other relevant source documents because the bank's archived records

(continued)

were a mess. It took time to reconstruct and locate other bank documents that we needed as evidence in the court case. This limitation of supporting evidence compelled us to file only a portion of the amount stolen from the bank. We were able to produce direct evidence of financial statement fraud of around 20 percent of the entire haul taken by Eddie; the rest was circumstantial evidence. Nevertheless, our direct evidence duly supported by original documents gave us a favorable judgment from the criminal court.

As a result of this case, we enhanced our review procedures on income and sundry transactions before posting to the system.

Recommendations to Prevent Future Occurrences

To strengthen internal control over access to and entries on financial statements, we recommended the following:

1. All accounting entries in the daily statements of condition should be supported by original source documents approved by the branch accountant.
2. All checks sent out for clearing should be duly accounted for and compared with the deposit slips. The review procedures on checks for outward clearing should be reiterated regularly to ensure all employees are following them.
3. Review procedures should be performed on all transactions.
4. Employees' code of conduct should be strictly enforced.
5. Job rotation should be practiced regularly.

About the Author

Antonio Ivan S. Aguirre, M.B.A., CFE, CPA, CSI, is a chief resident auditor under the Office of Internal Oversight Services (OIOS), United Nations. He previously worked with the largest bank in the Philippines as the head of special audit and acted on several occasions as an expert witness against numerous white-collar and organized crimes. Tony is also a strong chess player and a martial arts instructor.

Net Capital Requirements

KEVIN G. BREARD

Gertie was someone her contemporaries would have called "a tough old bat." My path crossed hers when she was a septuagenarian bookkeeper with white, thinning hair that resembled a threadbare gym towel. I was an outside CPA auditor in my early 40s.

In her office, next to the comptroller's adding machine, was a flattering college graduation picture of her in a black gown and mortarboard hat, with that cocked head and turn of the shoulders that only looks natural to a photographer. Gertie had graduated with a degree in business administration with an emphasis in accounting — an education unique for her time. Not many women were strolling on college campuses, let alone majoring in a "man's field" like accounting. In those days, if you poked your head into an intermediate accounting class, it would have resembled an Alpha Beta Pi fraternal gathering.

However, Gertie was self-assured and probably knew she was smarter than most of her male counterparts. When she graduated, she entered a world full of suits and quickly established her own work "uniform" of off-white blouses and Montgomery Ward knee-length navy skirts.

Gertie's first job out of college was working for C. W. Surebet Securities. After a few years, she married the owner's son, Clyde II, a World War II Navy veteran. He had seen dark days on the battlefield and in the market. The salty old sea dog was overweight with a badly pock-marked face and a balding head. Over the years, Gertie and Clyde II grew the business and Gertie wore many hats at the firm. She was corporate secretary, office manager and full-charge bookkeeper, somewhat typical of a small firm. Except for a brief stint of leave to raise her baby-boomer son, Clyde III, she devoted her life to the firm.

Surebet Securities

C. W. Surebet Securities was a family-owned broker/dealer in securities. When my firm was hired as the outside auditor, the office was located on

Montgomery Street in San Francisco. Surebet was founded in 1906, the same year of the devastating earthquake and fire, and was known back then as Worthington & Surebet Securities, Inc. The company's cofounder, Richard Worthington, was bought out by Clyde I shortly after the stock market crash of 1929. Richard thought the market would continue to go up; Clyde thought otherwise. To the victor go the spoils.

On Montgomery Street, the broker/dealers lined up next to each other, no different than car dealerships in some parts of the country. It was a high-rent district, the Bay Area's version of Wall Street. Surebet was located in one of those enormous rectangular skyscrapers to which Donald Trump would love to affix his name.

The small broker/dealer in securities had great capacity in the market, trading blue-chip stock and reputable municipal bonds. It was a full-service house with activities including:

- Proprietary trading in the firm's accounts
- Agency trading on behalf of clients' solicited or unsolicited orders
- Clearing trades for the other broker/dealers
- Serving as custodian and safe keeper of customer securities

Ah, but great capacity begets great solvency and liquidity requirements. In the industry, it is known as *net capital* — a calculation that begins with the firm's equity and then generally subtracts nonliquid assets, like furniture and equipment. There can be further subtractions if the firm has any security positions, known in the industry as *haircuts*. Surebet was subject to the highest net capital requirement of a broker/dealer, at least $250,000, and a portion of the annual certified audit was devoted to attesting to the net capital calculation. This was where things got dicey, every year. Surebet was always within net capital by the slightest margin. As outside auditors, if we proposed expensing rather than accruing a roll of postage stamps, it would wreak havoc on net capital.

The 1,200 square feet of office space Surebet occupied were divvied up between a reception area, two offices and a kitchen. Posh exteriors met impoverished office surroundings once you crossed the threshold. Although Surebet had once been a thriving firm, the staff had dwindled during the past decade. The office walls were stark white, and a splash of color would have gone a long way. The small, desolate lobby reminded me of a doctor's office because there were plenty of outdated magazines on the coffee table and the seating had seen better days. The waiting room sofa was concaved from years of use. I had the feeling that other than the nightly cleaning crew, not many outsiders crossed through the doorway.

The company's bookkeeping was not computerized; Gertie kept the books manually in handwritten, oversize, canary-yellow ledgers bound by black pressboard covers. Silver pegs with screw tops held them together.

I expected a green visor and constant late nights to be part of the package. In her mind, if it was good enough when Gertie graduated college a half a century earlier, it was good enough today.

The Securities and Exchange Commission (SEC) and the Financial Industry Regulatory Authority (FINRA) require broker/dealers in securities to be audited annually by an outside, independent CPA firm. Although the SEC usually focuses on publicly held companies, broker/dealers are one of the few exceptions. I was the managing partner of a CPA firm that concentrated on the securities industry, and Surebet engaged us for the annual audit.

Audits of broker/dealers in securities were physically due to the regulators 60 days after year-end, and requesting an extension was not an easy or automatic process. If an extension was approved and granted, it was only valid for 30 calendar days. Despite the difficulties involved, I decided to request an extension for my audit of Surebet that year because I felt I never had adequate access to Gertie's supporting documentation. I vowed that this year would be different.

The DITs Were MIA

Usually, we didn't have an opportunity to review the January bank statement; after all, it arrived in the mail in the middle of February and the audit was due at the end of the month (this was before online banking was popular). But that year we requested additional time and we were able to examine the January bank statement. I immediately saw that more than $100,000 of the deposits in transit (DITs) listed on the December 31 bank reconciliation had not cleared the bank until January 31. That was an awfully long time for deposits to clear. I wondered what the deposits were for, and I made a note to speak with Gertie regarding why the DITs were MIA for a month.

Officer Loan Account

What I knew and what I didn't know were equally disturbing, so I decided to make an office visit immediately. When I arrived at the grandiose building, I barely had to touch the well-polished revolving door for it to spin counterclockwise to admit me. After walking into the plush lobby, I was met with a bank of elevators. A security guard, who seemed to want to know too much about my visit, escorted me to the proper elevator. It was like a cross between being a VIP and a suspected felon.

Once I began working with Gertie, I realized she was doing her best to impede our progress. My team and I had prepared a list of items we needed for the audit — our document request list (DR list). Gertie was glacially slow or she stonewalled us over each item on our list. She often became contentious, barking at us, "Why do you need this?" or, "I gave that to you last year; why do you need it again?"

She had a frosty personality and I dreaded talking to her. In Gertie's mind, the audit was a pain and it was to be shared equally among client and auditor. From the beginning of the day to the end, Gertie always seemed to be in a foul mood. Her pack-a-day smoking habit completed the effect by giving her a raspy, intimidating voice. "What do you want?" she croaked one day as I knocked on her office door.

"I have questions about some of your journal entries and cash receipt entries."

"Which entries? Didn't I already answer your questions?"

"These entries," I said meekly. "Why did you reclassify meal and entertainment expenses to the officer loan account? And why would you offset an increase in equity against the officer loan account? Where is the backup for these cash receipts that are hitting the officer loan account?"

Gertie acted as if nothing were unusual, which made me suspicious and prompted me and my team to request all her books for the past three years.

Gertie's Recipe

When the books arrived, we rolled up our sleeves and began the investigation.

The first things I looked into were the cash receipt transactions from December that hadn't cleared the bank until the end of January. These cash receipts had been posted against the officer loan account, which would normally indicate that the officer had paid back funds that he owed to the company. But there were no copies of the checks for me to use to determine that this had happened.

Because it was very unusual for checks to take more than a few days to clear the bank, I requested copies of the checks in question from the bank for further investigation. It turned out that the supposed deposits in transit were dated January 30. The December deposits in transit were bogus cash receipt transactions Gertie had created and offset against the officer loan account. I figured that Gertie had created these phony transactions to inflate the company's year-end cash balance. Additional research, however, revealed otherwise.

Next, I began investigating the journal entries made by Gertie in which she increased the company's equity account, offsetting the increase against the officer loan account. There was no support for the entries, and Gertie wouldn't explain why she made them. It seemed likely that Gertie sought to inflate the balance in the company's equity account in order to maintain compliance with the SEC's net capital requirements.

Finally, I looked into the entries Gertie had made to reclassify meal and entertainment expenses to the officer loan account. There seemed to be no rhyme or reason to these reclassifications other than they were made to increase the company's bottom line and therefore its net capital balance.

Gertie's fraudulent postings to the officer loan account — to reduce meal and entertainment expense and to increase the equity balance — resulted in an unusually high balance in the officer loan account. This explained the mysterious deposits in transit — Gertie had created these fake deposits to reduce the balance in the officer loan account with the hope of avoiding detection of her scheme to increase the company's net capital.

The crux of Gertie's scheme was that she cooked the books all by herself — there was no sous chef in her kitchen.

Gertie's Well-Done Books

Bogus Transactions	Fraudulent Purpose
DR Officer loan (↑) CR Meal and entertainment exp (↓)	To increase the bottom line (and net capital) by eliminating expenses.
DR Officer loan (↑) CR Equity (↑)	To increase the equity balance (and net capital) by creating a phony officer loan receivable.
DR Cash (↑) CR Officer loan (↓)	To reduce the balance in the officer loan account to avoid detection.

Superstitious Rationalization

We gathered a mound of circumstantial evidence, but Gertie had her rationalization ready for us. She knew that Surebet was on the decline and could not meet its net capital requirements. However, she said that she was in a tough position because if she suggested closing the business, her family would have interpreted it as the preamble to their last rites. Slightly stunned by such an extreme reaction, I asked her to explain. Apparently, all the members of the Surebet family held a sacrosanct belief that retirement meant death was just around the corner. The superstition developed because the founding Clyde Surebet had died immediately after he retired. Clyde III expressed the family presumption by saying: "They'll probably find me hunched over my desk one morning." Although I had some sympathy for Gertie and her no-win situation, I knew I needed to report it to management. Gertie's husband, Clyde II, was clearly not the person to go to, and he seemed impervious to the rest of the office minutiae anyway.

I decided that Clyde III would be our point man. He owned and ran his own municipal bond broker/dealer but was very familiar with his mom and dad's business, as he had always been in the background. Clyde III was a whiz in math just like his mother. He was a university finance graduate and a card-carrying MENSA member who, thankfully, had better manners than both of his parents combined.

I explained to Clyde III that our CPA firm would need to disengage from the certified audit of Surebet's financial statements because, as auditors, we required that management have integrity and we could not tolerate dishonesty. However, Clyde III begged us not to drop his parent's company and negotiated with me. I eventually agreed to continue with the audit if we were allowed to increase our testing and scope of investigation, which would cost more money. As a part of our agreement, Clyde III said he would actively review the bookkeeping, especially the bank reconciliations.

My desire was to have Gertie fired and replaced, which I'm sure caused extreme internal conflict for Clyde III. The truth is that extricating Ma from a Ma and Pa business is often endowed with as much seriousness as impeaching a U.S. president. I think Clyde III reasoned that his mother was a good lady who had made an innocent mistake. Nevertheless, I had to report the irregularities to the SEC and other regulators, and the previous year's audit was amended and refiled.

The fraudulent journal entries reclassifying the expenses to the officer loan account were reversed, moving the expenses back on the income statement and off the balance sheet. The fraudulent journal entries that were made to the equity account were also reversed, as were the phony cash receipt transactions. The result was a sharp decrease in the liquidity and net capital of Surebet, resulting in the firm's dissolution.

Lessons Learned

Don't Put a Halo on Bookkeepers Your Parents' Age

Maybe it was my strict Catholic upbringing, but I was taught to put stock into the Ten Commandments. The one about honoring thy father and mother had a lot of traction in my childhood home. (It's enjoyed renewed interest as my wife and I raise our son and daughter.) However, don't let your respect of your elders blind you to the possibility of fraud. Auditors should maintain professional skepticism.

With So Many Moving Parts, Risk Needs to Be Properly Assessed

Surebet was as big as they come in terms of capacity of a broker/dealer in securities. One of the areas we focused an extraordinary amount of time on was how it differed from most of the other broker/dealers we had audited, because of the safekeeping and holding of customer securities. I had placed too much emphasis on counting the securities and the confirmation process.

As an analogy, it would be like a bank auditor taking an exorbitant amount of time to confirm what a customer kept in a safety-deposit

(*continued*)

box. After all, the items in a safety-deposit box don't appear on the bank's balance sheet, just as the securities in the vault didn't appear on Surebet's books. Also, we should have realized that Surebet was in an office it couldn't afford; the company was just hanging on.

Manual Books Require More Time to Examine

Today it is almost a given that a company maintains its accounting on a computerized system. During engagements, auditors request the electronic general ledger report, which can tell them valuable stories about a company. Electronic files eliminate manual number crunching and enable auditors to search for unusual entries, such as Gertie's credits to the expense accounts, more quickly and easily than they could in a manual system.

Recommendations to Prevent Future Occurrences

Follow Up on Deposits in Transit

Auditors should follow up on outstanding items. Had I been more tenacious when Gertie wouldn't provide support for the deposits in transit, I would have nabbed her fraud sooner. I should have requested a cut-off bank statement for the first week of January so that I could have verified whether the December deposits in transit had cleared. Had I discovered that they hadn't cleared, and had I spoken to the officer who had supposedly written the checks, I may have discovered Gertie's fraud then and there.

Don't Let Clients Talk You Out of Audit Procedures

I allowed Gertie to talk me out of requesting and auditing Surebet's cut-off bank statement for early January. This was a mistake that I now know not to repeat. Clients should not dictate what audit procedures the auditor follows. As a matter of fact, any attempt by a client to influence the audit procedures should be viewed as a red flag.

Don't Rush the Audit

Clients are often reticent about requesting a 30-day extension. Waiting to find out if your request has been granted can be very stressful and even just requesting one can make the broker/dealer stand out to the regulator. However, the 60 days available to prepare the

(continued)

(*continued*)

December 31st year-end report are excruciatingly difficult for auditors because there are so many federal holidays during that time. Nevertheless, the audit shouldn't be rushed. A solution is to allow 75 to 90 days for the audit to be filed or make the process more automatic.

About the Author

Mr. Kevin G. Breard is the founder and managing partner of Breard & Associates, Inc., CPAs (www.baicpa.com). The firm is a full-service accounting practice with expertise in the securities industry. Mr. Breard is a graduate of California State University, Northridge, B.S. Business. He has earned designations as a Certified Fraud Examiner (CFE), Certified in Financial Forensics (CFF), Certified Fraud Specialist (CFS) and Diplomat of the American Board of Forensic Accounting (DABFA). Kevin was born and raised in the San Fernando Valley, a suburb Northwest of Los Angeles, CA.

CHAPTER

Delaying the Inevitable

JOLYNN RUNOLFSON

Equipment Financing Company (EFC) was a large corporation with more than $2 billion in assets. Within its doors were three men who controlled the financial reporting for the company. At the top of the organizational chart was the CEO, Clifford Elmer, a dominating individual who enjoyed a high-spending lifestyle. By his account, he was a scrapper who had become a self-made millionaire by working hard and not accepting "no" from anybody. Separated from his wife, he had a new girlfriend and teenage children to support. With an expensive lifestyle and several households to fund, Clifford was focused on the success of EFC and also on expanding the business to increase his fortune.

Next in the hierarchy was the CFO, Curtis Franklin, a former banker and friend to all. Curtis was close to retirement and knew that his eight-year tenure at EFC would be his last stop before living the carefree life he had worked so hard for.

Last in the chain was the chief accounting officer (CAO), Calvin Atkin, a middle-aged certified public accountant who had worked his way up at EFC into a management position. Calvin had used his success at EFC to provide for a comfortable lifestyle that included a home in an exclusive neighborhood and private schools for his children.

Securitization of Loans

EFC's core business was financing high-cost medical equipment. The company would receive "warehouse" loans from larger lending institutions and turn around and lend the proceeds to healthcare providers to purchase their expensive assets.

As demand for EFC's loans grew, the company changed from holding the loans as receivables to moving them off the balance sheet using collateralized debt offerings. This new "securitization" allowed EFC to repay the warehouse loan and recognize the difference between the interest yield on the equipment loans and the bond yield given to investors in the current year. EFC then serviced the loans and monitored their status to comply with the bond covenants.

To further assist EFC's customers, management started a second division within the company to provide small-business loans backed by the medical practice's outstanding receivables. These were used by customers to keep their equipment loans current and to finance operations.

Early SOX Violation

EFC's public troubles began in May when the CFO and the CEO falsely signed the management's certification stating that the March financial reports filed with the SEC were presented "fairly . . . in all material respects," a requirement of all public companies subsequent to the Sarbanes-Oxley Act of 2002.

The certification was standard, but EFC's financial statements had been filed without the consent of the external auditors. Because of this, the auditors resigned the first week in June and issued a public statement about their resignation. Later that month, the SEC got involved. EFC claimed that the deficiency was a misunderstanding and that new auditors were being hired immediately. But that wasn't exactly true. Although new external auditors were courted, EFC's financial situation became dire and the financial reporting issues were placed on the back burner while management addressed the more immediate concern of a pending bankruptcy.

Investigating a Bankruptcy

By August the company had gone broke and the judge appointed an examiner. My firm was hired to assist in his investigation. When I arrived at EFC's offices, the first thing I noticed was how empty the building was. Around 50 percent of the employees had already been terminated. The remaining employees were very upset about the bankruptcy, not to mention confused with court filings implying fraudulent activities.

My team and I began by interviewing various members of the staff. We were concerned with allegations that the company had mortgaged its assets to more than one lender — a practice known as *double-pledging* — so we decided to identify why the company would do this. We went to each department head and asked how an originated loan traveled through the company and who was responsible for them after they were initially written.

We determined that the organization was separated into very specific departments for loan origination, documentation and workout. But this meant no one department was responsible for the current value of a loan. So when we questioned them about who determined whether an impaired loan was included in loan loss reserves, all the departments responded that the final determination was made by the CEO and CFO.

Several years prior to the troubles, EFC's external auditors decided that all loans more than 61 days past due would be determined "impaired." The calculation was the responsibility of the CEO and his staff and a loss was taken on the financial statements in the current period. Due to this policy, the company made every effort to keep loans from crossing the 61-day past-due status.

I discussed the workout process with several employees; they told me that if a loan was determined to be underperforming, it traveled to the workout department. They ascertained why the obligor was behind on his payments and facilitated the creation of a performing loan.

I spoke with members of the accounting department to understand if a loan that had been sent to workout could be resubmitted into a new securitization pool if it was again current. They said it could not because the securitization covenants would only allow a small percentage of such loans. What I found was significantly different than what they told me.

Bad Loan Workouts

I learned how to research loans with the tracking software so I could begin to identify specific ones that had missed payments during the past 12 months; this was the starting point to discover how the loans were adjusted during the workout process. I found several different options had been used.

The most common workout strategy in the loan documents could only be used if the original obligor was still in business. First, EFC adjusted the payments down to an amount that the debtor could reasonably pay. I found several recent loans where workout had increased the term; created interest-only loans with balloon payments due in future years; or used the business finance department, housed within the company, to make loans on receivables to generate cash to pay the debt. Because turning the nonperforming loans into new, performing ones was in the best interest of the financial statements, the workout department did not have the same rigorous standards the loan origination department had. I found the newly rewritten loans had higher default rates.

In addition to term changes, I found unpaid interest related to the loan — which the company had already recognized as income — rolled into the principal of the new loan so EFC would not have to recognize a revenue reduction in the period of the rewrite. This complicated the loan value because the underlying collateral, a rapidly depreciating piece of equipment subject to obsolescence, was not worth the amount of the new principal balance.

When the new terms for rewrite were agreed upon, the original loan was retired, which updated the general ledger. The subsequent note was issued a new number with no notations tying it to the previous underperforming loan. The documentation department was unaware that anyone in the company needed to distinguish between a rewritten and a new loan. This practice made it difficult for me to identify which loans were rewritten and which were original using EFC's loan-tracking software. I exported the information to a new database and began tracing the different loans for a ten-year period. I had to determine if the company had used this practice to circumvent the securitization covenants that restricted rewrites to make up only 3 percent of the pools.

One file I reviewed clearly did not comply with the covenants of the securitizations. The obligor started diagnostic operations with five separate loans from the company, and all of them commenced nine years prior to our investigation. The initial aggregate of the five loans was just under $2 million. Each of the debts was included in securitization pools and taken off the balance sheet to free up warehouse loans and facilitate additional equipment lending.

After just two years, all five loans were in default. The aggregate payments made totaled just $230,000. Because they were included in securitization pools, the company used performing loans to buy the past-due ones from the securitization, trading a performing loan for it. The past-due loans became an asset of the company and were included on the balance sheet at the full value of the principal and the past-due interest. The company's on-balance-sheet assets could then include ineligible loans for inclusion in future securitization pools; this strained the company's ability to provide adequate collateral for their warehouse loans.

To turn the nonperforming loans into viable debt for future securitization pools, the five deficient loans were rewritten into two new ones and given new numbers. In order for the company to avoid a loss for interest income that had been recognized in prior periods but not received, both the principal balance and the unpaid interest income was combined into the two new loans for a total principal balance of $2.1 million. The two new loans carried an aggregate balance in excess of the original purchase price, though the equipment held as collateral had depreciated substantially. This same process happened several times during the next seven years with the new loans going into various securitizations. When I started my investigation, the loans had values of $4.9 million with just the original equipment listed as collateral.

If a loan could not be rewritten due to the obligor's insolvency or history of unsuccessful rewrites, the company would sell the loan to a related party. These related-party relationships began with several diagnostic-center management partnerships. The idea was that EFC's partners would buy the loans in default and turn them into performing loans that could be inserted into securitization pools or listed as collateral on the warehouse loans. These related-party transactions were often written as non-recourse loans, meaning that if the related-party could not make payments, EFC would not take action against it for the unpaid amounts — the entire risk for the loan was born by EFC. The documents were also written with principal balances that included unpaid interest from the prior loan, just like those that EFC rewrote in-house.

Aside from the nonrecourse nature of the related-party loans, the inflated principal balance was often 50 percent greater than the underlying equipment's fair value, which was always the only collateral. This left EFC exposed for at least 50 percent of the balances; however, management did not report impairment losses on their financial statements. The rewritten loans were recorded as new ones, thereby disguising that they actually came from nonperforming loans from a previous obligor.

The Process in Action

One of the loans I traced illustrates just how this approach evolved. The obligor used a $14 million loan from EFC to purchase three diagnostic centers from the estate of a deceased physician. Five years and several rewrites later, the obligor declared bankruptcy. The loan balances totaled $19.6 million with a documented fair value from the workout department of $4 million if the centers were purchased in an operating state and $1 million if the assets were sold separately.

EFC brought in one of its related-party management teams to take over the loans and create "performing" ones that could be included in securitization pools. The new transaction included a $3.4 million line of credit balance, the equipment loan balances, a $2 million working capital loan, and an additional $1 million for miscellaneous expenses related to the agreement. This totaled $22.7 million.

The loan included various benefits for the obligor. First, it was non-recourse and was only collateralized by the $1 million fair value of the existing equipment. Second, the loan included an interest reduction of 5 percent. Third, the loan allowed various payments to be missed. Fourth, it provided for a balloon payment with options for payment stretched out over 24 months. And fifth, the loan was never scrutinized by the credit committee; it bypassed the credit approval process completely.

The result was a distressed asset put back in the performing asset category without any loss shown on the company's financial statements. In addition, management recognized interest income from the loans for the prior five years even though the amounts had not been received. At the time of our investigation, EFC had never recognized a loss on this loan.

Collecting Collateral

Although I found that most loans were kept on the "performing" list by rewrites and related-party transactions, the equipment was sometimes repossessed. When that happened, the accounting department would inquire as to the fair value of the company's new equipment. In most instances CEO Elmer and the valuation team would falsely estimate the repossessed equipment at the full value of the unpaid principal *and* interest to avoid any write-down of asset value or prior interest income. However, this wasn't done very often.

When I questioned members of the accounting department, they told me they were not qualified to value the equipment and relied solely on Elmer and the repo group. My boss and I also questioned the repo group about the aggressive valuations and the staff assured us the equipment *might* be worth that if EFC could find the right operator. However, they said the valuation ultimately fell to Elmer and Franklin.

Double-Pledging Assets

When EFC's balance sheet started to have an increasingly higher concentration of rewritten loans, Franklin worried that the warehouse lending institutions would reject the loans as collateral. And if Franklin could not use the loans as collateral, EFC would not be able to originate new performing loans. Also concerned about the lending institutions' auditors, Franklin began to list a single performing loan on multiple collateral schedules for different lending institutions, allowing EFC to have just $300 million in performing loans to cover over $600 million in obligations.

To list the loans on more than one collateral schedule, Franklin instructed the recording department to change the warehouse institution code in the loan tracking system. April Ramirez, the manager of the recording department, did not know that she and her staff were being used to facilitate fraud, and they dutifully recorded the changes as instructed. Because the warehouse institutions' auditors did not visit at the same time, Franklin had time to change the listed assets on different warehouse lines before the next auditor visited the company. With this change, the auditor would only review recently written performing loans showing compliance. When the first auditor left the company, Franklin adjusted the collateral list for the next auditor and submitted the change to the recording department.

However, the large volume of changes submitted by Franklin began to raise Ramirez's suspicions, and she started to do some investigating of her own. She found that the loans were listed on collateral schedules for overlapping periods of time, so Ramirez wrote a letter to Atkin, the CAO, informing him that the company had double-pledged assets and that loan values listed in the financial statements were not reflective of current values. Her letter was disseminated to the board of directors and in August the CEO, Clifford Elmer, was asked to resign.

Outcome

By the end of August, EFC filed for bankruptcy and Clifford Elmer had tendered his resignation. In October, the bankruptcy court appointed an examiner to determine what caused EFC's collapse and if there had been illegal acts committed when the company reported financial information to the SEC and various FDIC-insured lending institutions.

The court-appointed examiner also reviewed the loans, conducted several interviews with Franklin and obtained e-mails from Franklin to Elmer stating that the double-pledging was wrong and it would destroy both of their careers. Franklin, however, could not produce any written communications from Elmer verifying he received the e-mails.

The one element we could not produce in our six-month investigation was the actual amount that EFC should have included in their financial statements for loan loss reserves related to the nonperforming loans. The analysis would have meant I would have had to evaluate each of the loans — worth more than $2 billion — to determine which were rewritten or at risk of default. We were left with the option of simply showing the loans we had determined were uncollectable.

One morning I came into the office to continue my review of some credit binders I had been reading the day before. When I opened up one binder I found the information we were looking for had been left by an employee earlier that morning. The document showed that EFC had done an analysis of their loans six months before and estimated the amount of uncollectable loans to be $150 million. The document was one of the most important we included in the case report.

We issued the report six months after our investigation began, and, after reading it, the bankruptcy trustee asked Atkin to resign as controller and chief accounting officer. The liquidation plan was confirmed one year after the bankruptcy filing and the company was liquidated.

The SEC settled civil complaints against Elmer and Franklin — six years after the original bankruptcy filing — prohibiting both from acting as officers or directors of a public company. Neither admitted guilt for financial fraud. But that was only the SEC case, which was not criminal.

The U.S. Attorney's Office brought actions against Franklin for mail fraud and violating corporate financial reporting rules of the Sarbanes-Oxley Act. He was one of the first individuals indicted under Sarbanes-Oxley. He pleaded guilty to reduced charges and received a 30-month sentence, along with a $51 million restitution judgment payable to the banking institutions involved in the double-pledging scheme. It is unlikely that most of that money will ever be paid back.

Civil litigation is still continuing seven years after the bankruptcy filing. EFC's creditors have sued Elmer, Franklin and Atkin along with EFC's external auditors, board of directors and warehouse lending institutions.

Lessons Learned

Sarbanes-Oxley had just been enacted when EFC's fraudulent financial reporting was discovered. Both Elmer and Franklin were aware of the new law, as evidenced by e-mails turned over by Franklin; however, neither was deterred from signing the new attestations. Franklin eventually pleaded guilty to charges related to the new law, but Elmer was only charged civilly and received only a lifetime ban on his ability to function as a director in a public company.

Proving intent against CEOs has been difficult as cases related to the new law are just getting settled by the SEC. Although the evidence against Cliff Elmer was substantial, the absence of a written or verbal confession was enough to keep him from having to even admit guilt in his settlement. He might lose the civil litigation filed by EFC's creditors, but the long wait for a decision, plus the additional wait for the inevitable appeals, will not soothe their pain or their wallets.

Another important factor this case highlighted is the estimations that accountants make when preparing financial statements. We are asked to value a company's assets liberally, knowing full well that those estimates may never consistently hit the mark. This leaves the door open, as it did at EFC, for management to go with a best-case scenario. When this did not reflect reality, EFC's management found itself in a difficult position of taking a loss *and* increasing its loss reserves or masking the losses by misrepresenting the collectability of the loan portfolio.

At the time, the industry average loan loss was 9 percent. External auditors should have questioned a company that showed less than 1 percent. In retrospect, EFC should have been forced to show an allowance account for the loans written in the current period and not just actual losses related to loans written in previous periods. This would have avoided the temptation by management to conceal the loans when they were determined to be uncollectable.

Recommendations to Prevent Future Occurrences

One recommendation I would make is to include multiple departments in loan impairment decisions. Although EFC's workout department was knowledgeable about the medical facility and the earnings that could likely be used to service the equipment debt, their valuation of a loan based on an earnings calculation was not the conservative

(continued)

approach required when preparing financial statements. Also, the valuation of impaired assets should not have employed a top-down approach from senior management whose bonuses were directly tied to the performance of the company and, therefore, the valuations of the nonperforming loans.

A second recommendation is for external auditors to be more vigilant in identifying suspicious accounts. EFC's auditors should have questioned why the loan loss reserves were so far out of the norm for the industry. The auditors gave the company a list of traits a loan had to have to be included in the impaired asset list. In effect, this gave EFC's executives a checklist for what to avoid when a loan was underperforming and therefore taught them how to bypass the impairment list. The auditors should have asked for more information regarding why EFC did not fit the industry norm and they should have insisted on original documentation, not the computer-generated information management provided.

My final recommendation is for managers who might find themselves in Elmer's or Franklin's position. Loan losses should be tied to a reserve account created in the period that the loans are written. EFC's reserve for uncollectable loans was limited to what they wrote off, meaning the current financial period was affected by loans from past years. This enticed Franklin to begin to mask prior losses so the negative result would not hurt EFC's market capital.

About the Author

JoLynn D. Runolfson, CFE, CPA, of Vernal, Utah, is a Lecturer for Utah State University and consults privately for fraud examination, insolvency, business restructuring and litigation support engagements. Ms. Runolfson is a graduate of Utah State University and has more than 15 years of experience in both business valuation and forensic analysis.

17

Power and Corruption in the Publishing Industry

KENNETH BIDDICK

High-magnitude financial statement fraud rarely happens at the hand of only one individual. Sometimes though, the influence of a leader is so powerful that it defines the culture of the organization and can cause employees to commit fraudulent acts they would otherwise never consider. In such instances, the employee's behavior can extend far beyond his or her intentions — or so the accused will claim.

To be fair, there were many bad actors in this case who significantly contributed to the complex financial gamesmanship about to be discussed. In fact a judge hearing one of the many actions brought against the company identified the "Inner Circle" as a criminal organization. And not unlike in a criminal organization, the "boss" was generally removed from direct involvement. However, the actions of the perpetrators had to be approved or ordered, with knowledge somewhere in the chain of command.

If you define *powerful* as the ability to control and have undue influence, then Sam McFarland was the most powerful man in the largest publishing company in the past five decades. One of McFarland's key means of control was having the final say over salaries and bonuses, including controlling awards of deferred compensation funded in company stock. Employees were held captive by the practice of being denied their accumulated company stock if they left for any reason other than retirement.

A veteran and a law school graduate, Sam had a diverse skill set that made him well equipped to run an international company. Few people without the benefit of holding a controlling interest in stock get to run a publicly held business as their own, but McFarland was an exception. Growth and stability were the mainstays of both his career and marriage; he raised six children to share his traditions and values about leadership.

Sam began his career at International Publishing directly out of law school. He quickly earned the respect of his superiors and was given responsibility over one of the largest divisions, and eventually took control of the entire publishing house.

A True Success Story

International Publishing (IP) began its operations in a remote foreign outpost in the early twentieth century and moved to the United States in the late 1950s to take advantage of strong capital markets. After McFarland took over as CEO of IP, he maintained a focus on doing business in foreign markets while focusing on serving the interests of multinational media enterprises. IP went public shortly thereafter and expanded into print-media markets. By the end of the twentieth century, IP was the most respected company in its industry and was sought after as a business partner by its peers and customers. Stock analysts raved over IP's results:

> We believe that IP is likely to continue to post double-digit earnings gains over the next several years. First, the domestic market continues to be profitable despite one of the most difficult environments in recent memory. The cycle turn now at hand will add further momentum to IP's earnings. . . . Finally, IP has a deep bench of management talent, and we expect Mr. McFarland's eventual successor to come from within these ranks.

IP was under significant pressure to maintain its status. The company had operations in more than 60 countries, most as wholly owned subsidiaries, and had more than 20 business segments operating within these subsidiaries, but several were structured as LLCs, LLPs and joint ventures. McFarland and his management team began to use these entities for experimental ventures, unproven markets and products, or simply as a place to park losses and revenues that they did not want to recognize in a specific accounting period. The complexities of IP's operations were designed to create confusion and keep outsiders from piecing the puzzle together.

Let's Make a Deal

Size has both advantages and disadvantages. Being the largest and most influential business in an industry brings power as well as the scrutiny of regulators and analysts. Keeping these outside gatekeepers in the dark requires very coordinated and complex structures. McFarland maintained relationships with his industry counterparts in case the opportunity for a venture arose. IP was always making deals and it became standard industry practice for competitors to collaborate with each other to create new business structures. Generally, IP's partners were guaranteed a fee or some indemnification — which was never disclosed to the outside regulators.

This amounted to a scam, which began to unravel when McFarland and others on his management team became so cozy with their partners that they took turns winning print-media contracts. This prompted an investigation by the state's attorney general's office for potential collusion among industry players. It brought a wave of attention and the first in a series of high-profile accusations involving or directly targeted at IP.

IP was already the focus of stock analysts who closely followed the company's financial results. IP's balance sheet liability, deferred revenue, was out of sync with its revenue growth and the analysts began to question the possibility that revenue recognition might be too aggressive. McFarland's arrogance led him to execute even more transactions in response to the analysts' comments. He allegedly called another company's CEO and arranged a series of contracts to publish materials that would extend for several years and increase deferred revenue to meet analyst expectations. These transactions were so blatantly preconceived that analysts began to have strong suspicions that IP's accounting practices were without substance. This pressure made it difficult for McFarland to maintain IP's public market leadership and so IP's board began its own independent investigation.

The timing couldn't have been worse since new legislation, Sarbanes-Oxley, required a specific certification over internal controls for financial reporting. When the board's initial investigation found a lack of such controls, the first chink in the armor of IP's inner circle appeared.

One Thing Leads to Another

As a result of probes by the attorney general alleging collusive business practices and by the SEC for material misstatements of financial reporting — prompting the first restatement of IP's annual 10-K — the plaintiff's counsel representing institutional shareholders left little opportunity for IP's inner circle to control any spin on what turned out to be decades of manipulated business outcomes. This is where my company began its involvement in the investigation.

My firm, ENRG Advisors, specialized in fraud examination and forensic accounting and more specifically, financial statement frauds. Our managing directors and staff cut their teeth in the Big Four as auditors. Some of us actually uncovered frauds during our audit years and knew the pressure put on auditors to find justification for some clients' financial gamesmanship. When we were solicited to assist the plaintiff in investigating IP, we agreed on the basis that we would only consult with counsel. Being an expert witness against public companies and their auditors carries a stigma — we become the bad guys for making companies and auditors look like culprits, even though we're really investigating bad management and potentially complicit auditors.

With the result of the first investigation identifying serious manipulations of IP's financial reporting, the new Sarbanes-Oxley legislation required auditors to demand a second internal investigation. This time nothing was left to chance and IP made a second amendment to its 10-K, restating prior years' financial results and making outright admissions of improper accounting and material weaknesses in internal controls. IP was looking more and more like a breeding ground for financial statement manipulation.

The Specifics

IP managed its earnings in a number of ways, but the most prevalent was by parking mostly bad results outside the company and bringing them in at will. It is critical to note that all of the transactions were real. In some cases the accounting was window dressing, specifically the transactions that led to the first investigation, designed to affect the balance sheet without any risk of loss.

Since IP had many subsidiaries throughout the world, McFarland took full advantage of them to orchestrate off-balance-sheet transactions and, along with industry partners, parked operations in the entities that he knew would produce income as well as experiment with new lines of business. The premise was to ensure a steady year-over-year increase in financial performance for the parent company. Keeping a certain level of guaranteed income available allowed McFarland to make up for shortfalls in IP's core operations and maintain consecutive quarter-over-quarter earnings. Keeping the new operations off the books ensured that there would be no downward surprises. Negative results could be brought in when core operations exceeded expectations. This was a far superior way to manage earnings compared to the standard cookie-jar approach.

IP's board of directors needed to clean house so they forced the departure of many top executives. Although McFarland was not directly implicated in the board's investigation, it was widely perceived that his controlling influence led to how the company's financial results were reported. Many of the company's top executives and lieutenants extended McFarland's control by executing his commands without question. The rank and file followed directives out of fear or the hope of eventually becoming part of the "inner circle."

Corporate environments like IP's should be screaming red flags to auditors, but they also can intimidate the audit team. When IP revealed its financial statement manipulations, I was not too surprised to see the admissions of material weaknesses. Given the magnitude of amendments in IP's restated 10-K and the material weaknesses in internal controls, the class action filings were amended to include the previous auditor as a defendant. The pervasiveness of adjustments and admissions and material weaknesses in internal controls were too much to ignore.

Counsel retained us to perform two functions that would be staffed by two teams. One was made up of more than forty attorneys who were managed by our firm to code all the documents obtained through discovery. The second was a financial team of fifteen or so CFEs, CPAs, M.B.A.s and CFAs experienced in financial statement analysis, investigations and auditing. They would be responsible for drafting a summary memo for each issue we discovered. I was the consulting expert leading both teams and defined all of the critical matters and definitions for tagging the documents that would be evaluated by counsel. I provided the attorney-coders with the background and technical knowledge to identify important information with the appropriate issue tag and degree of relevance.

The financial team and I developed a standardized memorandum format to maintain complete uniformity regardless of who drafted the memo. Each began with a one-page executive summary identifying the restated financial issue, the technical violations, any known auditor involvement and the financial magnitude, followed by relevant quotations from documents identifying the intended manipulation. The memo would then provide a summary of the allegations; a list of individuals involved and their professional role; an introduction of the transaction and its intent to manipulate the financial reporting; a detailed analysis of the original financial reporting, how it was accomplished and the corrected financial reporting; any specific auditor knowledge and his direct role in approving the accounting, identifying the area as high risk and performing specific testing of the transactions; the results of the audit work; the financial impact by year and quarter of the improper financial reporting; and the technical violation of generally accepted accounting principles (GAAP) and generally accepted auditing standards (GAAS).

Our investigation began with two simple directives — prepare comprehensive memorandums on all of the disclosed restatements and identify the extent of auditor knowledge prior to the restatement and SOX-forced disclosures. We had a few roadmaps to follow with the two amended 10-Ks and two investigations performed by the independent law firms. We also had access to previously discovered documents, which the plaintiff's counsel maintained in a central electronic vault that all parties could access. On its face this seemed like ideal efficiency or, at the very least, to be saving a bunch of trees. Unfortunately, none of the documents were text searchable and there was absolutely no organization in more than one million documents. That is why the team of attorneys was coding documents based on the issue tags I developed.

The financial team developed a matrix of identified issues and their origins, which became a critical element in identifying additional discovery requests. It was clear that we needed a more organized document set, and the best solution would be the auditor's work papers.

Our requests to get an electronic version of the complete set of auditor's work papers for the past five years were not received well. Certain agreements among the parties had already been made regarding discovery and, without a clear and convincing reason, no request would be forthcoming. We were stuck sifting through the existing documents page by page, attempting to code them and build an inventory of audit work papers among all the other sources commingled in the mass of images. Eventually we coded enough of the file to clearly show the piecemeal nature of both the SEC's and the state attorney general's discovery set, indicating that not one entity or any one year had an intact set of auditor work papers. So we made our discovery request again and this time it was granted.

The electronic files came and kept coming. We asked for not only the auditor's proprietary audit software, but also each of their electronic desktops and e-mails. We needed to match all the individuals who appeared anywhere in the discovery set to make sure we actually received all the files. We were getting the raw data this time, so it was searchable and we easily identified missing information.

The great thing about electronic information is the organization, the ease of searching and the ability to go directly to areas of interest. Unlike the age of paper, without the benefit of computer forensics, you get a very clean set of work papers. The files did not have review notes, obvious changes to explanations or conclusions or side notes scribbled in margins. They were almost perfectly sanitized documents that, if taken alone, provide little understanding of how accounting manipulations counted in billions could have gone without detection. But then we had the desktop files and e-mails.

Secrets in the E-Mails

The more telling e-mails revealed chatter among staff members questioning managers' directives or asking the professional practice group (the audit firm's quality control and whistleblower team) to intervene. But one of the most revealing exchanges was between the audit manager and the engagement partner. The following excerpt provides a peek into the engagement team's hierarchy and how its character resembled the very entity it was supposed to be auditing.

> Can you tell me what you want recorded on the deferred revenue reviews? Maybe your team can enter the facts (say they consulted a specialist), and we all agreed on these transactions. I can add some commentary and mark it reviewed.

Although circumstantial, the manager who wrote the above e-mail had previously reprimanded a senior accountant for questioning the accounting, and that same senior accountant never returned to the engagement.

Another message we discovered was related to a very sophisticated series of transactions involving two investment banking houses and two straw customers to convert securities with unrealized gains into core publishing revenues while maintaining ownership of the securities.

> Glad it wasn't qtr end. Given 10,000 monkeys 100 years and each has a typewriter, eventually they would produce the works of Shakespeare. Given IP's funky transactions, 1 qtr and each funky transaction matures during the qtr. IP would produce a near thing.

Here IP is converting some of its unrealized gains in partnership investments by funding the distribution itself. Amazingly, it didn't recognize that it could have accomplished the same result by accounting for the investment under the equity method.

> Please send the cash out tomorrow. . . . We will receive the 20 million USD back on December 31. Book this as revenue.

One of IP's operating units had significant long-term contracts on the books that had not been reconciled for many years. SOX forced the issue into light by requiring a reduction to equity of more than $1 billion. Although this account was audited each year, the auditors never pressed IP to address the problems with its reconciliation by estimating a potential adjustment.

> The legacy problem is not getting attention in that office — we don't have enough staff. Out of 200 accounts, they cleared 10. At that rate, we will have to wait two decades before it is done.
>
> Adjustments required by our contracts were accrued but were not individually calculated. In addition, most of the sub-ledgers were useless as required account reconciliations were not done, nor were systems properly updated to reflect the deals on the books and records. A home office team of accountants and a small army of temporary accountants began working on the adjustment and account reconciliation backlogs in January five years ago.

Even with all the various schemes, occasionally some loose ends would need to be tied up. Handling this was simply a matter of the inner circle ordering a journal entry. These entries were sometimes referred to as "top-side adjustments" and always came at a quarter-end and were a major audit risk. Since they were generally estimates based on a judgment call, there was a lot of wiggle room. IP rarely had any documentation other than an explanation from a highly placed corporate executive. At the end of the period more than $400 million of these top-side adjustments were reversed by management, since they had already accomplished their goal.

Between all of the independent investigations, the SEC and the attorney general, we located 67 transactions that were manipulated to achieve a specific accounting result. We identified the most significant and consolidated several that covered a similar scheme, and prepared twenty detailed memorandums. We also prepared a consolidated memorandum covering all the issues related to the auditor's knowledge and handling of each issue. Between the two restatements, IP actually had lower earnings in the five-year period by more than $2 billion and reduced equity by approximately $4 billion.

Old Habits Die Hard

At the entity level, IP got off with little damage. The SEC settled for several hundred million dollars, the attorney general punished other industry players on the collusion issues, and the recovery of the securities class action claim was settled for a little less than $1 billion. IP suffered the worst damage to its management team; the company cleaned house and had difficulty replacing its talent pool. Ironically, however misguided McFarland was, he and IP would have been the industry leader without the accounting maneuvers.

The entire corporate management team was dismissed along with several second-tier vice presidents who played key roles in executing the improper transactions. The group involved in working out the details related to McFarland's deferred revenue arrangement was criminally prosecuted. McFarland defended himself vigorously and eventually all litigation against him was settled without any money trading hands. No criminal charges were ever brought against him, but he lost control of the company he helped build and spent more than $100 million in legal fees fighting the litigation for more than five years. A few years after being ousted as CEO, the 90-plus-year-old McFarland started a new company in the same industry, in that same foreign outpost where IP's journey began so many years ago.

The auditor settled the class action litigation for less than $100 million with the usual denials of any wrongdoing. IP continues to use the firm as its independent auditor.

Lessons Learned

In most cases, the tone at the top is a primary indicator of pressure to achieve mandated results. As anti-fraud professionals, we read and
(continued)

hear this everywhere because it is not only obvious; it is the very foundation for the integrity of financial reporting. IP's management team handed directives down the executive chain and even created committees for the sole purpose of enhancing earnings through transaction manipulations. Unmet results were temporarily covered by top-side adjustments, sending a clear message that "You're not off the hook because the quarter ended; we covered for your failure and you're expected to make up the shortfall."

Compensation policies incentivized employees to play their part and be loyal to the company above anything else. IP paid the majority of its bonuses in company stock through a deferred compensation plan solely controlled by McFarland. It was well known that if an employee left before retirement, his or her deferred compensation would be forfeited.

Independence in the audit committee, internal audit and outside auditors is critical to providing oversight of financial reporting and C-suite influence. Human beings generally do not act outside of their best interests. IP's internal auditor reported to the CFO and was compensated at the pleasure of the CEO. The audit committee was populated with other industry players or former officers subject to the influences of IP's stock performance. The CFO was the former worldwide relationship partner from IP's outside audit firm and the current engagement partner's mentor.

Recommendations to Prevent Future Occurrences

We can't expect change to happen when bad behavior pays such high rewards. All of the executives who were dismissed from IP were able to keep the compensation they took home, regardless of the years of financial manipulation. Although only three lower-level executives were found guilty on a criminal level, all the dismissed executives could (and probably should) have received sanctions through forfeiture of compensation. Regardless of any other recommendations addressed below, breaking the rules to achieve significant financial outcomes for their own benefit needs to become a zero-sum game for those responsible.

Audit committees need to be completely independent of the C-suite's influence. This may be difficult to achieve given the requirement to be financially competent and have an industry background. However, making sure the audit committee members have no reason

(*continued*)

(*continued*)

to cover for any executives is critical to providing a bona-fide oversight function.

Internal audit needs to report directly and only to the audit committee. This may simply mean that the audit committee retains its own staff to constantly monitor the financial reporting function. Other internal audit tasks would not be part of this team and could report to the appropriate executive or other standing committee of the board of directors.

Independent auditors also need to be immune to the attempts from management to influence their decisions, including audits of companies whose board members include the executives of an auditee. Until our industry changes how independent auditors are paid, any relationship might influence auditor independence. Auditors need to understand that their business won't suffer when they perform their work and report activity in violation of existing accounting standards. Pressure by executives to obstruct auditor business with board members who are at a high level at another auditee significantly magnifies auditors' awareness of the financial stakes at risk.

Significant transactions, including partnering relationships and minority interest holdings, require high scrutiny by internal auditors and experienced independent auditors to identify the substantive purpose of the arrangement. Although the accounting rules have been modified, such transactions will still be a vehicle of choice to park financial results and engineer accounting chicanery.

About the Author

Ken Biddick is a Certified Fraud Examiner, Certified Public Accountant and is Certified in Financial Forensics. Ken has been investigating financial fraud for 30 years. Since 1985 Ken has been a pioneer in utilizing computer data analytics in investigating suspicious financial activity.

CHAPTER 18

It Starts and Ends at the Top

KIMIHARU CHATANI

Akira Tanaka was an unassuming man who quietly climbed the ladder of success at Premier Electric, a well-known Japanese auto supplier headquartered in Tokyo. With his last child's entrance to a prestigious Tokyo university, he could focus on climbing the final few rungs of the corporate ladder to become an officer and board member, a feat that eluded most of his comrades who started with him some 30 years ago. He was summoned by the human resources department one lazy afternoon in late March to be "unofficially" notified of his new assignment as the CEO of Premier's largest foreign subsidiary, located in Flint, Michigan. He accepted without any hesitation; Tanaka was the ultimate "company man." Plus, during the past 30 years of Premier's operations, being named the CEO of the U.S. subsidiary virtually guaranteed future success at the company. Tanaka was an avid golfer on weekends and an accomplished singer on the Tokyo karaoke scene at night. Like many Japanese executives on the rise, Akira Tanaka was a chain smoker, a habit he picked up in college.

Akira Tanaka was an average-looking man with an infectious smile that made people comfortable and his engaging laughter put everyone he met at ease, a quality that he took advantage of everywhere he went. The day of his promotion was no different from any other day — after putting in a grueling 12 hours of work, he led his subordinates into the "night jungle" that was known as Ginza. Because of the good news, his smile was a bit brighter, his laughter a bit more confident, and his step slightly lighter as he entered his favorite watering hole. He told of his impending promotion to his troops and the hostesses in a loud and robust cheer. But in the midst of his celebration, he had forgotten to inform his wife of 25 years.

Tanaka was following in the footsteps of previous leaders at Premier as he took the reins in Flint. His future with the organization was now assured. Premier Electric was not very different from other major Japanese companies with foreign subsidiaries, in that the U.S. market was its largest outside Japan. The Flint office was considered training ground for future Japanese CEOs and board members. Most executives in these U.S. positions always had one eye on Flint operations and the other eye glued to Premier's performance in Japan. The goal was to successfully navigate this final hurdle before heading home. Most CEOs in the U.S. subsidiary valued the status quo and rarely ventured to take on major initiatives. Akira Tanaka was a typical of this group — he was in a survival mode as he boarded the plane to Detroit.

Growth and Decline

Premier Electric began humbly in 1920 as a manufacturer and supplier of electric bulbs for the emerging automotive sector in Japan. It was a small operation that relied on the ingenuity of the company's founder. His use of direct-mail campaigns in the early 1920s was considered revolutionary at the time, and helped him secure his very first client, a reseller of Christmas lights. The first big break came in the mid-1920s with a huge order from an automotive supplier in the United States. Premier Electric rode the wave of international sales that allowed it to open its first manufacturing plant in Tokyo. World War II propelled Premier Electric to establish other facilities around the country in support of the military. After the war, the company aligned itself with one Japanese automotive company and began exclusively servicing that carmaker. It was a time of unencumbered expansion as it followed the automotive company's global expansion into the United States, Europe and Asia. The company established its second U.S. manufacturing presence in Flint, Michigan, in 1986. That location became the U.S. headquarters, with more than 2,000 employees.

Akira Tanaka, like other CEOs before him, recognized the need to mold and nurture his chief financial officer to ensure that his own operational performance as the CEO was stellar. Tanaka had not worked with Kenji Yamashita, Flint's CFO, before his foreign placement, but he knew of Yamashita's reputation as solid "finance guy" with "unquestioned loyalty"; both phrases were music to his ears. His success was tied to Yamashita's and both executives knew it. Yamashita's first four years in Flint were uneventful, as the company more than exceeded sales and net income expectations, and was about to erase an accumulated deficit that had troubled the company for years. The U.S. economy was expanding and Premier continued to develop its presence in the United States. It was a great time to be a captive provider of headlights to one of the fastest growing auto manufacturers in the largest car market in the world.

One day Tanaka called Yamashita into his office and met him with dead silence while handing him a stack of documents. The recession that hit Japan and derailed Premier Electric's surge in the market had now caused the company to stall. A stern directive was sent to the overseas subsidiaries to buckle down, cut expenses where possible and expand sales to meet the revised, aggressive financial goals.

Yamashita instinctively knew that the orders from headquarters were nearly impossible to satisfy, but it was his responsibility to try. As he left the office, Yamashita gave Tanaka a reassuring smile but didn't notice the grim expression on Tanaka's face as he closed the door. Yamashita did not yet understand the gravity of the situation.

Creative Inventory Procedures

The basic goal in manufacturing is to sell goods and move inventory for profit. This is an obvious mission at all levels of the organization — one that is clearly understood from the assembly lines to the bookkeepers to the executive suite. Although it was operationally a single company, Premier Electric was legally split into two separate and distinct entities — Northern and Southern. For whatever operational reasons, "sales" and "purchases" were recorded when goods crossed this invisible line. During previous audits, these intra-company transactions were, for the most part, ignored because they were nullified in the intra-company elimination entries. Thus any supporting internal transfer documents were ignored during the audit process. In hindsight, this structure should have served as an initial warning to auditors.

Premier's operations in the United States depended on meeting specific quotas and net sales set by the parent company. Japanese regulations of corporate financial reporting to the Tokyo Stock Exchange required Premier Electric in Flint to submit guaranteed financial results to its parent company in Tokyo before its books were closed. These, in essence, served as an accurate forecast of impending results and could not be revised. Only Akira Tanaka was authorized to guarantee the financial number submitted to the parent company. In addition to being CEO, Tanaka was also a first-year appointed board member of Premier. It was extremely important that operations in the U.S. subsidiary continued to succeed and grow under his leadership, for both individual and organizational recognition. With a stalled economy, the Flint transplant was under great pressure.

During Tanaka's third year as CEO of the Flint office, it was business as usual, and the audit team began preparing for their annual visit in February. It was my third year as the audit partner on the engagement with a Big Four accounting firm. Other than the previously mentioned, uniquely split company structure, early rounds of the audit revealed no major concerns. Executive interviews claimed no serious financial performance issues, and access to accounting records and schedules were provided on a timely basis — with one exception.

Premier used an inventory reconciliation schedule to settle physical inventory against what was officially recorded on the books. This paperwork was typically shared at the start of an audit; however, this year Tanaka held back key inventory schedules for reasons that we didn't know at the time. The audit team, however, proceeded with a plethora of other to-dos on their checklist. The manager on the engagement should have been curious about why a standard inventory reconciliation schedule/cut-off schedule was one of the last items to be produced, right before the closing of an audit. Curious, but not necessarily suspicious, because the timing of audit schedules often changes — along with the basic focus of the audit. It is a somewhat fluid process. But the audit manager's trust must have kicked in and allowed him to overlook the anomaly, and I only stumbled upon it during my final review of the audit. Call it what you will — auditor's instinct, experience or suspicion — but this outstanding item just did not make any sense to me. I called a client meeting with Yamashita and the controller, Marsha Brown, to get an update.

Unwelcome News

I met with my audit team during a routine review. Knowing that it was unusual for the inventory reconciliation schedule to remain open at this stage in the audit, I walked over to Jim Daniels, who was responsible for inventory. I'd known Jim for several years, and he was a very dedicated veteran of Premier. He had red hair and a freckled face that always turned red when he was embarrassed. When I asked Jim for the status of the inventory reconciliation, he explained that there were reconciling items that he was investigating with the controller, Marsha Brown, and the CFO, Kenji Yamashita. I had known Marsha and Kenji for a long time: Kenji and I were golfing and happy hour friends and maintained a strong client-auditor relationship. Both Marsha and Kenji were chagrined at the bottleneck in finalizing the inventory reconciliation, but assured me that it would be resolved within the coming week. The audit manager, Kevin Lawson, had been assigned to the engagement prior to my arrival, and he knew the client's business inside and out. His review of the inventory schedules indicated several items of significant value still open; they were accounted for as "inventory in transit" with an affiliate. Kevin felt that the open items would be cleared during the inter-company reconciliation that remained. All seemed well on its way to resolving itself as the audit headed to an uneventful close once again.

Nevertheless, I somehow knew that this year-end audit would be different and my auditor's instinct pulled me to the inventory binders and their contents. A cursory review revealed a routine audit; however, one schedule of an inter-company in-transit reconciliation schedule caught my attention. Although the schedule addressed inventory transfers before and after year-end to ensure that inventory was stated fairly in accordance with U.S. generally accepted accounting principles, something didn't match up. Bills of lading typically signify transfers of inventory and ownership between parties in a transaction. The numbering of inter-company inventory transfers I spotted was out of sequence with the remaining bills of lading, raising a red flag. I called Lawson and Yamashita to express my concern that inventory could be misstated by several million dollars, which would not only wipe out net income, but could also significantly impact Premier Electric's financial statements.

Lawson was called away to another meeting, and Yamashita and I continued the discussion in private to review the implications of my findings. He felt that the errors were unintentional and not cause for alarm, but he ultimately agreed that only one or two individuals above the CFO position had the authority to be involved in transactions of this magnitude. He asked for a few days to consult with the COO, Hiroshi Koyama. I told Yamashita of my suspicion that the only one with the motive, means and opportunity to conceal a potential fraud was Akira Tanaka, the CEO.

Yamashita confided to me that the annual budget had been revised several times during the year and with each revision it became harder and harder to achieve, placing a heavy burden on Akira Tanaka and the Flint operation. Yamashita felt that Tanaka was under tremendous pressure and stress as he was summoned to Japan frequently. Tanaka's behavior was nothing out of the ordinary, according to Yamashita, expect for occasional outburst of temper followed by a visit to his favorite Japanese bar in Chicago. When Tanaka was under stress, he often made the three-hour trip from Flint to Chicago with his trusted staff members.

Yamashita reassured me he thought that Tanaka was above board and, as a rising star at the organization, would not risk falsification of financial results to achieve short-term glory. It was uncharacteristic of Tanaka and there was no need for him to take on that burden when the entire organization was under the same economic pressure.

I saw Yamashita burning the midnight oil with the audit team, crunching number after number, all the while his expression becoming darker and darker. We all sensed that we were in the eye of the storm and the momentary calmness would soon be replaced by a fury of unimaginable proportions. We were in for the ride of our careers.

Undeliverable Promises

Several days later, Yamashita and Koyama came over to inform me that Tanaka had been summoned to Tokyo unexpectedly. The mood of the conversation was somber and I instinctively knew Tanaka's fate, once a promising rising star of Premier Electric. Several weeks after my discovery, I learned that he was "transferred" to a small subsidiary in Japan and that his career at the company was effectively ruined.

Apparently he had received private communications from Japan demanding a stronger financial performance from the Flint plant in return for a faster promotion. He had pushed his team to drive down costs and defer expenses, but it was not enough to meet the results he had promised at the beginning of the year. Tanaka used internal bills of lading signifying inter-company transfers of inventory to falsify sales as though they were made to third parties. He understood the timing and focus of the audits and he tried to prolong and conceal the inevitable questions from the audit team and his internal staff members. He was hoping, unsuccessfully, that the audit team would not scrutinize the internal bills of lading.

Tanaka was able to further conceal the fraudulent transactions by setting up a fictitious third company to confirm sales made at year-end. These were made to entities no longer doing business with Premier, in amounts that Tanaka hoped would not raise concerns for an inexperienced auditor. The customers' addresses were all P.O. boxes under Tanaka's personal control. He was hopeful that he could intercept the accounts receivable confirmations and respond to the auditors to avoid suspicion. But Tanaka did not realize that the audit team would closely examine transactions near year-end that were made to post office boxes.

Yamashita and Koyama later learned that Tanaka had promised year-over-year sales growth that could not be legitimately sustained. Based on our findings, I reported Tanaka's falsification of his financial statements to our Japanese audit partner. After much discussion involving the senior executives at Premier in Japan, we extended our audit of the Flint operation and reexamined all suspicious transactions. Fortunately for Premier Electric, Tanaka appeared to have limited his falsifications to the inventory. The only saving grace for Akira Tanaka was that he was not prosecuted for his actions while in the United States.

Lessons Learned

Kevin Lawson, the audit manager, and I learned that the skeptical lens of the auditor must be present on all audits, regardless of familiarity with the client or management. Each engagement must be evaluated within the context of the overall economic and political situation of the company and its executives. Close coordination with the parent company's audit team on internal communications, directives and unusual meetings or arrangements should be shared with members of the extended audit team.

A case study summarizing this audit was made available at all levels of Premier Electric across disciplines and geographies. Because of this case, we instituted a cross-disciplinary audit team that includes a member of our forensic practice. We have also instituted cross-functional

(continued)

training where fraud examination and forensic interviewing, among others, are made available to audit teams in training sessions. But the most important lesson reinforced for me was possibly the simplest: It is critical that personal relationships do not cloud auditor judgment.

Recommendations to Prevent Future Occurrences

Fraud is often attributed to a rogue staff member or an unassuming person in management who quietly and under cover tries to skirt both ethics and policies for personal gains. But in many cases, the fraud originates from a single person in charge of an entire organization.

CEOs are supposed to be trustworthy and uphold leadership standards. As CEOs come under greater scrutiny and regulatory calls for more transparency increase, the need to examine all levels of the organization should be reactivated. The motto of the CEO should be, "The buck stops here."

My relationship with the company and the CEO (also an up-and-coming board member at the parent company) extended over a number of years in both business and personal settings. I had considered myself to be one of Akira Tanaka's trusted business advisors. The company, a well-known U.S. subsidiary of a foreign manufacturer, had a practice of releasing "approved financial results" to its parent company before the start of an audit, which in the end proved to be Tanaka's downfall.

All audit firms, including the one I worked for at the time, should reevaluate training programs from the ground up. We should train highly technical auditors in the disciplines of information systems, fraud examination, forensic interviews, business intelligence and analytics. The days where auditors just crossed the t's and dotted the i's are over. Today's auditors must possess curiosity and proper training to follow up on leads like detectives would. Our profession might be witnessing the dawn of a new breed of accountants — the fraud examiners.

As the global economy converges and becomes more interdependent, along with the potential conversion of U.S. GAAP with International Financial Reporting Standards (IFRS) in the near future, more burdens will be placed on the shoulders of our profession to add an understanding of the global economy and accounting convergence to the growing list of auditor capabilities and competencies.

About the Author

Kimiharu Chatani, CFE, CPA, CFE, CFSA, CIA, is a former Audit and Consulting partner at Arthur Andersen, AT Kearney and BearingPoint. He is bilingual in Japanese and English and advises global executives on audit, fraud examinations, business and systems strategy, business process improvements, business continuity management, IFRS and other complex enterprise initiatives.

CHAPTER 19

The Triple-Three

LEONARD RANG'ALA LARI

Admittedly, this is not a large case. But it shows that the application of proper audit techniques can be applied to uncovering frauds, both big and small.

The depositors and shareholders of Raboss Sacco, a savings and credit cooperative in Kenya, will never forget John Ojok, who was also known as "the triple-three," because he had three wives (in Kenya, polygamous marriage is legal under customary law). The triple-three was known as a hardworking and intelligent pharmaceutical marketer who cared deeply about his work. His employer, Raboss Pharmaceutical, considered him an asset, and his public relations and marketing skills earned the firm a sizeable number of customers — both the distributors and retailers of drugs.

It was therefore not surprising that, when the triple-three was made the chairman of the board of Raboss Sacco, he was initially described as a "successful chairman." Ojok's power was bolstered by the fact that he selectively issued loans on incredibly favorable terms to specific Sacco shareholders. These loan beneficiaries in turn guaranteed Ojok their votes in the shareholders' annual general meetings. Other board members often felt that there was no point in disagreeing with Ojok because his ideas always seemed to be voted through.

During his free time away from the pharmaceutical company and his board duties, Ojok discreetly ran a transportation business called Eastland Commuter Connection with the treasurer and vice chairman of Raboss Sacco — who also happened to be his two best friends. The side business provided commuter-transportation services among various Nairobi neighborhoods with a fleet of taxis and minibuses, each of which cost a pretty penny.

At 45, Ojok, a loving father of three children with each of his wives (nine children in total), was perceived as friendly and selfless, particularly

177

among patrons of the bar he regularly visited. Even the bartenders liked him. He and his best friends/business partners, Mike Omolo and Jack Mango, were regular bar customers and shared similar social characteristics. More often than not they could be found near the female customers. Ojok was a trained pharmacist with a degree in pharmacy and a certificate in marketing. His partners in the transportation business each had a certificate in pharmacy and technical knowledge of financial accounting.

All the wives of Ojok, Omolo and Mango were self-employed, except Ojok's first wife, who worked full-time as a primary-school teacher. The other wives jointly owned a grocery store chain with locations throughout Eastland, the middle-class suburb of Nairobi that they all lived in. It was a popular neighborhood known for its social amenities and high population density. The income each family made from the grocery stores was predictable, due to the large local population, but the profit margins were small.

The three men sent their children to expensive private schools. Ojok had three children in high school and the rest were in primary school. His partners each had two kids in high school. The cost of so many tuitions added up quickly for the men and was one of their main motivations for starting Eastland Commuter Connection.

The unique, friendly and humorous attitude of the triple-three and his partners earned them good professional reputations. But their voracious appetites for hard liquor, concubines and extravagance were always lurking in the background.

Establishing the Rules of Play

Firmly entrenched in Raboss Sacco's board of directors and assured of their power, Ojok, Omolo and Mango convinced the other members to hire a part-time accountant to help with Sacco's finances; the accountant, predictably, shared behavior and personality traits with the three friends. Mwangi Njeri was a qualified accounting technician who served on the board until 2002, when Sacco's directors received a mandate to hire bookkeepers competitively from the market.

Biki Maura, a supervisory member of Sacco's board, was frustrated with the way oversight was conducted at the savings and loan institution, particularly because he could not get the necessary documents to conduct the board's quarterly reviews of the financial statements. Maura asked aloud one day, "How long are we going to have to put up with this triple-three trouble?" Maura was starting to sense that the board was being run by a group of bullies, and he wasn't alone in his suspicions. Unfortunately, for the time being, Ojok's unwillingness to provide documentation to Maura severely impeded the quarterly and annual reviews conducted by the board's oversight committee.

Drugs, Money and Rumors

Raboss Pharmaceutical was a registered Kenyan company that specialized in the development and distribution of pharmaceutical drugs for the consumer market. It had been in operation for decades when the owners decided to expand and allow employees to form a subsidiary savings and loan operation. Their reasoning for starting a business so outside the realm of the pharmaceutical industry was that the savings and loan could motivate and attract its customers from Raboss Pharmaceutical's staff. At the time, the pharmaceutical company employed more than 500 people.

Raboss Sacco was registered as a cooperative financial institution in the 1980s and, when I began my investigation, it had 300 Raboss Pharmaceutical employees. The Kenya Cooperatives Societies Act states that an "individual person shall not be qualified for membership of a cooperative society unless his employment, occupation or profession falls within the category or description of those for which the cooperative society is formed." This section of the law was the basis for Raboss Sacco's creation as a subsidiary of Raboss Pharmaceutical.

Just before my company's appointment as Sacco's external auditor, information reached Sacco members that the affairs of the board of directors were being handled poorly. The alleged misbehavior included board members using bank checks for personal expenses and issuing Sacco loans to friends and family members, based on personal biases, which was contrary to the bylaws and contributed to a backlog in outstanding loan applications. The members used the circulating gossip to force an appointment of a new auditor. Sacco's management solicited my firm's audit services for annual audit and I accepted. When I began to plan the audit, I knew that an understanding of the entity was a key component of our planning process, and Sacco's supervisory team was a major source of information for the audit team.

As the supervisor of an audit team of three, my job was to ensure that the external audit work was approached with skepticism and that the substantive testing was done accurately. We attempted to test all the controls that mitigate risks before carrying out any focused, substantive audit procedures or testing. Specifically, we looked for proper segregation of duties with respect to cash handling, as well as controls surrounding the collections process and loan originations.

During my initial meeting with Sacco's management team, I raised questions about the possibility of fraud; it is a standard audit practice. The executives — all of whom were also board members — were hesitant to make any accusations, but they did express a belief that fraudulent transactions had occurred. I asked about the chain of command and separation of duties among the managers and staff, but it quickly became clear to me that Raboss Sacco had no formal organizational structure. I also learned from initial interviews that most of the company's financial records were maintained manually, with the exception of members' statements (e.g., payment schedules for loans, shares and interest), which could be extracted from Raboss Pharmaceutical's computerized payroll system. Clearly, Sacco's activities were not properly segregated from those of Raboss Pharmaceutical if one company could access the other's personnel records.

The Importance of Planning

Ours was essentially a routine annual financial audit and we followed the auditing standards established by the International Auditing and Assurance Standards Board. In the process of identifying the client's risks of material misstatement, we performed a preliminary analytical review of various financial statement components. We then calculated variances from the prior year for each of these accounts. When we found differences exceeding 10 percent, we made a note and sought an explanation from Sacco's management.

Next, we completed an internal control checklist, which helped us assess the corporate governance environment and:

- Checked Sacco's organizational structure to confirm whether the responsibilities of various levels of management and their decision-making process were well-documented and made sense given the size and industry of the organization.
- Verified that managers prepared strategic plans and confirmed any operational functions that were outsourced.
- Made sure there was a risk management policy in place.
- Discovered who performed authorizations of loan applications.
- Learned which staff members had the responsibility of record keeping and custody of assets.
- Verified whether reconciliations of various accounts (e.g., bank reconciliations) were present.
- Confirmed the general information technology control environment.
- Determined whether detailed annual master budgets were properly prepared.

We then conducted our fraud-specific checklist, which involved a review of the board's special reports and meeting minutes. These documents were particularly telling about how the board meetings were run. Just from reading them, it was clear that Ojok, Omolo and Mango controlled the topics discussed and the decisions made by the board.

Next we met with the supervisory committee and other non-management personnel (including some shareholders) at Sacco. Our goal was to determine whether there was pressure from board members or management to override internal controls. Further, we reviewed the general ledger with an aim of identifying:

- Transactions that were outside the normal Sacco operations
- Transactions that involved issuing excessive loans or defaulting on loans
- Improper interest and loan amortization
- Unsupported increases in members' shares capital and deposit balances

Moreover, our team calculated various ratios to gain further understanding of the business and assess certain fraud risks, and performed procedures to determine the strength of the internal audit committee of the board.

We looked at the prior year's audit report to confirm either the lack of audit qualification (acceptance) or the existence of an audit report qualification (or nonacceptance) in the financial statements. The sustainability of Sacco services (going-concern test) was also reviewed. As expected, the prior year's audit report contained an unqualified opinion and no mention of unusual issues.

We then turned our attention to large journal entries posted close to year-end that mainly affected the following accounts: loan, share capital and members' deposits, interest income, cash book balance and loan defaults.

Also, we conducted inquiries into loan application forms and security for Sacco's general filing system. We paid close attention to how quickly management responded to our requests for documents and information during the audit. It was, to say the least, a very slow process. Obtaining documents from the client was like getting a root canal: it was painful, took a long time and no one really wanted to do it. Additionally, we noted the incidence of unusual delays in processing and issuing loans to applicants who met all the terms and conditions of the loan requests.

The final phase of our audit strategy involved meeting and communicating with management through letters, which culminated in an audit report. Two management letters were issued — one for the interim audit work and another for the year-end.

In summary, the overall audit planning strategy addressed the essential aspects, including the degree to which our audit work could rely on internal controls and the level to which the institution complied with policies, procedures and laws.

Loans in Default

During the audit review, I observed that Sacco's unamortized interest was added to the loan listing balance. The details to separate the two items were not provided to us, except for irregular journal entries posted at month-end to transfer interest earned to the income statement. This procedure enabled creative accounting to take shape, leading to a difficulty of separating loan control (ledger) account balances and loan listings (schedule) at year-end. This aggressive accounting affected all three years we reviewed.

Our audit indicated that loans totaling $15,897 could not be reconciled. Someone with knowledge of Sacco's controls and the means to circumvent them had to be behind the unreconciled amount.

This confirmed the existence of loans that had not been deducted or posted to Raboss Pharmaceutical's payroll, which was the standard procedure. A ratio of the loan ledger to the schedule that is higher than 1:1 is considered a red flag or a potential loss in practice because it can indicate loans extended but not properly recorded.

Our investigation of the transactions at year-end (cut-off test) revealed no timing differences, which confirmed our hypothesis that loans were being fraudulently manipulated. The existence of unsupported journal entries at year-end, which affected mainly the key accounts, was a further affirmation of intentional bookkeeping errors.

An interesting discovery from our interviews and the available records indicated that some of the defaulted loans had been issued to Ojok and his two partners. Other members of the board and employees at Sacco confirmed that Ojok, Omolo and Mango delayed the processing of legitimate borrowers to grant each other loans, which they used to operate Eastland Commuter Services. These fraudulent loans were then misstated on the year-end financial statements as current receivables to disguise the fact that they were in default.

Finally, the audit fieldwork revealed defaulted loans totaling $13,462. These were not supported by loan application forms and, therefore, it was impossible to identify the concerned guarantors to institute the recovery. However, our interviews and circumstantial evidence pointed to three culprits — Ojok, Omolo and Mango.

Shortly before our audit concluded, Ojok died unexpectedly from what medics termed a "lifestyle disease." His untimely death became the talk of the Raboss Pharmaceutical's personnel for some time, and it was followed shortly thereafter by the deaths of five close female coworkers, all from the same unspecified disease. Ojok never confessed to playing a role in the Sacco scheme.

Revealing Ratios

Raboss Sacco's confirmed net loss resulting from the defaulted loans that remained unrecovered upon Ojok's death totaled $5,128. Out of the total loss of $13,462, the savings and loan was able to recover $8,334 from Omolo and Mango. The $15,897 worth of unrecorded loans remained a subject of in-depth investigation, although we knew there was little chance of recovery.

A summary of the ratios we used in this audit process is below:

Type of Ratio	Year 2	Year 1	Year 0	Comments
Loan members schedule balance/ loan ledger balance	0.904 < 1	0.860 < 1	Not Disclosed	A value less than 1 increases the odds of fraudulent financial statements.
Dividend and members' bonus rate	5%	5%	6.2%	This shows an almost constant rate, which was not reflected in the actual performance. Thus, it was suspect.
Net profit/total assets	5.8%	4.57%	5.86%	A figure below 10% is below the standard of excellence.*
Members' loans net of provision for bad loans/total assets	65%	86%	83%	Acceptable standard is 70–80% — value outside the two extremes is a sign of bad performance.
(Share capital + members' deposits)/ total assets	86%	94%	92%	Acceptable standard range is 70–80%. Any % outside the range is a sign of bad performance.
Loans defaulted	$16,025	$ 2,820	$5,380	Incomplete details provided
Total revenue	$14,100	$10,380	$8,590	Incomplete details provided
Total operating costs	$ 4,100	$ 4,320	$2,564	All expenses for year 1 & 2 were supported.

*Source: World Council of Credit Unions, Ratios Toolkit Series, No.4 (2002).

Raboss Sacco calculated interest rates using a flat interest-rate method, which fixed the interest rate calculated on total loans. The interest repayment therefore remained constant throughout the loan tenure.

During the exit meeting at the cooperative's premises, I separately interviewed the key suspects — Ojok, Omolo and Mango. I asked each of them if they thought there was a chance the bank's bookkeeper had manipulated the financial records, and they each gave vague and varying answers that allowed for the possibility of fraud. Their explanations touched on all three key items: interest earnings, loan accounts and share capital accounts. To my surprise, however, no culprit was ready to blame the other.

After I submitted the final audit management letter, I offered my qualified audit report to the Sacco management committee for acceptance and subsequent registration with the cooperative societies' regulator, as required by law. The report indicated cases of:

- Misstated loans to Sacco members, including loans to officials
- Overstated interest earnings

- Forced loans account balance
- Forced share capital balance

Further administrative lapses in judgment, such as biases in loan issuance, were disclosed. After the society's annual general meeting in March, the entire management team was let go. Attempts to recover the losses were instituted against the surviving fraudulent officials, Omolo and Mango. In the subsequent audit year, I was given access to more of the necessary documents and uncovered and reported even more related losses.

Ojok, Omolo and Mango had each worked at Raboss Pharmaceutical for more than 15 years at the time of Ojok's demise. Separately, each had served on the Sacco board for at least nine years running. They were valued employees who worked their way up the ranks to become powerful board members. Without professional skepticism, we may not have uncovered problems. Long tenure and a position of trust should not clear someone of suspicion if the evidence is pointing toward him.

Lessons Learned

I and a team of three other auditors learned much about the unique nature of Sacco's fraud. The audit revealed how management can collude with bookkeepers to manipulate loans, shares and interest schedules. And although clichéd and repeated constantly, the importance of good internal controls cannot be stressed enough. It also became clear that delayed issuance of loans to institution members was a good indicator of misdeeds, as were clues pertaining to signatories' endorsement of checks from pubs (or other personal expenses) and cases of intentionally misplaced loan application forms. We also learned how some accounting ratios are good tools in detecting financial institution frauds.

Recommendations to Avoid Future Occurrences

The following recommendations were highlighted in our management letters:

- Insist that qualified bookkeepers are procured competitively. Irregularly hired employees can compromise the quality of operations. Those employed without following acceptable standards are more susceptible to taking shortcuts.

(continued)

- Ensure production and reconciliation of loan, shares, cash book and interest schedules on a monthly basis. A lack thereof is a major red flag in these types of institutions. Therefore, maximum internal controls should be in place to avert fraud.
- Use specific accounting ratios, such as dividends, to test the financial trends. Those above the industry average are likely symptoms of manipulation, and this is particularly notable when the growth rate is not in tandem with increase in total assets and the rate of loan recoveries.
- Institute key controls over the custody of loan application forms to avoid "losing" records. These forms act as legal proof of who the guarantors were. The loan register should show records of items such as the date of the loan, the interest rate, loan term, loan redemption date, reason of taking the loan, loan number, list of loan repayment and names of the borrower(s).
- Timely response to rumors of unsupported changes in the lifestyles of officials is an important step in preventing and detecting fraud. The introduction of a whistleblower policy or anonymous hotline can also help to this end. Full compliance with lending policies and a company's bylaws are also essential. Irregular journal and ledger entries should be carefully examined. Further, unamortized interest must be accounted for independent of loan balances.
- Ensure the management team's mandatory adherence to principles of good corporate governance, such as transparency, accountability and integrity. Training on the basic interpretation of accounting reports to both managers and members should also be emphasized.

About the Author

Leonard Rang'ala Lari, CFE, CPA, is a Deputy Director of Audit at the Supreme Audit Institution (Office of Auditor General in Kenya). He has more than 16 years of experience in both external and internal audits in both government and private sectors. He earned his master's of commerce (forensic accounting option) and is a member of the ACFE and the Institute of Certified Public Accountants of Kenya (ICPAK).

20

What Is 1 + 1? What Do You Want It to Be?

ROBERT BARR

Elliott Z. Maroni was a native of Houston, Texas, who moved to Austin to attend college. Shortly after finishing his freshman year, Elliott, known to his friends as "EZ," dropped out of school at age 19 to open a stereo store in a vacant grocery store. He named the store Austin Stereo and designed it to be similar to the stereo stores his family owned in Houston. In his first year in business, EZ sold $1.5 million worth of stereo equipment, and Austin Stereo was considered a big success.

Two years later, EZ sold his store to the family business, Houston Stereo Enterprises (HSE), a high-end stereo components retailer in Houston. EZ's store became HSE's first location outside Houston and the company grew from six stores to more than eighty within five years. EZ was highly involved in HSE's business operations, particularly purchasing the products carried in the stores. He was very skilled at getting discounts from his vendors to keep inventory costs down and margins high.

EZ wanted to begin carrying discounted electronics merchandise, including telephones, kitchen appliances and other consumer electronics items in the HSE stores, but other family members wanted to stay solely in the high-end stereo equipment that had made HSE successful. So EZ, along with a friend who also worked for HSE, resigned from the family business to start a discount electronics business. He used the money he saved from the sale of his Austin store and substantial funding from his father to start the new business. He named the company Maroni Electronics Corp., but it was known as MEC.

Martin Lambert was EZ's best friend from high school and had been his college roommate. Martin also dropped out of college with EZ to work in his stereo store and never returned to school. He moved back to Houston with EZ to work for HSE, and followed him again to MEC. Although Martin had no financial experience, EZ named him the chief financial officer of MEC.

Jimmy Scullin was another high school buddy of EZ's. He attended a small university and graduated with a bachelor's degree in accounting. After college, Jimmy worked in the accounting department of an oil and gas exploration company but, even after six years at the company, was still considered a junior accountant who showed little ability to advance. Jimmy had taken the CPA exam twice a year since graduating from college, but had never passed a single part of it. EZ hired him to be MEC's controller.

EZ's father, Charles Maroni, provided 50–60 percent of the capital needed to start MEC. He purchased about 5 percent of the company's stock and made loans (all of which were repaid fully in three years) to help get it started. Charles had been involved in HSE, but mostly as an investor; the company had been run by his four sons. A few years after EZ founded MEC, the family sold HSE, and Charles had nothing to do. So EZ hired him to be MEC's chief operating officer. He carried the COO title happily, although he conducted little or no real business activity with MEC other than showing up at the offices several times a week and collecting a paycheck. He had no decision-making authority at MEC.

EZ Street

EZ started Maroni Electronics Corp. to be a wholesale distributor of consumer electronics merchandise. He decided to go the wholesale route because he did not want to be in competition with his family's retail stereo business and he believed wholesale would allow him to make more, and better, deals with his customers. EZ used his initials as his name and told his contacts that not only were they his initials, but they showed he was easy to do business with.

MEC's management used January 31 as their fiscal year-end because the end of January was the slowest part of the year, and it allowed the company to take inventory and close the books on a timely basis. In the first three years of operations, MEC experienced significant growth due to EZ's marketing skills and a fortuitous period of economic growth nationally. Also, there was a substantial increase in revenues due to high inflation at the time.

EZ held an initial public offering for MEC stock two years after the company started and a secondary offering a year later. Subsequent to the secondary offering, EZ still owned approximately 51 percent of MEC's shares. EZ had planned another registration statement a few years later to sell a large amount of his stock.

Friends and Family

The board of directors included a few outside members, but they were a minority — three of the seven positions. The other members were EZ, Martin Lambert, Jimmy Scullin and Charles Maroni, the company's management team. Although there were outside directors, it was clear to everyone that EZ ruled the roost and no one was willing to question his authority.

MEC also had an audit committee consisting of three members: EZ, Martin and one outside director. EZ was the chair of the audit committee and made all of the decisions for the audit committee, just like he did on the board of directors.

Because MEC sold discount electronics, a large portion of the business was in obtaining and selling closeout merchandise. EZ would purchase 100 percent of a manufacturer's discontinued inventory at discounts of up to 80 percent. Although obsolescence was speedy in the closeout products, there was enough demand for EZ and his staff to move the products with relative ease. Because MEC was well known for carrying closeout merchandise, the company had no premier retailers; most of its customers were smaller, discount retail stores in Houston and throughout central and eastern Texas.

Fewer than ten years after EZ started MEC, Houston experienced a severe economic recession that caused high unemployment and brought about the failure of many retailers. However, MEC continued to show significant increases in sales and profits and was projecting substantial growth, even though overall sales in the region were showing precipitous declines.

One year MEC reported revenue increases of 311 percent — up from $21.3 million the year before to $87.8 million — but beginning with the first quarter of the following year, MEC began showing significant operating losses for the first time in the company's history. Before MEC reported the results for that quarter, EZ filed the registration statement to sell his founder's shares and traded a large number of his shares. He used the cash to purchase a controlling interest in another publicly traded entity in the consumer electronics retail business.

Each quarter during the year after the registration statement, MEC showed losses. Although EZ was still the CEO, he spent most of his time in New York working on his new investment. The sales for the next year showed an almost 60 percent decline from the prior year. Shortly after the first year of losses, there was substantial shareholder litigation against MEC and its auditors for not disclosing the significant losses incurred at the time of the registration statement. Later that year, MEC's management filed for Chapter 11 bankruptcy, the creditors' committee forced a change in management and a turnaround specialist was hired to manage the business.

Sorting Through the Mess

I was brought in by the turnaround specialist to look at the auditors' work papers and assist in the investigation of MEC's accounting records. Counsel from both sides of the case had concerns about the financial reporting. From discussions with company insiders, I learned there had been some gossip about the executives misrepresenting MEC's financials. When I was brought in, no one knew if there had been fraudulent financial reporting, but no one was confident there had *not* been fraudulent financial reporting, either.

I started the investigation by looking at some large sales transactions that occurred near year-end in each of the two years prior to the last registration statement. All of these transactions were traced to all of the supporting documentation for the transactions.

Window Dressing in the First Year

On November 30 of the first year, MEC purchased $2.5 million worth of computer monitors from Star Electronics, a subsidiary of Walton Sound. November 30 was the fiscal year-end for Walton Sound. Our research found that there were also some other unusual facts surrounding the transaction. First, Walton Sound was a publicly traded company on the West Coast. EZ was a member of the board of directors of Walton Sound, and the CEO of Walton Sound was a member of the board of directors of MEC, which made this appear to be a related-party transaction. Also, MEC never took possession of the inventory.

Two months later, EZ sold the entire inventory of computer monitors to Walton Sound for the same $2.5 million that MEC had paid Star Electronics. The sale was made on the last day of MEC's fiscal year and recorded as revenue on the books, accounting for 11.88 percent of revenues for the year. Again, the transaction was not disclosed as a related-party transaction. I discussed the transactions with MEC's purchasing manager and sales manager, but they were unaware of the sales. Further investigation showed that both the purchase and the sale were recorded by Martin Lambert, and neither had gone through the normal processing for purchases or sales.

Fictitious Revenues in the First Year

On January 30 of the first year, MEC recorded $370,440 in sales on six separate invoices to Third Generation, a regular retail customer. My investigation showed that there were significant discrepancies in the records for this transaction.

First, there were no shipping documents related to the sales because the merchandise was allegedly shipped directly to Third Generation by the company's vendor. MEC was never able to get any copies of such shipping documents.

Second, MEC's auditors sent an accounts receivable confirmation to Third Generation, but it was returned with exceptions because Third Generation's accounts payable clerk said that they had not made any such purchases. The exceptions were worth 8.93 percent of MEC's total accounts receivable. When the auditors asked EZ about the exception, he said that because the items were shipped on January 30, Third Generation would not have received them by January 31, hence the exception. The auditors never followed up with Third Generation.

Third, MEC never tried to collect on the accounts receivable, even though Third Generation had always paid promptly. Subsequent to filing the Form 10-K on April 26, MEC issued credit memos on all six invoices, indicating that the merchandise was returned but provided no receiving reports to back up the claim. Additionally, MEC's receiving department had no records of any returned merchandise from Third Generation.

I discussed the sale and return transactions with MEC's sales manager but, as with the Walton Sound transactions, he was unaware of the Third Generation sales. After a bit of digging we discovered that Martin had recorded the sales and the credit memos outside the normal processing protocols.

Fraudulent Journal Entries in the First Year

Physical inventory was taken on January 31, so Martin made one-sided entries — moving the inventory from one MEC warehouse to another — to hide the fact that inventory never actually left the warehouse. In legitimate inventory transfers, the sending warehouse debited the inventory suspense account and credited inventory for the transferred items. Then the receiving warehouse debited their inventory and credited their suspense account, resulting in a zero balance for MEC.

In January, the main warehouse transferred in inventory related to the Third Generation sale, but there was no transfer from another warehouse. In addition, there were no inventory transfer forms to document the transfer, only entries made in the system by Martin. He then made a journal entry to debit the inventory suspense and credit cost of sales to make the inventory suspense account balance zero. When the sales were entered, the revenue and cost of sale was recorded and the inventory quantities in the warehouse remained unchanged. The result was $370,440 in revenue with zero cost of sale, accounting for 27.5 percent of the company's pretax income for the first year.

The Potato Chip Theory of Fraud

A potato chip company once had an advertising slogan, "I bet you can't eat just one." The Potato Chip Theory of Fraud indicates that committing fraud is similar to eating those chips. Once someone successfully commits a fraud, it is easier to commit another one. At MEC, not only did the same frauds occur the next year, but they were worth even more.

Window Dressing: A Repeat Performance

The following year, MEC's revenues were up 311 percent and its pretax income had increased from $1.3 million to $5.9 million. Similar to the year before, MEC purchased $6.9 million worth of handheld televisions from

Walton Sound on November 30 and sold them back to Walton on January 29 for $7.1 million. The $7.1 million was recorded by MEC as revenue. When computed, the price increase was exactly the price of the goods plus interest at 10 percent for the time MEC "owned" the inventory. Again, the inventory was never shipped or delivered from Walton Sound and remained at their warehouse the entire time. This sale accounted for 8.1 percent of MEC's total revenues that year, but this was obviously not a normal sale, nor was it reported as a related-party transaction.

I looked at the purchase and sale documents and was not surprised to find that they were recorded by Martin Lambert. Again, the purchasing and sales managers were both unaware of the transactions.

Fictitious Revenues: Even Bigger in the Second Year

During the last three days of the second year, MEC recorded unusually large sales of one type of computer monitor — worth $200 each — to three high-end retail store chains, none of which were existing MEC customers. The three stores were Mark Brothers, a high-end department store; Gilland's, a moderate-level furniture and appliance chain; and Crescent, a now-defunct retailer of home electronics that had tried to become a "big-box" retailer but failed. I traced each of the sales invoices to the original documentation and saw that EZ and Martin recorded the sales. The books did not show purchase order numbers for the transactions. The sales were supposedly as follows:

Mark Brothers	$3,562,500
Gilland's	$1,452,000
Crescent	$3,350,750

We had a number of reasons to question these sales. MEC had never done business with the three companies prior to these huge sales, nor had it ever stocked anywhere near that number of computer monitors at one time. MEC's warehouses would not have had sufficient room to store that many monitors — they would have required 100 percent of the company's warehouse space. We also questioned MEC's ability to deliver the monitors, which were supposedly sent across multiple states. And finally, EZ and Martin were recorded as the salespeople on the transactions, although they were never listed as salespeople on any other MEC invoices.

MEC had six delivery trucks and, when deliveries were made, the drivers were required to obtain signed receipts. There were no delivery receipts for the sales to Mark Brothers, Gilland's or Crescent. Also, based on the capacity of the trucks, it would have taken almost 1,400 truckloads to deliver all the monitors. Many of the delivery locations would take days to reach, and it was simply physically impossible for the six trucks to deliver that quantity of merchandise in the last three days of the fiscal year. I asked the drivers about the orders, but none of them had ever made a delivery to Mark Brothers, Gilland's or Crescent.

I also called the accounting departments at the three companies and found out that none had any record of ever doing business with MEC.

The Cover Up

Martin and EZ again made entries in the inventory system to hide the fact that sales of computer monitors had never been made. In fact, MEC never had the inventory in stock to make such sales. Just like in the previous year, Martin recorded fraudulent inventory transfers without moving products or preparing the necessary forms, and then made a journal entry to hide the fact that no inventory changed warehouses. The end result was $8,365,250 in revenues with no cost of sales, turning MEC's pretax losses for the first 11 months into a significant pre-tax profit by the end of the fiscal year.

None of the receivables from these computer monitors sales were ever collected, and all of the sales were later reversed.

Registration Statement

In early May of the second year, EZ filed a registration statement for his un-registered stock and sold about 80 percent of it. He used the proceeds to purchase a controlling interest in a consumer electronics retailer and eventually took over as the CEO, all the while maintaining his CEO position at MEC. Immediately after taking over at his new company, EZ fired all of the existing management and insisted that the company take a physical inventory. Within three days of taking over, EZ discovered the inventory was overstated by at least $50 million, and his new company was forced to file bankruptcy as a result. A few months later, MEC had to file bankruptcy as well, because it became clear that all the fraudulent revenues were uncollectible.

No charges were filed in the MEC case. The FBI and Department of Justice were busy investigating and prosecuting the case against EZ's new company and when we presented the MEC case, they figured EZ had probably learned his lesson.

Lessons Learned

Lack of Board of Directors Oversight

MEC lacked oversight by a legitimate board of directors; the board members did not question the abilities of a CFO without a degree and
(*continued*)

(*continued*)

with absolutely no financial or accounting experience, and a controller who was unable to pass any part of the CPA exam or the lack of any professional accounting staff at the company.

The board of directors also did not sufficiently review MEC's financials. They never questioned the unrealistic revenues and results in the last month of the year or the window-dressing sales that were not made in the normal course of business. Board members didn't question how the company had losses through 11 months of the second year, but ended up with $5,903,201 in pretax profits from unrealistic incomes in the last month of the year.

Had the board of directors questioned any of these items, the fraudulent financial statements should have been detected much earlier.

Auditors Lacked Professional Skepticism

The external auditors also appeared to lack professional skepticism because they failed to question the year-end sales to Walton Sound with the inventory that MEC never took possession of and sold back to Walton months later. Also, instead of questioning the large, fictitious sales to Third Generation at year-end, the auditors simply accepted management's explanation without verification. They didn't consider if the sale of more than 40,000 computer monitors, all delivered in three days by six drivers, was even possible.

Recommendations to Prevent Further Occurrences

Have an Independent Audit Committee

The audit committee should comprise outside directors and members of management should not be allowed on the audit committee, especially the CEO. The audit committee should review the results of the operations of the company monthly, quarterly and annually for anomalies. In the case of MEC, the audit committee should have questioned the unbelievable profits that were recorded in the last month of the fiscal year, particularly as it was the slowest month of the year. Committee members should also have questioned the inventory purchases and sales to and from the same company (a related party) with little or no gross profit. Had the audit committee looked at these transactions,

(*continued*)

they would have realized that these did not qualify as revenues in the normal course of business.

Additionally, audit committees should consider whether management personnel are qualified for their positions, and maintain strict oversight of the accounting and financial reporting of the company.

Board of Directors

A company's board of directors should be independent enough to question any extreme growth in sales and profits. MEC's board was all too happy to accept the 311 percent growth in sales from one year to the next, despite the fact that the local economy had declined by 22 percent during the same period. An objective, ethical board of directors is essential to preventing similar occurrences in other organizations.

About the Author

Bob Barr, CFE, CPA, is a senior manager in the audit and litigation consulting and forensic accounting practice of Harper & Pearson Company, P.C., in Houston, Texas. In addition to auditing, his practice provides support services to attorneys in commercial litigation, including expert testimony on a broad spectrum of accounting, fraud and damages issues. Mr. Barr has over 30 years' experience in public accounting. Mr. Barr also teaches a graduate-level Fraud Examination course at the University of Houston.

CHAPTER 21

Take Two

MATTHIAS KOPETZKY

George Sizler was an experienced man. He had a past checkered with financial statement fraud allegations and even a conviction for falsification of public documents. However, not many people in business today and in charge of the current investment industry are old enough to know about his very special history. George Sizler was well over 70 years of age and his conviction happened almost 30 years earlier — an entire generation ago. His anonymity among modern professionals afforded him a second chance to embark on his quest for money. This time around, he was determined to learn from his past mistakes and planned to work from the second row. He would leave the risk-taking to the young and greedy hotshots dreaming of founding the next Microsoft, Google or eBay.

This time he saw himself as the elder consultant sharing his profound knowledge with a group of mediocrely successful small-business owners. He promised them a deluge of investor money to buoy their struggling businesses and offered them his expertise as proof. They were IT entrepreneurs hoping to escape their garage or basement offices and start the next big thing on the Internet. Naiveté grew into solid egoism when these business owners started to realize the true rules of the game. Some of them left Sizler's scene early enough to escape the public prosecutor's searchlight. Others played a minor role on the edge of the scheme and actively pulled out when they realized they weren't going to receive any investment funds for their projects. Only a handful of them developed into active players in the ringleader's circus.

There was also a separate group of Sizler advocates — the support network. First was Mary Pfister, his loyal secretary, who covered for Sizler, produced all the documents he needed and handled the cash and people. Sizler was not very tech savvy and wrote most of his ideas and orders by hand. Pfister was his translator to the modern tech-based world. The second leg in his support system came from a CPA named Henry Braun who offered him a helping hand. He gave Sizler advice on tax issues, produced necessary expert opinions and borrowed the name of a well-known CPA firm for use in brochures and other client communications.

Naiveté and Ego

Invest Consult Ltd. was at the center of a network of high-tech companies that shared lofty, unrealistic goals, like revolutionizing the Internet. Invest Consult's network heralded the ultimate mobile-ticketing devises, geographical information systems (GIS), neuronal networks and many more avant-garde IT ventures. In all, more than twenty small companies depended on Invest Consult to provide investor services and marketing advice. The investors were lured in with promises of hefty tax deductions and the potential to be part of the next big thing on the World Wide Web. George Sizler was the owner and CEO of Invest Consult; he invented different investment vehicles but didn't take in money from investors directly. In most cases Sizler backed small, struggling corporations, so investors could see the history and true entrepreneurial spirit behind them. Sizler put the companies on financial life support with Invest Consult's capital, so the business owners trusted the company with the money they received from investors.

Only in rare cases would the entrepreneurs pull the plug early, when they realized that the promised investments had not made it into their company accounts. They stopped the acquisition process and ended their relationship with Invest Consult Ltd. But those few lucky ones were the exception to the rule of money-dependent, underfinanced, struggling companies that were sold as rising stars to investors.

Different Pieces of the Same Puzzle

The first red flag was raised by tax inspectors looking into Invest Consult as a result of the huge tax deductions that investors were requesting. They reported investment losses because the Internet firms associated with Invest Consult were losing significant capital during their startup phase. New Internet companies usually burn money in their first few years, so this was nothing new. But the tax inspectors wanted to know if the startups had legitimate business models or if they were set up to just realize tax deductions for the investors.

Being part of a business venture means that the entity's financial results become part of the investor's income — and help determine his or her tax bracket. Losses on paper can easily exceed the original amount someone invested. Moving these losses to the tax return can create a significant shelter for the investor, often as high as or higher than the original investment. If the investor contributed $100 but eventually lost $300 on the investment, his tax burden would be reduced by $100 (assuming an average tax rate of

33 percent). Sizler reckoned that investors wouldn't complain about their lost investments as long as they could keep their tax shelters. The intended losers in this model were the Internal Revenue Service (IRS) and honest taxpayers.

When tax inspectors started to looking into Invest Consult, Sizler played games with them. Because every investment vehicle associated with Sizler's company was a separate case for the IRS, he started to move the registered offices of the companies around the country to make it hard for investigators to grasp the totality of the case. Different field offices were responsible for different pieces of the puzzle, turning the investigation into Sizler's version of the fabled blind men touching the elephant. When tax inspectors in Albuquerque started an audit, Sizler moved the registered office to Boulder, where new tax inspectors had to learn the case. This usually won Sizler months to continue operations and, in the end, it was years before the IRS realized the scope of the case and established a national team to investigate it.

The district attorney also started looking into Invest Consult using a team of specialized police departments in combination with the privately held investigation company where I worked as a CFE. Our team's mission was not only to investigate the tax issues but to question the investment group as a whole. Did it offer legitimate investment opportunities with real business models or did it create ghost towns — nice facades with nothing behind them?

Unpaid Suppliers

We started by collecting the annual financial statements from seven years ago onward. In analyzing the accounts of the companies we realized quickly that the case was much bigger than a simple tax question, and that it was much older than seven years. Because Sizler and Invest Consult started new investment vehicles almost twice a year — which meant new ideas, business models and managers acting on the front end — each single venture never made it on the IRS's radar for long. Each startup firm was too small and the investors were too widely dispersed across the country for red flags to be spotted.

Before starting a new venture, Sizler would intentionally move it into the jurisdiction of one of the big IRS regional offices. He knew that investigators in the larger hubs were used to big-ticket tax fraud cases with expansive networks of perpetrators. A small, new company with a few investors wouldn't be worth their time or effort; they had bigger fish to fry. However, in one case Sizler forgot to move the venture's jurisdiction, and it stayed in a relatively small regional IRS office. These units often employed highly engaged and curious inspectors for whom a million or two investor dollars would be remarkable and worth taking a closer look. And so this misstep by Sizler set the ball rolling.

The venture that Sizler forgot to relocate, Market Maker, was a firm purportedly specializing in market research and analysis. After a brief search into the history of the company, it led us to a chain of investment vehicles sheltered by Invest Consult, each appearing to share a goal of gathering intellectual property and market research. Each company in the collection of small businesses appeared to spend most of its operating capital on purchases of intangible assets, like geographical data, neuronal networks, customer lists, supplier lists and others, all of which were generously written off in the few first years. This created significant accounts payable to suppliers on their books. Normally suppliers diligently pursue their accounts receivable, because they have expenses, too; however, the suppliers to Invest Consult's protégé firms did not seem to care about the funds owed to them. But there was no record of payment from the startups or Invest Consult to their suppliers, and there were no records of complaints from them. This was a glaring red flag to us.

Curiously, the accounts payable of Invest Consult's companies were only paid up to the amount that investors had contributed. The balance remained unsettled and was written off years later, usually during bankruptcy proceedings. We realized that these companies had few assets, if any.

On the profit and loss statements, these intangible-asset transactions equaled enormous operating expenses that burned up the investors' money and created very large accounts payable. As soon as the investors got their tax deductions, the startup companies declared bankruptcy and ceased operations. This pattern raised questions in our minds:

1. Did the intangible assets actually exist?
2. Were the suppliers real companies?
3. Did they make nominal deliveries without recording them in their books?
4. Why did we find certain staff contacts being shared by different suppliers? By chance?

Suppliers accepted nonpayment from Invest Consult ventures without complaint and even entered into further transactions with Sizler's other companies. This astonished us, and we decided to open a special investigation into these suppliers. Most of them were outside our jurisdiction, which meant we needed a Letter Rogatory to access legal and financial information about them. Some were already under investigation by tax investigators in their region but others were unknown to outside officials. None were registered and the IRS did not have a history for any of them.

Dual Cash Accounts

Under these circumstances we were displeased but not surprised to discover transactions worth hundreds of thousands of dollars paid in cash. Or so the books stated. There was a special account named Cash Account B in the books of almost all of the investment vehicles and of Invest Consult. Although it is not that unusual for a company to have two cash accounts, the situation was odd to us because huge amounts of money had moved through each company's Cash Account B, and every transaction followed the same process: Invest Consult received funds from investors in cash or via bank transfer, and then the money was withdrawn from the bank — usually the whole amount — and "deposited" into an investment vehicle's Cash Account B. Then, often for weeks, several hundreds of thousands of dollars sat around in a cash account, without earning interest, seemingly forgotten.

Meanwhile, each company's Cash Account A functioned much as we expected — experiencing deposits and withdrawals of relatively small amounts and petty cash transactions. When Cash Account A started to run out of money, someone rushed to the bank to get more petty cash to fill it up. We thought it strange that someone would go to the bank to withdraw funds for Cash Account A, rather than simply transferring some of the hundreds of thousands of dollars that were unused in Cash Account B. We concluded that Cash Account B was fictional and that the sums recorded to the account balance had left the respective companies a long time ago — or never made it into the account in the first place.

The Cash Connection

So now we had suspicious (possibly fictitious) suppliers and two cash accounts that were handled completely differently, one with several hundred thousand dollars untouched for weeks and one with the usual petty cash transactions. The suspicious suppliers received their payments in cash. During our questioning of Invest Consult's personnel (the individual investment vehicles normally did not have employees), we learned that Cash Account A was handled by regular staff members, but only Sizler and Mary Pfister had access to Cash Account B.

Next we asked Sizler to provide evidence of the third-party deliveries of intangible assets; we expected him to have records and descriptions, programing codes and databases, customer or supplier lists — standard proof that intangibles actually exist. However, Sizler was unable to provide any such evidence, but we did find a few resource guides on his bookshelves with titles like, *How to Present Intangible Assets, How to Get a Patent* and *Intangible Assets: The Next Big Thing in Taxes.*

Even if we had thought the deliveries were legitimate, we would have doubted the ability of one supplier to provide completely different intellectual property to multiple, disparate companies, but that is what Sizler claimed happened. Most of the so-called intellectual-property suppliers turned out to be fictional or unable to provide reasonable proof that they had the capacity — quantitatively and qualitatively — to deliver the claimed "know how." Other suppliers turned out to be completely uninvolved; they had not heard of Sizler, Invest Consult or the individual companies to which they had supposedly sold intangible assets. We found that most of Sizler's suppliers were affiliated with a man named Pjetr Chechov from Bulgaria. He was a plumber in his younger days and later specialized in delivering software services and consultations to Internet startups, in particular the Internet startups of Invest Consult Group. He also received regular, large transfers from Cash Account B of Invest Consult and its many small enterprises. We tried to get access to Chechov's financial records, but international regulations made it too difficult. We did, however, review Sizler's personal bank records with this new information in mind, and noticed a distinct pattern. Each day following a transfer to Chechov from a Cash Account B, Sizler received a deposit from Chechov. Sizler's deposits were usually worth between 75 and 85 percent of Chechov's payment.

Sizler Loses Again

Our investigation was raising more questions about the legitimacy of Invest Consult's investment vehicles, which gave the IRS enough reason to deny the tax-shelter claims of Sizler's investors. As a result, a large number of them started filing complaints against Invest Consult. Just weeks after we learned of Chechov's existence, we learned that he supposedly died in Bulgaria under unknown circumstances.

In the midst of the investigation, Sizler was taken into pre trial custody, where he remains today, awaiting his court hearing. His group of CEOs of the investment companies pleaded guilty to or denied knowledge of the fraudulent transactions and falsified financial documents.

Most of the transactions were conducted in cash by Sizler and always via Cash Account B, which the court later saw as conclusive evidence that Sizler did not use most of the investors' money for business purposes. During initial proceedings, Sizler didn't even attempt to prove that the transactions recorded in Cash Account B were for legitimate business expenditures.

Lessons Learned

Intangible assets always present a challenge for correct valuation in balance sheets. The arm's-length principle is most in danger if suppliers of such intangible assets are affiliated companies not held in arm's-length positions.

Financial data, especially balance sheets, are the main fraud tools for carrying out tax-shelter investment scams. Normally the IRS — and
(*continued*)

taxpayers in general — are the victims of such schemes. As soon as the IRS starts to investigate and negate the tax shelters, the damage moves to the investors, who have to pay back-taxes and start to realize that they are invested in bankrupt or ghost companies.

Reasonable supplier relations have distinct behaviors:

- Even if information is the (intangible) product being sold, legitimate transactions will have plenty of evidence regarding the content and value. Investigators can find written descriptions and maybe electronic evidence. The delivery of intangible assets is usually accompanied by reams of legal papers regarding the description of the sold goods, the method of transfer of possession, inherent guarantees and methods of payment.
- Suppliers who have actually delivered an intangible asset usually want payment in reasonable timeframes.
- Suppliers who do not receive timely payments usually start to actively demand them. If their efforts fail, suppliers will normally seek legal assistance.
- In case of bankruptcy of the customer, suppliers usually participate in bankruptcy proceedings as creditors.

How petty cash accounts are used in reality:

- Usually do not contain large amounts of money. The danger of theft is too high for companies to bear such a risk.
- Normally are used only for small, everyday expenses like postage, small travel expenses, direct deliveries of merchandise and so on.
- Do not earn interest, so it does not make financial sense to hold large sums of money in them.

Large payouts from petty cash accounts — although theoretically possible — are very unlikely in serious business situations, not to mention impractical. I had to wonder how Sizler was supposed to have removed $100,000 from the bank without advance notice. Was the money in one plastic bag or two? How big was the suitcase? How high was the stack of bills?

If I had asked him, I'm sure he would not have known how to answer because, in reality, those funds were not moved all at once, as the books suggested, but were the result of a series of smaller transactions that were covered by false entries in the accounting system. For example, Cash Account B had recorded a series of small deposits over a long period of time, eventually accumulating to $100,000 in cash. One day

(continued)

(*continued*)

Cash Account B shows a payment of Pjetr Chechov for $100,000, which depletes the account. We can assume that those small deposits to the cash account never occurred; Cash Account B was fictional, created for the illusion that the money was held by Invest Consult until Sizler had a plausible excuse to "transfer" it to his "supplier," Chechov.

Recommendations to Prevent Future Occurrences

The following are suggestions and important facts offered in the hope that they will help prevent or detect a similar fraud.

1. Intangible assets pose an accounting threat in knowledge-driven companies.
2. It is shortsighted of investors only to think of tax deductions and not question the actual business model. Companies need a valid business to keep their tax deductions and be able (at least theoretically) to earn money with their investment.
3. Investors have the right to check the balance sheet of the companies in which they are invested. Sometimes it is also necessary to have a look into the account balances to get an idea how the daily business is run.
4. The balance sheet only shows a snapshot of a certain day. There are a lot of ways to hide transactions between balance sheet cut-off dates.
5. Frequent changing of auditors is an important measure to deter fraternization between auditors and management and prevent professional bias.
6. Unusual account development needs to be questioned, and explanations need to be checked thoroughly, even if they seem plausible.
7. Investigators need to get to the bottom of big write-offs or big account balances that have not changed during many years, even if they are on the creditor side.
8. Graphical representations of cash accounts often show a kind of liquidity "sediment" that can be interpreted to mean the cash balance is falsified by the amount of the sediment bottom line. For example, if the account balance never falls below $12,000 and money is transferred into the account to prevent it from dipping below that, it's likely that the $12,000 doesn't exist.

About the Author

Dr. Matthias Kopetzky, CFE, CPA, CIA, is a specialist on economic crime detection and prevention in Austria/Europe. Regularly he acts as an expert witness in Austrian courts. He is, together with Dr. Joseph T. Wells, author of the German version of *Corporate Fraud Handbook* and he teaches in different universities in Austria and Germany. He is member of the board of the IIA-Austria and treasurer of the national chapter of the ACFE in Austria.

CHAPTER 22

Wade's WMD

MICHAEL SPINDLER

World Machine Distributors (WMD) had undergone a significant period of growth during a time of economic expansion. WMD had developed expertise in industrial machinery and maintained an inventory of hard-to-find spare parts by buying equipment from factory foreclosures and other open market purchases. Wade Johnston, the company's CEO and largest shareholder, drove the company's sales and had developed relationships with many suppliers. As equipment lines were discontinued, he would buy up the inventory of spare parts. Maintaining this line of inventory required capital, so as the company grew, Wade decided to hold an initial public offering of the company's stock, thereby becoming a public company with SEC filing requirements.

Although WMD had become a public company, it was still very much "Wade's" company. He had a volatile personality and he ruled with an iron fist. His employees were not very interested in crossing him or questioning his directives. If provoked, he would fire employees without consultation with department heads or human resources.

Breakfast at Denny's

Our work began with an initial interview with a whistleblower, Clive Ingram. Clive had told the external auditors that crimes had been committed (although he wasn't exactly sure what crimes they were). The external auditors notified the company's audit committee and informed them that an independent investigation into the allegations must be conducted. The company's board of directors formed a Special Committee and legal counsel was retained. I led the external forensic accounting team that was retained by counsel to conduct the investigation into the allegations.

Simply stated, Clive had started a firestorm. Yet no one knew who it was that had lit the fuse, and company management was very interested to learn who our source was. Crimes would be committed in attempts to find out his name and also to intimidate him. The phone in our conference room at WMD's office was bugged in an attempt to listen to our calls and to learn his identity. One person was fired on the mere suspicion of being the informant. We managed to protect Clive's identity throughout the course of our investigation and never divulged his name, except, ultimately, to the Securities and Exchange Commission and the Department of Justice.

Our story begins on a Saturday morning over breakfast at a Denny's restaurant far away from the company and its employees. Clive was uncomfortable and reluctant to tell us his story. He was scared. The CEO was a large, domineering individual and people did not normally take actions that were not in furtherance of his interests. This didn't surprise me. A domineering CEO can be a red flag of financial statement fraud, since his or her personality can erode the effectiveness of internal controls designed to prevent, detect and deter such frauds. After spending some time to build Clive's comfort and develop a rapport, he told us what he knew. It wasn't much, but it was enough for us to commence an investigation.

He told us he had suspicions about accounts receivable related to certain customers. He believed that certain accounts were being falsified. He identified one in particular, a South American customer, and several others that he believed we should look at. We asked if the accounts receivable were uncollectible and what impact they had on the accounts receivable reserves. He said that he believed that regular payments were made on the accounts. He also had no documents to support his allegations. He said that we would never be able to prove anything, because "they" could create any document we asked for. He wished us luck, since we were going to need it.

Men in Black

On Monday morning, the head of the Special Committee, the audit partner from the outside auditing firm and I met with the CEO to explain that allegations had been made that certain accounts were being falsified and that we had been retained to conduct an investigation into the matter. This meeting occurred shortly after the movie *Men in Black* had been released and we later learned that the CEO had jokingly told his employees that the "Men in Black" would be arriving that morning to conduct an investigation into rumors and innuendo. We had each unwittingly worn black suits that day, which made him think we had better sources within the company than we actually did at the time.

Expecting an angry outburst, I was surprised that the CEO responded with an icy calm. I suspect this was due to the fact that the audit partner had explained that the audit firm would resign if we were unable to conduct the investigation. He understood this was something to which he was forced to submit. However, he made it clear that he was not pleased about the circumstances. He explained that this was the second time that the auditors had questioned his integrity. (An earlier allegation had been made and resolved, apparently.) He explained that this would be the last time the auditors should make such allegations impugning his character. He said that he believed he knew who our whistleblower was and that it was a disgruntled employee with personal issues who didn't know what he was talking about. Wade said that he was responsible for the well-being of his 300 employees and their families. He had to think of them and shouldn't be bothered by unsubstantiated allegations of troubled individuals.

Not surprisingly, the meeting ended awkwardly following his speech. His assistant directed me and my team to a conference room next to the CEO's office to do our work. The room wasn't set up for us to have access to the computer systems and I was a bit suspicious about the location they had provided for us. Why were we placed next to the CEO's office? Did he want to eavesdrop on our conversations? Did he want to monitor our investigation? To test this, I searched through the company's building and found some empty offices that had system access. I suggested that we could work in those offices. The assistant told us that we couldn't do that, since the CEO had insisted that we work in the designated conference room. I had my confirmation that something wasn't right about the arrangements.

Reflecting upon events thus far, I had my concerns. The CEO hadn't attacked the allegations, but instead chose to attack the whistleblower. It is my general observation that innocent people address the allegations and guilty people attack the person making the allegations. I also noticed that his reference to being responsible for the families of his employees sounded like a potential rationalization for any improper acts — providing one leg of the fraud triangle. His domineering personality most likely provided the second leg of the fraud triangle — opportunity. But what was the need — the third leg of the triangle? There was much left to learn at this early stage.

Interesting Patterns

We began our analysis by downloading sales data from WMD's servers. We sorted the sales transactions in various ways, arranging sales chronologically and also by sales invoice number. Our first revelation occurred when we noticed an interesting pattern in how the invoices were numbered. When a sales invoice was issued by WMD, a five-digit invoice number was assigned in numerical order. In theory, the chronological sort should have revealed a series of invoices in numerical order. However, we noticed that there were a series of invoices that had invoice numbers that had more than five digits. These invoices with longer numbers would always have the number 1 in the sixth position or beyond. We then examined the invoice folders for those clients who had invoices with numbers that were longer than five-digits.

We determined that those invoices were originally issued with five-digit numbers in chronological order. As the original invoices approached 90 days of age, the invoice was canceled and reissued with the same invoice number, but with a 1 added at the end. Indeed, one could determine the correct age of an invoice by counting the 1s at the end of the invoice, as though they were tree rings.

We then analyzed the company's accounts receivable aging reports and confirmed our suspicion — by performing an invoice credit and rebilling the invoice, the receivable was in effect "refreshed" for aging purposes. This served to avoid recording accounts receivable reserves, since the company calculated those reserves based on the aging of the outstanding invoices. This was our first solid indication of financial statement manipulation.

The Chocolates

During the initial stages of our investigation, the CEO maintained his gruff demeanor with us. He had told his employees about the investigation and that he expected we would be gone quickly. It was apparent to us that the employees felt intimidated and they were uncomfortable talking with us. As often happens, employees will watch the situation closely. They will be reluctant to come forward unless and until they have the sense that the investigation will be successful in uncovering wrongdoing and that changes will occur as a result. Their fear is that if they were to come forward, the fraudster would somehow survive the investigation and know who spoke out against them.

It had become clear to WMD's workforce, based on the questions we were asking and the documents we were examining, that we were not going to disappear as easily as the CEO had indicated. There was a palpable shift in the atmosphere at the company. People were more willing to visit with us. The CEO fired an accounts payable clerk on the suspicion that he was the whistleblower, thereby creating a second whistleblower. We could feel that the employees were rooting for us.

One day I came into the conference room and noticed a box of chocolates on the table. I asked where they had come from and was a bit shocked to learn that the CEO had brought them to the team to thank them for their efforts. Clive told us that the chocolates were a sure sign that Wade had now become very worried about us. We all agreed that, although they looked delicious, it probably would not be a good idea to eat any of the chocolates.

Falsified Documents

We began to examine the supporting documentation for sales to selected customer accounts. These were the accounts mentioned by the whistle-blower plus accounts where the billings had been "refreshed." Even with the accounts receivable aging manipulation, there had still been accounts as of the most recent quarter-end that had been questionable and were at risk of requiring a reserve. There were four accounts in particular that had been the subject of collectability discussions with the auditors. The auditors were informed that the company had agreed to acquire some spare parts from these accounts subsequent to the end of the quarter and, since those purchases were larger than the sales, they would be able to realize the receivable through an offset of the resultant amount payable from the purchase. This explanation apparently was sufficient for the auditors to agree to forego a reserve requirement.

As we examined sales and purchasing documentation for these four accounts, we noted some disturbing issues. We were examining invoices for all of the company's purchases from the first customer. Many of the invoices were for small dollar amounts — most were under $10,000. The purchase the company had told the auditors about was for nearly $200,000 — conveniently larger than the amount of the receivable. When we compared the large invoice to the other purchase invoices, we noticed that the invoice contained a field for the airway bill number for the shipment to the company. The airway bill number for the large invoice was exactly the same as an airway bill number on an earlier invoice. We also noticed that many of the fields were similar across the two invoices. For example, some numbers were transposed on the invoice number, but the digits were the same. This also held true for the invoice amount. It appeared as though the earlier invoice was the source used to create the larger invoice. We also noted this for the second of the four customers; although the airway bill numbers were different, the numbers appeared to be similar.

The purchase invoice for the third customer was dated on a Sunday and the purchase invoice for the fourth customer bore a stamp that indicated it had been received on a Sunday. We knew the company was closed on Sundays. When fraudsters create false documentation, they don't always check to see whether their fake dates make sense. We now had reason to believe that all four documents had been falsified. We suspected that the IT director created the false invoices and when we confronted him with the evidence, he admitted that he had created them at the direction of the CEO.

Early that evening, I notified legal counsel for the Special Committee of the status of our investigation and what we had uncovered. We agreed that the evidence indicated the need to expand our investigation and conduct a complete analysis of the accounts.

The Midnight Deposition

The next morning, we were discussing the status of the investigation in the offices of our accounting firm, away from the inquisitive ears at the company. I received a call from legal counsel for the Special Committee, who said the company had requested a "cooling-off" period in the investigation and that he wanted to let me know of what he had done last evening. He apparently had been invited to a deposition, at around midnight, at the company's offices of the IT director. The IT director had apparently repudiated what he had told us about the invoices. He indicated that he had a transcript of the deposition. I asked him to come to our offices so we could read through the transcript and so that we could discuss the investigation. He arrived shortly thereafter and I quickly perused the transcript.

According to the transcript, the IT director admitted to creating the false documents, but he said that he had done it solely to embarrass the CFO. He knew that if he placed the false documents in the customer files, we would find them and assume the CFO had been cooking the books. Moreover, he had only created the documents a few days prior and, thus, they could not possibly have been used to mislead the auditors. In light of this new information, counsel for the Special Committee asked us if we still felt as though the scope expansion was necessary.

I pointed out to counsel the inconsistencies between the transcript and what the IT director had told us in our interview. I also pointed out that nowhere had the IT director indicated what had become of the original documentation, if these were merely falsified copies of what were, theoretically, legitimate transactions. The telling blow to the company's attempt at a cover-up came in the form of a JIC file. The senior auditor had maintained a file that was separate from the audit workpapers. It contained documents that weren't needed for the workpaper files, but he held on to them, "just in case" (JIC). The four false documents were in the JIC file, thereby establishing that they had, in fact, been provided to the auditors and had been created well before the timeframe indicated in the transcript. When confronted with this evidence, the Special Committee agreed that we should be provided with unfettered access to conduct the investigation as we deemed necessary.

Confessions

Let us return to the fraud triangle. You'll recall that we had a potential rationalization from the CEO (his responsibility for the 300 families of his employees) and his dictatorial approach provided the opportunity. But what was the need? As we analyzed the company's accounts, we noticed additional unusual activity with accounts receivable. The bank would collect on accounts receivable and notify the company of what had been received. When we examined copies of the checks received and compared them to the company's accounts, we noticed that the company that made the payment wouldn't necessarily be the same as the company account to which the cash was applied. Were they misapplying cash to avoid more aging problems? It didn't appear that way, since the payment amounts were so specific and matched the amount due to the penny, although from a different customer. Could one entity be paying on behalf of another, such as a parent company making a payment on behalf of a subsidiary? That didn't appear to be the explanation, either. When I read through the company's debt agreements, I found my answer. The company's debt facility was asset-based. They could borrow against their inventory and accounts receivable. However, not all accounts receivable were eligible. The non-account-matching cash payments we noted had been made by customers that were not eligible for borrowing and applied against accounts that were. It appeared as though we had a classic case of bank fraud — the company was creating false invoices by taking actual sales but changing the customer on the invoice to an eligible account so that the invoice could be sent to the bank to borrow against.

After this revelation, the CEO appeared and, continuing his suddenly friendly state, asked me if we could have lunch together. After we had settled into our seats at the restaurant, he asked me how the investigation was going. I told him that we were making good progress. I told him that it appeared to me as though the company found itself in a cash crunch and, since he was responsible for the 300 families of his employees, he had to falsify invoices to make them eligible for borrowing under the company's line of credit in order to keep the company going. He looked at me and said, "you've asked me a direct question and I cannot tell a lie — yes, that is exactly what we did." (Generally, I've found that obtaining confessions are quite easy when the perpetrator knows that you have already figured things out.)

We followed up with the IT director, who admitted that he gave false testimony in his midnight deposition. The evening of his deposition, he had gone out after work for some adult beverages at a local watering hole when his cell phone rang. He was told to return immediately to the office, where he was informed that a stenographer was coming to the office to produce a transcript. He was going to be asked certain questions and he was told what he was going to say. Although he was drunk at the time of the deposition, he said that he threw in some false information so that we would know his testimony was untrue when we read it. He also said that he had intentionally used the same airway bill number when he created the false invoice so that he could demonstrate later that it was false if he needed to. He also confessed to us that the phone we had been given to use in the conference room next to the CEO's office had been bugged at the direction of the CEO, who was eager to learn who the whistleblower was. This attempt was unsuccessful, since we never talked to the whistleblower at the company or on company phones.

One mystery remained. We had been told that the CFO was completely unaware of what had been going on. Many people seemed to be protecting him. I reasoned that it would have been difficult, if not impossible, for this all to have occurred without the CFO's knowledge, but we didn't have any evidence that actually linked him to knowledge of the plot. I was talking with him a short while after we had uncovered the fraud. I told him, "You know, I'm really impressed. This was pretty complicated, since you had money coming in from one account, but it had been recorded under another account, so you had to switch it so the account could be relieved in the false account, but if a customer ever called about the status of their receivable, you would have to figure out where each sale really belonged! I don't know how you managed to keep it all straight!" To which the supposedly uninvolved CFO replied, "Yeah, it wasn't easy, but I was able to track all the false invoices with this spreadsheet here!"

The Outcome of the Investigation

Based on their inability to rely on the representations of management, the auditors resigned and pulled their past audit opinions. The CEO also resigned, as it was a requirement of the new audit firm before they would agree to serve as the company's auditors. However, the new auditors also resigned when they learned that the CEO was still directing the company's activities from off-site.

The CEO was indicted on fraud charges and pleaded guilty. At his sentencing, the judge made particular note of the midnight deposition and said it was one of the most egregious cover-up schemes he had ever heard. He sentenced the CEO to three years in jail.

Lessons Learned

Throughout the investigation, the fraud triangle proved useful in guiding us. By focusing on the perceived needs of the organization and its leadership, we were able to form a fraud hypothesis and focus on key areas to prove or disprove the hypothesis. Understanding the rationalizations of the CEO also started the wave of confessions we needed to confirm our assessment of what had occurred. Finally, we were able to protect the whistleblower's identity through careful communications among our team members.

Recommendations to Prevent Future Occurrences

In large part, this fraud occurred because of the dominance of the CEO and the lack of meaningful controls and oversight around him. After the CFO admitted that he was aware of the fraud that had occurred, I asked him what he thought of the fraudulent activity.

(continued)

He said, "I figured it was Wade's company and that was what he wanted to do." Well, it certainly wasn't "Wade's company." Even though he owned part of the company, it was publicly held, so there were shareholders and other stakeholders who were victimized. Even if he had wholly owned the company, it wouldn't have excused sending false documentation to the bank to improperly obtain loans.

The SEC filing for the company's IPO contained a biography of the CEO. It made reference to his background and his college degree. One problem — he never obtained the degree he claimed. Someone who will lie about a college degree will quite likely lie about other matters, especially with the right combination of pressures and opportunities to do so. This highlights the importance of doing complete background checks on potential employees. The CEO should never have been placed in that position of responsibility. Once there, he should have been subjected to appropriate oversight.

The AICPA publication *Management Override of Internal Controls: The Achilles' Heel of Fraud Prevention* indicates that the audit committee can address the risk of management override by:

- Maintaining skepticism
- Strengthening committee understanding of the business
- Brainstorming to identify fraud risks
- Using the code of conduct to assess financial reporting culture
- Cultivating a vigorous whistleblower program
- Developing a broad information and feedback network

About the Author

Michael Spindler, CFE, CPA, CFF, is Executive Director — Litigation and Forensics with Capstone Advisory Group, LLC, in Los Angeles, where he focuses on forensic accounting investigations and litigation support.

Fraud Under the Sun

A CASE STUDY OF ACCOUNT MANIPULATION IN THE RENEWABLE ENERGY SOURCES INDUSTRY

OSCAR HERNÁNDEZ HERNÁNDEZ

Julio Panin was born in the heart of the Salamanca district, one of the most elegant and wealthy areas of Madrid. He was the eldest of four brothers and his father, Aurelio Panin, was a distant descendant of the Marquis of Garcillan, a key figure in Spanish politics at the end of the nineteenth century.

Aurelio Panin spent his life enjoying the substantial fortune accumulated by his ancestors over the decades. The inherited wealth allowed him to set up a series of import and export businesses and delegate their management to associates, some of whom had dubious reputations. In this way, he could dedicate the majority of his time with his two greatest passions: hunting and clandestine poker games that took place in one of the basements in the Casino de Madrid.

Julio Panin had a happy and comfortable early childhood; however, one rainy afternoon in October was engrained in his memory forever because his father, half sobbing, gathered his wife and four sons to tell them of the family's ruin and that he faced going to prison due to the activities of his business partners.

From that moment on, Julio Panin's life changed forever. He was forced to leave his exclusive Jesuit school, one of the oldest and most prestigious in the Spanish capital, to assume the role of head of the family. The family's move to one of the working-class areas on the outskirts of Madrid dealt a great psychological blow to the young Panin, who had inherited the pride of his father and iron will of his mother but no wealth of his own. He decided that he would not rest until he regained his economic and social status.

At 17 years of age he started studying civil engineering at the Universidad Complutense de Madrid. At 23 he married Maria Ruzafa, a childhood friend and daughter of a wealthy banker. Panin worked as an engineer for many years in the privately run companies owned by his wife's family. Then he decided to make a career change and moved to Germany for nine months to study the latest innovations in renewable energy, specifically solar energy.

On his return, he capitalized on the network of contacts passed down from his father and father-in-law to secure the necessary investors to set up a pioneering company in Spain, taking advantage of the exceptional light conditions on offer in the country and marking the transition into a new phase in the Spanish energy industry.

This led to the foundation of SunElectric.

Bright Future

SunElectric was started with capital stock amounting to $120 million. Its main shareholder was ATR Inversiones (Grupo ATR), an industrial group located in Southwest Spain, with an extensive equity investment in the transport sector and a risky bet in new technologies.

SunElectric owned two factories in Galicia (Northwest Spain) and its main offices were in the financial heart of Madrid. It also owned five commercial offices in large Spanish cities and satellites in Chicago, Buenos Aires, Paris, Brussels, London and Berlin. SunElectric employed more than 2,000 workers, of which more than 1,900 worked in factories in Galicia. The finance and administration department comprised 30 people.

The main activity of SunElectric was to manufacture and assemble solar panels for the production of electric solar energy. The principal raw material, silicon, was mainly imported from China and Russia.

SunElectric had a Research and Development Department located in a suitable building in the industrial complex in Galicia. SunElectric's market was approximately 50 percent domestic and 50 percent exports to countries in the Mediterranean arc and central Europe. The company enjoyed spectacular profits as a result of the exponential growth of the renewable-energy sector in Spain at the start of the twenty-first century. Julio Panin worked his way to President of the company and was responsible for keeping the shareholders at Grupo ATR informed of SunElectric's position.

The financial responsibility rested with Armando Cortes, the Financial Director, and Andrés Burguillo, the Financial Sub-director in charge of accounting. At the close of the year, the company registered the highest net revenue in their history, $180 million, representing a 15 percent increase from the previous year.

With these good prospects, Grupo ATR launched a market-exit strategy for SunElectric. For this, it selectively searched for investors, personally led by Panin, to attract new shareholders to the company. For several weeks,

Panin was occupied full time with meetings with potential buyers and banks, and he was able to find several strong candidates for new shareholders.

SunElectric and Panin selected a capital-risk company called Adventure Money that belonged to a wealthy Catalan family. In the last years, the owners had been searching for new industries in which to invest profits from various real estate and banking activities. Adventure Money subscribed for the entire capital increase of the company for $140 million.

Suspicious Resignations

Everything suggested that it was going to be a relatively calm end to the financial year. The past few months had been fairly busy, but the initial symptoms of the financial crisis were now starting to take effect on the Spanish economy.

One Monday morning in July, the head of our investigation department, Carlos Longares, called an urgent meeting in his office. He had just received a call from one of the most important law firms in Madrid. He said, "Team, Ruiz & García & Asociados have just rung, and it seems that one of their clients may have a problem with their accounts."

The same afternoon, we met with two partners in the offices of Ruiz & García, Juan Ruiz and Pedro Rivas. "Gentlemen, we have called you because one of the companies of Grupo ATR, one of our main clients, is having problems. Two of their directors have voluntarily submitted their resignations in the past 48 hours, just before the initial meeting with the auditors regarding the field work," said Rivas. "The internal auditors of the group have detected a series of inconsistencies in the reported figures from the past few months that do not tally. Since the group thinks that something strange may have taken place, we have contacted you."

We arranged a meeting with Miguel Larrumbe, Director of Internal Audit at ATR, and he provided us with a short memorandum outlining the problems detected by his team. They mainly related to the sales figures and credit notes from the three months prior to the close of the financial year when they were planning the capital increase of SunElectric.

According to Larrumbe, two weeks later they unsuccessfully attempted to analyze the questionable documents with Panin but, "It was strange because when we met with Julio in our offices to discuss the latest sales figures, his attitude, normally affable and open toward me, changed." The next day Larrumbe received a call from his secretary informing him that Panin had handed in his notice for medical reasons (depression). The following day, Panin's right-hand man, CFO Cortes, also announced his resignation.

Larrumbe gave us a brief description of the problems he and his team detected. They had noticed that the number of sale payments had significantly increased in recent months. Likewise, they had detected considerable differences between the booked inventory and the physical count.

A Key Witness

Our deadlines, as always, were very tight. The new shareholders of the company had been informed by Grupo ATR of potential problems in the sales figures, which meant that the person in charge of industrial investment for Adventure Money was nervous. Without further delay, we created various procedures that we wanted to put in place throughout this investigation.

Our first decision was to meet with the subdirector of finance and the head of accounting, Andrés Burguillo, who at this time was the highest ranked director in the company and, in view of the duties of his position, a possible witness to the irregularities detected. I knocked on the door frame of his open office.

"Good morning Mr. Burguillo."

"Good morning, nice to meet you," he responded, accompanied by a nervous movement with his left arm.

"As Grupo ATR has already told you, my team's aim is to analyze in detail the latest sales of SunElectric, because certain inconsistencies have been detected, in addition to the sudden and immediate resignation of Mr. Panin and Mr. Cortes."

"I am in charge of the situation and am willing to collaborate with you in every necessary area."

We had a three-hour-long conversation. As time went by, he began to relax and the tension that was present at the start of the interview was gradually dispelled. I tried to send him a calm message and help him understand that the smartest thing that he could do was collaborate with me and my team. The feeling I got from this first interview was that I was dealing with an honest man who was committed to his work and his colleagues. I also deduced that during the past few months, his life had not been made easy by Julio Panin. Burguillo left me with the following statement:

"I am very grateful that you have given me the opportunity to recount what has happened in the company during that last few years. The truth is that my staff and I have had a very tough time, and on more than one occasion we planned to report the situation; however, we did not have the courage to do it."

I closed my first meeting with Burguillo by scheduling a series of interviews with him and various people in the financial, commercial, R&D and logistics departments of the company.

The next day, we went to Ruiz & Garcia for advice on accessing Panin's and Cortes' computers to make a forensic copy of both hard drives. Then we informed the legal department at SunElectric of our intentions and they referred us to Rubén de la Rosa, the head of IT who, we later found out, was one of the five closest family members to Panin within the company.

Rubén, without trying to conceal his annoyance at our impromptu visit, told us, "Both Julio and Armando always used a laptop. I don't know if they were their personal computers or if they were owned by the company. In any case, I am not aware if the machines are even currently on our premises."

Faced with this situation, we decided the next best option was to access their secretaries' computers. Our experience has told us that some managers delegate certain tasks to their assistants, such as the management of their mailboxes. Fortunately for us, this seemed to be the case at SunElectric.

The brief conversation that we had with Panin's secretary, Andrea Gutierrez, confirmed her unwavering loyalty to her boss of seven years. After five minutes of tense conversation, Gutierrez called an abrupt end to our interview. "Julio raised this company out of the ground, and everything that's gone wrong here is due to certain people who do not support his success."

As a result of Gutierrez's reticence, we requested authorization for our team of forensic technologists to analyze her computer, along with the computer of Estela Jimenez, Cortes' secretary. For good measure, we added Buguillo's secretary to the list. Within 24 hours, the hard drives were copied and ready for analysis.

We revisited the notes that we had taken during our interviews with Buguillo and his team and, after rereading key sections, we realized we had overlooked a statement from one of the company's accountants. It seemed that Julio never parted company from his blue notebook. So with the goal of finding this blue notebook, we conducted a thorough search in Julio's office, but we could not find it anywhere. Momentarily defeated, we turned our attention back to the analysis of the secretaries' computers.

This time we had good fortune on our side. One of our forensic technologists mentioned that during the analysis of Gutierrez's hard drive, they had detected the use of a thumb drive on the day Panin left the company. With a bit of luck, the contents of the drive would have been recorded on Gutierrez's hard drive. And it was, in part — we managed to locate one of the folders from the thumb drive, which contained a series of Excel documents. After a preliminary analysis we concluded that it contained various sales invoice records, expenses, payments, and so on.

Making Headlines

At the end of the afternoon, Carlos Longares, head of our investigation department, called us into his office. "Team, we need your early results; shareholders of SunElectric are getting nervous and want us to deliver a first draft summary of our work in 48 hours."

This situation was complicated by an unexpected circumstance. As always in this kind of investigation, confidentiality is paramount. We presented ourselves to SunElectric's employees as statutory auditors, not forensics auditors, in the hopes that the company would continue to operate as normally as possible.

However, that hot morning in July, we were sitting on the third floor in our client's offices when Marcos Martínez, responsible for sales in South America, showed us that day's *El Diario Financiero*, one of the most important financial newspapers in the country, with this headline splashed across the front page:

> Shareholders of SunElectric Investigate Irregularities Committed by Previous Management

Chaos ensued, bringing with it calls, comments, dirty looks and whispers from employees, customers and others. The discretion we had maintained over the previous few days had been blown completely sky high.

It was time to reinforce the strategy and analyze all we had gathered thus far. In this kind of investigation, it is very important to understand how to manage customer expectations while not leaping to rash conclusions. These are key elements in the success of any similar inquiry.

The support we had from Ruiz & Garcia was essential now that the news had been leaked to the press; the damage to the company's image had been significant. Despite the confusion, we were beginning to get an idea of what we were dealing with. We reorganized meetings and sped up the process of analyzing the hard drives. At the same time, we opened another line of investigation to review the financial analyses of the company accounts, which would complement the information we had previously gathered from interviews, e-mails and the computer files from the secretaries' computers.

While we were moving forward, the shareholders of SunElectric held a meeting with the company's statutory auditors to bring them up to speed. Their audit partner exclaimed, "No way! It must be a misunderstanding." As the evidence of the irregularities was summarized for the statutory auditors, their faces painted a picture of enormous surprise. They offered their services in our investigation straight away.

Over the following few days we went back to interview Andrés Burguillo. Through past experiences in similar situations, we knew to be careful with statements made by workers who had been subjected to the tyranny of their superiors. However, in this case, our team members all felt that Burguillo was sincere. Furthermore, we believed that there were still lots of doors to be opened, and we should therefore treat our conversations with Burguillo as a priority source of information.

The last investigative procedure we undertook was to search for close ties among Panin, Cortes and their families and SunElectric's suppliers. All the procedures we had planned at the start of the job were in place and the first results were already coming in quickly.

Packaging it for the Investors

As a result of the different lines of investigation we opened, results were beginning to emerge and shed light on a whole series of complex and intertwined irregularities. The plot had been masterminded by Julio Panin, who had managed to sustain it for several years, thanks to the fear-based participation of other managers. The nature of most of the suspected frauds all seemed geared to the same objective, to show the accounts of the company in the best light possible. This served to keep the shareholders from meddling with management and to reassure banks and potential investors that SunElectric was a wise investment choice.

It should be emphasized that all of this was achieved behind the backs of the statutory auditors, who had been deceived by Armando Cortes. He had past experience as an auditor and was a knowledgeable expert on auditing processes. He also enjoyed "helping" conduct SunElectric's audits.

Manipulation of Recorded Income and Costs

One of the accounting irregularities Panin and his team committed was to deliberately manipulate recorded levels of production on the solar farms that SunElectric operated throughout Spain. For example, a solar plant in the Murcia area was 25 percent installed at the end of the fiscal year, a percentage equivalent to the level of costs incurred by the company. According to Spanish accounting standards, the company might then have had an income equivalent to 25 percent of the total estimated costs. However, Panin recorded an income equivalent of 80 percent. We identified that the excess of income incurred by the company, connected mainly to five projects, amounted to $14.8 million in one year.

False Invoices for Delivery

To further manipulate income figures, Panin issued invoices and the subsequent accounting details for false sales of solar panels. We identified the fake invoices by comparing a list of invoices to a list of delivery confirmations. The sales that did not have corresponding delivery records were considered false. We also confirmed that we were on the right track by comparing our results with the information that our IT team found on various spreadsheets from the thumb drive files on Gutierrez's computer. In total, the fictitious sales amounted to $42.8 million.

Misclassification of Expenses

Panin also falsified SunElectric's expenditures — to present a higher net profit — by accounting for the purchase of raw materials (mainly silicon) as fixed instead of current assets. The amount capitalized was more than $7.3 million. We discovered that Panin had also registered financial expenses worth $1.5 million as fixed assets, thereby creating a fictitious level of higher net profits for the company.

Overvaluation of Stock

Together with SunElectric's logistics team, we identified a series of finished products (solar panels) that were clearly defective and not released into the market but were still recorded on the books for $1.65 million. Panin and his management team did not take these into account, therefore artificially increasing the net profit. One of the Excel files on the thumb drive included a list of inventory items, some of which had been considerably marked up. This served to further overstate SunElectric's stock value by $9.65 million.

Nonrecoverable Investment

From our interviews with R&D staff members, we learned that SunElectric supported a flagship project to develop solar panels that required significantly less silicon. However, according to the engineers we interviewed, the test results showed there was no feasible technology to accomplish such a goal. As a result, SunElectric lost 100 percent of the financial investment. When the loss was brought to Panin, he chose not to record the research loss on the books. The total amount devoted to the project was $653,000.

Conflicts of Interest and Other Consequences

We found that various SunElectric suppliers had personal connections with Panin or Cortes, and these companies invoiced SunElectric for a combined $4 million for goods not purchased in the past three years. As a result of all our discoveries:

- The new investor, Adventure Money, decided to pull out the investment.
- Grupo ATR and SunElectric lost hope of succeeding in the market-exit strategy.
- Panin is currently on trial for falsification of public documents and embezzlement.

Lessons Learned

At the time, this investigation was one of the most complex cases of account manipulation that my team and I had faced. As we had learned from previous experience, this kind of fraud practiced by senior management tends to progressively increase over time. The

(*continued*)

perpetrators don't follow a detailed plan designed from the start. Rather, the circumstances prompt more fraudulent recordings year after year.

Our experience also led us to conclude that the process usually starts with a precise and deliberate manipulation, such as misstating the end-of-year turnover figures with the hope that an expected boom the following year will compensate for the falsified books. However, the economic situation of the company does not become as positive as initially anticipated, making it necessary to continue manipulating accounts the following year, and the following, and so on. Thus a vicious cycle is generated, a snowball effect that becomes harder and harder to control.

We have also seen how the combination of a very stubborn leader mixed with the grant of freedom from the shareholders can create a highly explosive environment for the company. Other typical characteristics of this kind of management are that they surround themselves with people whom they trust, mainly friends and family from whom they can expect total loyalty and no questions. It must also be emphasized that standard audit tests, repeated yearly, can teach management what documents will be requested and how to better falsify them to conceal a fraud.

We learned to be especially careful with companies seeking new investors or launching a stock market exit strategy. In such situations, auditors should pay special attention to the sales figures, credit notes and work-in-progress projects, especially on the records of the last months of the year.

Recommendations to Prevent Future Occurrences

After our investigation into accounting irregularities committed by several former directors at SunElectric, we made the following suggestions to prevent similar occurrences in the future.

Install a Fraud Hotline

I believe that if the company had provided an anonymous fraud hotline, the irregularities would have been made apparent to the shareholders of SunElectric much earlier. Various members of the financial department told us in our interviews with them that, "Several times we were tempted to report what we were seeing, but we were scared we'd lose our jobs."

(continued)

(*continued*)

Institute an Internal Audit Department That Reports Directly to the Shareholders

SunElectric's shareholders fully supported Panin because he had won them over with his charm and personal prestige and, as a result, he had unfettered freedom to make unethical decisions and doctor the company's books. If there had been an internal audit department that was independent of Panin and the general management team, SunElectric could have enjoyed a stronger control environment and reduced levels of risk.

Institute a Policy of Segregation of Duties

Internal audit departments at other organizations should learn from the weaknesses at SunElectric. After analyzing control failures, companies should institute an official policy of segregation of duties that avoid the accumulation of too much power with one executive.

Analyze Management Background

Although an analysis of Panin's background would not have been sufficient to detect his personal traits, implementing such a practice might help SunElectric avoid hiring another Panin in the future. I strongly believe hiring of reasonable managers, without delusions of grandeur, helps companies achieve reasonable and legitimate growth.

Institute a Code of Ethics Approved by the Shareholders of the Company

Implementing a code of ethics and sharing it with all the employees helps prevent the behaviors identified in this investigation. Managers should work to create an environment of best practices and instill a solid code of values for themselves and the employees.

About the Author

Oscar Hernández Hernández is a manager at Deloitte in Barcelona, Spain. He has a business administration degree from the Salamanca University and a master's degree in accountancy. For the past seven years, Oscar has worked in the forensic department of Big Four companies around Spain. He has specialized in fraud investigations, including account manipulation and asset misappropriation.

Franklin County Contractors:

A CASE OF CONCEALED LIABILITIES

PATRICIA A. PATRICK

Richard L. Franklin, III, was the owner of Franklin County Contractors (FCC). He was a good-looking man — one of those men who looked as though he spent a lot of time on a yacht with his year-round tan and expensive yet casual clothes. But then, Richard did spend a lot of time on his yacht. Richard was born into a very wealthy family with extensive real estate holdings. His family was one of the wealthiest in the state. Richard had looks and brains, and he graduated with good grades with a degree in engineering from an Ivy League university.

After Richard's father died, Richard's mother gave each of the Franklin children several large tracts of real estate. Richard's tracts included several stone quarries and asphalt plants, as well as significant commercial and residential real estate holdings. Altogether Richard owned and operated about eight companies to manage his real estate holdings and business enterprises, and he even owned a company to manage the private plane he flew to his vacation homes. Richard had several accountants and each of them oversaw the books for one or more of his companies. FCC was one such company, which Richard had formed to complete state highway construction contracts.

Alan Baker had been the controller of FCC for more than ten years. He had a bachelor's degree in accounting but was not a Certified Public Accountant (CPA) and therefore was not bound to uphold any formal licensing requirements. Alan also did not possess any professional designations. Thus, he was not bound by any professional codes of conduct either.

When Alan resigned from FCC, he said it was "time for a change." The real reason Alan resigned did not become clear to me until many months after I replaced him as controller. I had been working for a large nonprofit organization for the past five years and was looking for a challenge. I contacted my former employer, a public accounting firm, and learned that FCC was looking for a controller. I had participated in the FCC audit years ago and recalled that Richard Franklin owned the company, but I did not know anything about FCC's current situation or its past. I accepted the position as FCC's new controller, but had very little accounting experience. Still, I was excited to assume my role in the fast-paced industry of highway construction. I was also aware of my professional responsibilities and planned to carry out my duties with the highest integrity.

Throwing Stones

FCC was the general contractor for dozens of state government construction contracts for large sections of interstate highway. As the general contractor, FCC bid and managed construction contracts, using the assistance of subcontractors, as needed.

FCC owned a large stone quarry and asphalt plant. It also employed about 300 semi-skilled, seasonal laborers to complete the highway construction jobs and about two dozen other job-related employees, such as superintendents, purchasing agents and estimators. FCC employed about five office staff to perform the accounting and administration functions. Richard owned a large fleet of heavy equipment, including tri-axle dump trucks, front-end loaders, backhoes and asphalt pavers. This equipment was used on the highway construction jobs, but on the advice of his lawyers, Richard formed the heavy equipment as a separate corporate entity to avoid legal liability, in the event that FCC was sued.

FCC was privately owned and operated by Richard, and I would not be exaggerating if I said that Richard ran it with an iron fist — he had a very bad temper and frequently flew into uncontrollable tirades. Richard wasn't violent and never struck anyone during these rages, but he did humiliate his victims and subject them to prolific profanity. Richard frequently fired employees during these rampages but did not remember doing so later; he often had to rehire the terminated employees the next day to keep the jobs moving. Since no one was immune to his ire, I did not take the outbursts personally and simply waited silently until Richard was finished. Some people became offended and walked off the job, refusing to put up with the abuse. Others argued or simply stood and cried.

Shortly after assuming my role as controller, I learned that FCC had a long history of questionable behavior, which included alleged and confirmed unethical and illegal acts with a direct and indirect impact on the financial statements. I saw these acts as red flags of fraud and organized them into the following categories: (1) management characteristics, (2) operating conditions, and (3) industry conditions.

Management Characteristics

FCC had a weak control environment and poor tone at the top — management's personal integrity and attitude toward internal controls. The independent auditors annually cited FCC for internal control weaknesses, but Richard failed to correct the problems. Most of these problems revolved around a lack of separation of duties and a failure to restrict access to blank documents.

For example, FCC frequently paid duplicate invoices and did not use a voucher system. That would have prevented the payment of duplicate invoices by requiring proper approvals and documents for purchases, but Richard never insisted the staff use it. Instead, Richard often signed handwritten checks with little or no documentation for employees claiming "emergencies" at the jobsites. Richard also had several signature stamps and allowed various employees to stamp his signature on handwritten checks. This resulted in checks that were written but not processed in the accounting system. FCC also failed to control access to blank purchase orders. Boxes of blank purchase orders were stored in an unlocked closet and laborers frequently stole blocks of purchase orders and used them at local hardware stores. We challenged these liabilities in court, but always lost. These weaknesses, along with the ongoing lack of separation of duties, led me to conclude that FCC had a poor tone at the top.

FCC had also committed a variety of tax and regulatory violations. Some of these violations were confirmed; others were suspicions based on rumors or hearsay. One of the known violations involved corporate income tax evasion. Several years ago FCC received a state tax audit and was found to have understated its net income by several million dollars. The company was put on a payment plan to reimburse the state government for more than $300,000 of back taxes, fines and penalties. Pursuant to this plan, every month I had to hand deliver a $13,000 check to the state office of the attorney general for FCC's back taxes.

I frequently heard rumors that Richard instructed the laborers to illegally dump the leftover asphalt from paving jobs. Asphalt is a petroleum product that must be disposed of in a certain manner. However, disposing of asphalt properly involves substantial costs. The fleet manager and laborers often hinted that it was better to not know how Richard got rid of his excess asphalt from jobs.

FCC also frequently failed to comply with certain provisions of government contracts. As controller, I soon realized that FCC had a tendency to miss project deadlines. Richard also complained about paying the laborers Davis Bacon wages on the government contracts. These are the prevailing wage rates required on contracts that receive funding from the federal government. Davis Bacon rates are set by the federal government and are based on job title and geographic area to ensure that employees on government contracts are paid fairly. The bids that FCC submitted to the government included Davis Bacon wages, so FCC was reimbursed for those. Still, Richard tried to circumvent the wage rates if possible.

Operating Characteristics

FCC was having serious cash-flow problems. It could barely make payroll or pay its current liabilities. Vendors and subcontractors called incessantly to be paid on overdue invoices. FCC could barely pay the $13,000 a month due to the attorney general for back taxes or make payroll. And I could not pay vendors until these two priorities were met. As controller, most of my time was spent managing cash flows and dealing with frustrated vendors.

FCC also had significant debt and debt service costs. The financial statements indicated that FCC had about 65 percent debt financing, exceeding the maximum amount of debt recommended by most credit-rating agencies and banks. Most banks recommend debt in the range of 45 to 55 percent with the maximum amount at 62 percent. Sound financial management practices advise against the use of long-term debt to meet short-term operating needs (long-term debt should be used only for long-term items, such as capital improvements, acquisitions and construction contracts). Thus, FCC was already overleveraged with debt and seeking more just to stay afloat.

Adding to these strains, FCC needed an unqualified audit report to qualify for the bank loan that Richard was planning to apply for soon. If FCC received a "going concern" audit report it would not qualify for the new loan. A "going concern" audit report would signify FCC's insolvency and raise doubts about its long-term viability to lenders, vendors, subcontractors and the state government. FCC was unable to pay the principal on its debt and was just barely able to pay the interest on that debt, but this was currently known only to insiders. A "going concern" audit report would let outsiders know the extent of FCC's financial problems. Richard was not going to let that happen if he could help it because we needed the bank loan to stay operable.

Industry Conditions

Highway construction is a highly competitive industry. State highway construction contracts must be entered into via a competitive bidding process and the government is required to generally award the contracts to the lowest bidders. FCC routinely submitted the lowest bid on contracts and simultaneously managed more than a dozen highway contracts, totaling more than $10 million. The jobs did not generate enough cash flows to keep FCC operable, but the underlying reasons for this were unclear. Perhaps Richard bid the jobs too low to cover the job-related costs, or maybe Richard mismanaged the jobs. It is also possible that FCC's fixed costs were too high relative to its revenues due to FCC's excessive use of debt. Whatever the reason, the jobs did not generate enough revenue to pay the subcontractors, vendors and debt service costs.

The industry was also highly regulated. As the general contractor on government contracts, FCC was required to comply with contractual requirements. These included paying Davis Bacon wages, meeting project deadlines and using asphalt and concrete that met the government's established product quality standards.

Unexpected Job Duties

My responsibilities at FCC included supervising the accounting department and overseeing the cash, accounts payable, accounts receivable, inventory and payroll functions. I also hired and fired all the accounting and information technology staff.

Things at FCC were always hectic. During my two years, we moved our office location three times and converted our records to a different computer system during each of these moves. Accounting software and information technology for job-costing was changing rapidly at the time and FCC was constantly seeking an accounting system that could accurately capture job-related costs. These changes resulted in accounting-related improvements, but also created chaos in what was already a very hectic operating environment. The constant changes made it difficult for the accounting department to keep up with its daily activities and to produce reliable financial statements.

My job as the new controller was much more hectic than I had anticipated. I had heard that managers spent most of their time taking phone calls and putting out fires, but it was the nature of the distractions at FCC that raised my suspicions. Most notable were the constant phone calls and surprise visits from vendors and subcontractors, claiming that FCC owed them money on jobs that were completed before I was hired as controller.

Most of the subcontractors claimed we owed them as much as $300,000 for products such as concrete barriers and services such as line-painting. The vendors alleged that we owed them for everything from equipment rentals to hand tools. Most had clear memories about the circumstances surrounding their transactions and claimed we were putting them out of business by not paying the invoices. It was not unusual for them to cry on the phone and insist on meeting with me. This led me to believe there could be some truth to their claims.

I could not understand why FCC had all the outward signs of insolvency (e.g., cash-flow problems, lack of liquidity, near inability to make payroll and high debt service costs), but its financial statements reflected relative solvency. These inconsistencies prompted me to look into the claims of the subcontractors and vendors further.

Escalating Debts

I decided to unilaterally investigate the claims of the subcontractors and vendors, and began by digging around in old desk drawers and file cabinets. With little effort, I began to find packs of unrecorded invoices, vendor statements and correspondence wrapped in rubber bands and stuffed into file cabinets. The invoices seemed to support the claims of the subcontractors and vendors, and many were accompanied by correspondence from the creditors asking to be paid. These documents provided the evidence needed to show that the work had been completed but not paid, just as the subcontractors and vendors had alleged.

I verified the invoices with the superintendents who oversaw the work. The superintendents said that, as far as they knew, the work had been performed satisfactorily, but Alan almost never paid subcontractors. The superintendents said sometimes Richard feigned problems with the work to avoid or delay paying the invoices. The superintendents believed the subcontractors should be paid.

After verifying each invoice with the job superintendents, I recorded the related liability. Over the course of a year, I recorded more than $4 million in unpaid liabilities. Because Richard had such a volatile temper, I did not discuss my actions with him, but did give him monthly financial statements, showing an ever-increasing amount of debt. Richard did not complain or ask about the debt, although FCC's financial statements now reflected the true extent of its insolvency.

The End?

A few months later, FCC applied for a bank loan, using financial statements that reflected the full extent of its debt and was turned down for the loan. The bank's decision was fatal, as FCC could not continue without the loan.

Shortly afterward Richard asked to meet with me "to discuss the debt on FCC's books." I assumed that Richard was planning to remove some or all of the debt that I had recorded so he could try again to secure the loan. Recognizing that my meeting with Richard would most likely end in a disagreement about the debt and my resignation or termination, I immediately began to look for another job. As a CPA, I knew that I could not misrepresent facts or subordinate my judgment to others. Thus, my position on the debt was firm.

Richard finally came to my office about two months later (I had already secured a new job by then, but had not given notice to Richard). Richard went through the open accounts payable file and reviewed each invoice, tearing up many of the subcontractor and vendor invoices that I had previously verified and recorded on FCC's books. He then deleted the liabilities from the general ledger. I told Richard that I could not be involved in this activity and left the office before he finished deleting the liabilities from the general ledger. I learned later that he had instructed the accounts payable clerk to assist him after I left and together they deleted most of the liabilities.

FCC never did get a bank loan, but was not forced into bankruptcy by its creditors either. Over the next few months FCC slowly went out of business. Rather than file for bankruptcy protection, FCC simply ceased operating under its current name and reemerged under a new name. No one at FCC was ever charged with fraud. I heard through the grapevine that Richard had used several million dollars of his personal money to pay some of FCC's subcontractors and vendors. However, some did not get paid anything and others did not get paid in full.

Richard did not satisfy his existing bank loans before going out of business, and these loans totaled more than $1 million. I believe the banks did not force FCC into bankruptcy because they wanted to give the company every opportunity to pay its debts. As long as FCC stayed in business the banks had some hope of being paid.

FCC was able to complete its existing highway construction contracts before going out of business and sought small paving and excavation jobs while it was wrapping up those contracts. However, FCC was unable to perform enough small jobs to meet its current liabilities and debt service costs, and this apparently contributed to its decision to close.

Lessons Learned

This experience taught me several valuable lessons and had a significant impact on the direction of my career. First, it was not the first time and would not be the last time I would find myself having to stand firm against an employer asking me to compromise my integrity. Thus, it is usually not a question of "if" we will be asked to engage in wrongful activities, but one of "when" it will happen. To avoid becoming involved in acts of wrongdoing, I reflect upon how I will react before I am confronted with such situations. This helps me to respond calmly and appropriately during times of stress.

Second, I was a CPA and member of the American Institute of Certified Public Accountants (AICPA) at the time, so I turned to *Rule 102 — Integrity and Objectivity* of the AICPA Code of Professional Conduct for guidance. Rule 102 states that a member cannot knowingly fail to correct an organization's financial statements that are materially false and misleading, when he or she has the authority to make such corrections. It also prohibits members from knowingly misrepresenting facts or subordinating their judgment to others when

(continued)

(*continued*)

performing professional services. It applies to CPAs working in public accounting, but I decided to interpret the rule broadly and to hold myself to its standards in all aspects of my professional life, including the work I performed for an employer. This provided me with inward direction for my actions and outward justification for my behavior.

Third, this experience significantly influenced how I channeled the remainder of my career. Afterward, I kept myself prepared for the possibility of having to make significant sacrifices to maintain my professional integrity, including resigning from my position and jeopardizing my financial security, if necessary. To maintain the flexibility needed to resign from an employer who attempted to pressure me into committing wrongful acts, I began to carry as little personal debt as possible and began pursuing professional accomplishments to stay competitive in the job market. I also avoided employers who were likely to put me in compromising situations and learned the importance of investigating prospective employers well before accepting positions with them. Of course, the Sarbanes-Oxley Act of 2002 now prohibits audit firms from recruiting candidates for their audit clients, so I no longer seek employment through my former public accounting firm.

I accepted a compliance examiner position with a government agency immediately after leaving FCC and spent the next 15 years in a variety of governmental positions, investigating financial fraud. I became a Certified Fraud Examiner and now uphold the Association of Certified Fraud Examiner's Code of Ethics, which requires me to exhibit the highest level of integrity in the performance of my professional assignments and to refrain from unethical conduct. I continued to seek higher education in fraud-related areas and eventually earned a Ph.D. in Public Administration. I now teach principles of fraud examination and auditing at a state university, and have published numerous articles about the prevention and detection of fraud. You could say that my experiences at FCC had a major impact on the direction of my career.

Recommendations to Prevent Future Occurrences

Stakeholders such as external and internal auditors, controllers, fraud examiners and other financial investigators can perform several procedures to prevent and detect unrecorded liabilities. These include

(*continued*)

gathering the best evidence possible, using the most effective procedures available to detect fraud and exercising greater levels of professional skepticism.

Auditors and fraud examiners can use the "evidence hierarchy" to
evaluate the appropriateness and sufficiency of the evidence supporting liabilities. The appropriateness of evidence asks whether the evidence is good enough (quality). The sufficiency of evidence asks
whether there is enough of it (quantity). The quality of the evidence
was at issue in the FCC case.

- The best evidence is generated by the auditor (e.g., the auditor
  directly observes or calculates the evidence, performs test counts
  of the client's inventory, etc.).
- The second best evidence is generated by a third party and given
  directly to the auditors (e.g., the auditor sends confirmations to
  vendors and the vendors reply directly to the auditor).
- The third best evidence is generated by a third party and delivered to the auditor through the client (e.g., the client gives the
  auditor its bank statements).
- The fourth best evidence is a document produced by the client
  (e.g., the client gives the auditor an internally generated report).
- The poorest quality evidence is a verbal representation by the client (verbal representations must be corroborated with documentary evidence).

Given Richard's motivation to understate liabilities, the best
possible evidence should have been used to test liabilities. This would
have been a document generated by a third party given directly to the
examiner, such as the confirmation of liabilities.

Confirmations are the best way to detect the understatement of
liabilities. They are used to identify discrepancies between a balance as-
serted by a client and a balance based on evidence provided by an external party, such as a bank, customer or vendor. Confirmations are usually
used to test the existence of large asset balances for possible overstatement (e.g., do these accounts receivable really exist and is the balance
this large?), but confirmations should be used to test the possible understatement of liabilities when: (1) the client's internal controls are poor,
(2) its cash flows are weak and (3) vendors do not send monthly statements. FCC possessed all these conditions.

The examiner should begin confirming liabilities by obtaining a
list of the vendors used by the client over the past few years, including
the accounts with closed and zero balances. The examiner sends

(continued)

(*continued*)

confirmations to the vendors with small and zero balances. The examiner should use blank confirmations, so the vendors will have to write-in the amounts owed. This is the best way to learn the amount the vendors think is due to them. The examiner will compare the balances indicated by the vendors with those of the client and thoroughly investigate the discrepancies.

Auditors and fraud examiners should also exercise high levels of professional skepticism when conducting their engagements. Professional skepticism helps the examiner identify the client's red flags of fraud and make accurate assessments of the risks. Skepticism also helps the examiner see how the tests to detect fraud may need to be adjusted in terms of the nature, timing and extent of those tests, where: (1) *nature* refers to the effectiveness of the tests and the quality of evidence gathered, (2) *timing* refers to when the test is conducted and (3) *extent* refers to how much testing and evidence is needed. In short, professional skepticism encourages the examiner to gather sufficient and appropriate documentary evidence.

About the Author

Patricia A. Patrick, Ph.D., CFE, CPA, CGFM, is Associate Professor of Accounting at the Shippensburg University of Pennsylvania. Patricia has published in *Fraud Magazine, Journal of Public Budgeting, Accounting and Financial Management, International Journal of Public Administration, Journal of Ethnicity in Criminal Justice, Journal of Criminal Justice, Security Journal* and *Security Management*.

CHAPTER

The Fall Man

NEARCHOS A. IOANNOU

Climbing the Social Ladder

George Papadopoulos was a hardworking individual who prided himself in starting at the bottom of his company and working his way up to CEO within 15 years. He was educated in the UK, qualified as an auditor in one of the Big Four firms and returned home to Cyprus to practice the audit profession.

In due course, he met Jane, the daughter of a wealthy manufacturer, and they eventually got married and had two daughters, Laura and Maria.

He was then hired by his father-in-law as a junior manager in C.Case Limited, a factory that produced packing material. Marrying Jane had changed his life dramatically — he had gone from the son of a civil worker to the son-in-law of a wealthy businessman. George and his family lived in luxury, and the factory was the driving force behind their lifestyle.

He took out a number of significant loans to support his lifestyle and, because he was in a position to repay his debts, the banks did not hesitate to loan him more and more funds. His monthly loan repayments amounted to $10,000. For the ordinary person, this would be a lot, but for George it was just a fraction of his monthly income.

C.Case

C.Case Limited was established in the early 1930s to manufacture shipping cartons for cigarettes and any other packaging involving cartons. It became one of the largest carton manufacturers in Cyprus and employed 3,000 people in its three plant locations. The company had strong internal controls in all the major operation cycles: revenue, inventory, purchasing and payroll.

The heads of the departments had been with C.Case for a number of years and they tended to pursue the interests of the company as a whole rather than their own. Overtime was common for them as it was often necessary to meet deadlines and production needs.

The company was heavily reliant on exports, especially to the Middle East. It had incurred significant capital expenditure in reaching its targets, which were the major cigarette exporters in the Middle East.

The Numbers Don't Add Up

I had been C.Case's external auditor for a number of years and observed that the company's key ratios relating to liquidity were deteriorating rapidly, mainly because it was not in a position to meet its short-term obligations; C.Case was experiencing financial constraints and cash-flow difficulties.

To overcome the financial troubles, C.Case's management needed to secure additional funding from a major financial institution; therefore, it had to show decent profitability and liquidity ratios. As a result of the loan application, a senior bank official was observing C.Case's spending. The official constantly monitored the entity's receipts, and significant payments like executive bonuses were only issued after his approval. As the auditor in charge of the engagement, I was instructed by my partner to pay particular attention to possible overstatements of revenues, because C.Case could be trying to make its financial statements more attractive to lenders.

My audit team and I were crammed in a tiny room (those in the audit profession should know the feeling quite well), so I was able to lean over my desk and ask Anna, a senior staff member who was also working on the assignment, to analyze revenue recognition because it was the most significant item in the financial statements.

Later that day, Anna called me over and said, "The numbers don't add up, Nearchos." I immediately reviewed the results and saw that she was right — she found a huge discrepancy in sales between 2008 and 2009, to the extent of 40 percent.

Such a difference was not justified by the sales revenue and volume of the previous periods. To justify further investigation, we used auditing software that identified the relationship and correlation between figures that should interrelate, like sales and cost of sales. The results were alarming — the two figures did not add up. At that point Anna and I knew that fraud or serious errors had occurred. Because I knew C.Case's internal controls so well, I also knew this fraud could only have been perpetrated by someone high in the firm's hierarchy.

Sales Deviations

I decided to meet with C.Case's sales manager, James, first to find out if there was a rational reason for the sales increase. For example, I thought maybe they had a one-off contract with a large cigarette manufacturer that didn't exist last year. But the sales manager verified that no such contract existed. I asked James to provide me with the sales budget so I could identify any significant variations between the budget and the actual figures. James called in his secretary, who immediately furnished me with the information I needed.

I asked James to explain C.Case's procedure for investigating significant deviations between budgeted and actual data. He told me that at the end of each quarter, all the budgets with actual data are reviewed by the CFO, Angelo Marinos; he looks for deviations and, if he finds any, asks the responsible department head to explain the deviations and provide supporting documents. This procedure sounded solid to me, so I took James off my suspect list. I came to the conclusion that somebody else within the organization was cooking the books to inflate revenue on purpose.

Based on my interview with James, I decided to pay a visit to Angelo Marinos to pinpoint the loose end in C.Case's internal controls. And I have to admit, when I arrived in his newly furnished office on the fifth floor, overlooking the Mediterranean Sea, I was envious. I thought about my view — of Anna's desk and computer monitor — and how much nicer Angelo's was.

After the normal greetings, I asked him to show me how he monitored the irregularities of each department. He pulled out a new MacBook and showed me various spreadsheets that interacted with each other. Once a variation reached a pre-determined threshold, an internal investigation to identify the source of the problem would begin.

I asked Angelo what procedures were initiated in response to the significant variation in revenue that Anna and I identified. He said, "Don't look at me. I'm just the guard of the whole process. If I identify something and the explanation that I get is not convincing, I immediately pass the investigation file to the CEO for review and further action."

I ended my meeting with Angelo because I had strong indications that the saying, "The fish smells from the head up," was being proven at C.Case.

I immediately reviewed the internal control procedures on the authorization and approval of postings in the sales ledger. I instructed my team to document in detail the control procedures and identify the control activities that each procedure was supposed to meet.

I also issued specific instructions to deal with any lack of segregation of duties and the ability of management to override the existing controls. I knew a hole had to exist in the control environment, and the identification of it would definitely lead us to the main suspect.

I then conducted an interview with the company's warehouse manager, because inventory was a major item in the cost-of-sales figure. I requested the inventory-ageing analysis to understand whether stock had been materially misstated in the financial statements. The warehouse manager agreed and furnished me with the inventory-ageing list.

Upon investigation I realized that there was a significant amount of spare parts in the inventory.

Spare parts were used in the printers and other machinery but, as auditors, we did not have the necessary exposure to assess whether these spare parts, which were physically present, were actually useable.

Old Friends

I then remembered John. John was the chief engineer of the company and, since he and I were both openhearted and easygoing individuals, we became work friends. He would buy me coffee at C.Case and I would do the same the following day and so on. Furthermore, we both supported the same local soccer team.

I called John and kindly asked if he could pay a visit with me to the company's warehouse, particularly the spare parts section; it was a section he knew well.

When we walked into the warehouse, we saw a huge storage shed full of spare parts. John said, "Oh my God, I didn't know that we had such a huge supply of spare parts. Let's have a closer look, Nearchos."

We opened the shed doors and walked in. We must have spent at least three hours in that dull container going through the parts.

When we finally finished combing through all the parts, John turned to me and said, "Nearchos, you know what is wrong with the majority of these parts?"

I said, "They seem to be brand new and well preserved."

"Yes, they are well preserved all right, but the majority of these relate to equipment from the 1980s, all of which is obsolete!"

And then it struck me right away. Not only was the revenue materially overstated but so was the closing inventory, a key element of the financial statements; its misstatement has a pervasive impact on the financial statements.

The inventory controls were operating effectively, so this was another brick in the wall suggesting that an override had to exist at the executive level.

All the evidence was pointing to George Papadopoulos, the CEO, and I knew we had to prove his involvement somehow. I had to carefully plan a meeting with him to push him into a confession with the facts and figures.

I called George's personal assistant to arrange for a meeting, but she told me that he was abroad for ten days, in Monaco on vacation.

One thing that I have learned well through my experience was that if a person lives a luxurious life, then he will do everything in his power to preserve that lifestyle, including conduct fraud or deliberately misappropriate assets.

I told his personal assistant, Julia, to inform me when George was available for me to see him. Meanwhile my audit team worked day and night to prepare the file with my evidence that indicated George's involvement in a scheme.

Off-Hours Meeting

Almost a month later, Julia called me and said that George could see me on a Saturday morning, when the factory was closed.

When the rainy Saturday morning arrived, I walked into George's office and he greeted me. "Hi, Nearchos, how are you? Hope everyone is treating you nicely here at the office. Maybe on my next trip to Monaco, you and your wife can join us for the weekend."

The invitation puzzled me; George hardly knew me but was inviting me and my wife to join him for the weekend, all expenses paid. However, as an auditor, I knew I had to safeguard my independence and integrity. That's one of the first lessons auditors learn. George had indirectly tried to bribe me and jeopardize my integrity.

I said, "Thanks for the offer, but I have to decline. The rules of professional ethics forbid me from accepting." The smile on his face suddenly disappeared.

I asked George about the procedure for budget variations, as if I didn't know. He verified what the CFO said — that at the end of each quarter, if significant variations were noted by the CFO, he would contact the department head for an explanation. If the manager did not have an acceptable reason, Angelo would ask George to initiate an investigation. After explaining the process, George mentioned that records of such investigations were only kept for three months, according to company practice.

I was in a difficult situation since I could not prove that the deviation letters from the CFO had reached him. I also could not prove what investigative procedures George undertook or if he did indeed try to hide it.

I tried to make him remember if he had received any concerns from Angelo about the significant revenue deviations noted. He told me that he was too busy to remember such a thing but that he could not recall any significant issues about the revenue.

I asked him whether he was aware that stock was materially misstated since the inventory included spare parts relating to obsolete machinery. He looked astonished, and said that if that was true, he wanted to rectify the issue as soon as possible. He claimed to want to ensure that the financial statements reflected the truth about C.Case.

He also stressed that he was very strict about procedures at the operational and strategic levels, so I asked if the three-month retention period was written down in the company's staff manual or procedures manual.

George said it was a fairly new policy, adopted due to the lack of storage space, and that it was not written down formally yet but he intended to do so in the near future. I asked if the directive was circulated to the department heads, and he said not yet, since he has been away so much recently.

I knew the interview was going nowhere, so I decided to end it. I still considered George to be the main suspect, and saw his explanation of the three-month holding period as a significant lead, and I was eager to investigate it. I remembered that Angelo Marinos, the CFO, told me that all his findings were sent to George both in hardcopy and by e-mail.

I immediately went to Angelo's office and asked him to send me the e-mail he sent to George about the revenue deviations. Marinos told me that he wasn't just sending e-mails to George at the end of each quarter, as per the instructions. Angelo was going above and beyond — he e-mailed his concerns to George on a monthly basis.

The Evidence in the E-Mail

This was the breakthrough I was looking for. I knew the monthly e-mails sent by the CFO were the nail in George's coffin.

I obtained the printout of last months' deviation warning from Angelo and called Julia again to arrange another meeting with George. The day of the meeting arrived, and I entered George's office. I told him, "George, I just need to go through a few details regarding the exception procedures."

George said, "No problem, Nearchos. Our procedures are an open book."

I told him that the three-month holding period was not advisable and informed him that I would list it as an internal control weakness on my management letter at the end of the audit. He agreed that the three-month period was not rational.

I then returned to the sales issue and asked if he had initiated and concluded an investigation on the sales deviation. George said such investigations occur on a quarterly basis, and last quarter's data had already been shredded.

I asked if he had received any other warnings of sales deviations and he said that he didn't recall that he did, to which I responded, "Well, sir, your CFO thinks otherwise." I pulled the e-mails out of my briefcase and showed them to him. They were in date order and all e-mails concluded with the phrase "please advise." However, Angelo had not yet received a reply from George.

George was stunned; he was speechless for a second. Then he turned to me and said, "Yes I remember now . . . but I didn't pay that much attention since the deviations were immaterial."

"Immaterial?" I asked. "Is a 10 percent deviation from budgeted figures immaterial? Unless your budget was not well prepared, the deviation is material, because it exceeds the 2 percent deviation threshold set by the CFO."

I told George that he needed to tell me the truth because his lack of action regarding a significant deviation reported by the CFO was an obvious act of negligence. I had to report it because fraud was suspected. Also, since I came across it during my normal audit procedures, the relevant authorities had to be informed.

George then almost broke into tears. He said that C.Case was his baby, and that it was experiencing severe liquidity problems due to an inappropriate strategy adopted, and the only way he could receive more bank funding was to demonstrate strong financial statements.

I almost felt sorry for the guy, but then I realized that if the company was his baby and he wanted to save it, he could have waived his year-end bonus of $200,000 and his other associated benefits that reached a staggering $5,000 per month. He also could have reduced his monthly salary from $20,000 per month. He should have lead by example, considering he was the captain of the ship.

But no, he chose trips to Monaco, a luxurious life and to pursue his own interest and benefits rather than acting on behalf of the shareholders and trying to maintain or increase their wealth.

The One Who Got Away

Once we had all our supporting documentation in hand, together with George's written confession, we turned over the evidence to our legal counsel. George settled out of court and paid a large amount in damages to the shareholders.

However, we were not in a position to accuse the brains behind the operation. George claimed his father-in-law (the president of the firm) came up with the scheme and forced George to participate. That might have been the case; his father-in-law had a dominant personality. Unfortunately we didn't have any evidence against him, and had to leave the situation as it stood.

Lessons Learned

It all came down to lifestyle. George maintained his lifestyle at the expense of C.Case. He wasn't acting as an agent of the company — he was pursuing his own personal interest. A glamorous lifestyle that is not justified by the corresponding revenues is one of the clearest indications of fraud.

(continued)

(*continued*)

As an audit team, we learned a lot from the investigation, identification and conclusion of this serious financial statement fraud. For fraud to exist, certain conditions are usually in place. C.Case demonstrated a lack of internal controls and the possibility of management to override the few controls in place.

I also learned that auditors should be friendly with all the employees at a client's firm. When needed, staff members might be in a position to push the case forward. For example, my engineer friend John gave me my first big break in this case.

Also, we learned that even though auditors are watchdogs and not bloodhounds as far as fraud identification is concerned, they still play a major role in identifying fraud and safeguarding the interests of the shareholders and the public in general.

About the Author

Nearchos A. Ioannou, CFE, FCCA, was born in Cyprus and obtained a bachelor's of accountancy with honors from the University of Dundee in Scotland. He qualified as a Chartered Certified Accountant in 2004 and a CFE in 2007. He worked for Deloitte for five years, serving local and international clients, and was a core learning facilitator. In 2009 he formed Exertus Services Limited and is the Audit Director. He is a part-time lecturer for the Association of Chartered Certified Accountants. He is married to Elena Ioannou and has one daughter, Zeta Ioannou.

CHAPTER

26

The Happy Life

TAMER FOUAD GHEITH

It is a rather common human desire to want to meet famous people in your community, especially if they have made major contributions to the society. However, most people don't expect that they will ever get the opportunity to meet their local celebrities. That's what I thought about Frank Marino. Frank was a handsome, tall and elegant man who always looked cool, calm and collected. In his mid-forties, he was the experienced executive director of Happy Life, a charity organization. Frank earned his bachelor's degree in business administration from a respected university in his hometown of Venice, Italy. He married in his early twenties and had three daughters and two sons.

Frank used his family contacts to get high positions in government agencies at an early age. Frank's hard work, dedication and intelligence earned him excellent appraisals from his bosses and, as compensation for his efforts in serving the government, Frank was appointed the executive director of Happy Life.

Frank's ambition and strong desire to maintain a certain social position exerted pressure on his personality and professional objectives. Frank started to worry about the future and asked himself, "How can I maintain the same lifestyle for my children? What they will do after my death or retirement?" Frank felt that his new position was an excellent opportunity to achieve great wealth and ensure his children's security. But he also felt that such an opportunity might not appear again.

Network of Collusion

Frank started his first day at Happy Life by beginning to establish a close network inside the organization. He selected two favorites with the goal of helping him get the best from their jobs, which in turn would assist in satisfying his needs. The first recruit was Peter De Luca and the second was George Easton.

De Luca was a short, nervous man who put a lot of pressure on himself. He was poorly educated but came from a family with good political connections, which helped him find excellent job opportunities. However, due to his lack of skills and technical expertise, Peter often failed to meet his job responsibilities and lost many positions. After a particularly embarrassing firing, Peter succeeded in using family relations to join Happy Life as head of finance.

George Easton, Peter's right-hand man and the assistant director of finance, was a short, talkative man in his fifties who had worked at Happy Life for ten years. He knew the financial issues of the charity and informally dominated the accounting staff through a network of employees, including Jack Rodriguez, the cashier; Andrew Gillis, the cash and banks accountant; and other junior accountants responsible for recording the various subsidiary ledgers. George controlled the purchasing and fixed assets functions, among others, due to a lack of knowledge and experience of the heads of those departments. George used his communication skills to gain the confidence of management and the department heads at Happy Life. His powers exceeded the primary responsibilities stated in his job description.

Happy Beginnings

Happy Life was a charity organization established in 1942 by Henry Philips "to provide a happy life to children who are coping with the loss of their parents and help them face the challenges life presents." Within a few years, Happy Life was successful in achieving its goals and, with time, started to gain support from local government officials, including the mayor. This resulted in receiving money from government as well as private funds from inside and outside the city. Then the management of Happy Life began marketing the organization's excellent reputation internationally.

After Henry's death, Happy Life was taken over by the local government, and gained even more public respect. Many high-profile government employees took positions in Happy Life. Despite the dramatic increase in the funds granted to Happy Life, the organizational chart and internal regulation remained elementary and the charity employed fewer than 50 people.

Happy Life provided full support to orphaned children until they reached the age of 18. Once they reached that age, the charity connected them with the proper government associations for housing and employment assistance. Happy Life followed the individuals' progress until they were able to secure employment.

Performance Concerns

Once or twice a week, the local newspapers and popular magazines ran articles about Happy Life and its various activities and social programs. But these stories made me wonder where the charity received the funds to finance its publicity campaigns. Wouldn't it be better to use that money on programs for children rather than attempts to raise awareness in the community about the organization? But I learned that Happy Life's management had made public relations a priority because they thought it would generate more donations.

However, a few years after Frank Marino was hired as the executive director, problems inside the organization started to affect management's dealings with other parties, including major granters, suppliers and even children who received benefits. These issues were informally communicated to the higher authorities. As a result, the city's director of social affairs requested reports on the financial and operational performance of Happy Life, but management failed to provide them. The social affairs' director asked David Jones, the chairman of the Central Investigative Governmental Authority (CIGA), to send an audit team to provide a report for the minister.

The chairman of CIGA sent a memo regarding the audit assignment to a CIGA manager named Albert Fraise. Albert was an expert in government audits and agreed to meet with the chairman to discuss the matter. The initial objective of the assignment was to provide technical support to the management and employees of Happy Life. However, the principle objective soon became providing assurance on the integrity of Happy Life's management and its employees. Also, the chairman requested a report on the entity's compliance with the applicable local laws and regulations.

I was an experienced auditor, so Albert asked me to be in charge of the assignment and requested that Michael D'Angelo work as my assistant auditor. Michael had extensive audit experience and a tough personality, especially when it came to obtaining sensitive information from a client, but he was also known for his finesse.

Albert called an audit meeting to start the job and discuss the objectives and expected outcome. He began the meeting by saying, "I've heard many stories of bad practices at Happy Life. However," Albert added, "Please do not rush to conclusions; let the facts speak for themselves. I want to first focus on the executive director, Frank Marino. The audit team should compare his actual authority and responsibilities with those stated in his job description." Albert said, "You can examine his employee file along with a random sample of employees' files. The initial purpose of the audit is to look at Happy Life's accounting department. To start, let's examine a sample of employees' personnel files to determine the company's organization and completion of the files."

Client Meeting

Albert assigned me the task of initiating communication with the client and arranging an audit meeting with the executive director, Frank Marino. On the day of the meeting, I drove out of town to Happy Life's headquarters with Michael; it seemed like they didn't get a lot of visitors. Since it was located outside the city, many auditors and governmental regulators were reluctant to make the trip. As we approached the gate, a security guard walked up to our car and asked for the purpose of our visit, with whom we were meeting and requested to see our ID cards. We gave him our information and he made a call. After a while, he returned our ID cards and gave me an entrance permit. This procedure gave me comfort about Happy Life's security and, to be honest, my snap judgment was that there would be nothing amiss. However, I remembered Albert's words, "Do not rush to conclusions. . . ."

I met with Frank and explained the purpose of our visit. Frank was very friendly and asked his secretary to call Peter De Luca, the head of finance, and George Easton, his assistant. Frank told them why we were there. I could tell they were both surprised, but they tried to hide their feelings with faint smiles and promises to provide us with the necessary information as soon as possible.

Employee Tips

I started the audit by meeting with key employees. I made a list of my audit requirements, including asking for the comparative financial statements for the past two consecutive years, and delivered it to Peter; it took him a full week to provide me with the information, which I duly noted, because it seemed excessive. I also requested Frank Marino's job description because I noticed that many of Happy Life's financial decisions were signed by him; normally someone higher than Frank would approve such matters.

One approval was for generous, regular reimbursement allowances to select employees. The stated purpose was to compensate employees who made exceptional efforts to support Happy Life by spending their personal money on items for the charity. However, when I reviewed the supporting documents, I found that they were often being reimbursed for personal items like clothing, meals and entertainment. Also, based on my review of the monthly payroll, allowances were not given to other similar employees. This inequity prompted me to start interviewing the workers who were not receiving allowances, and they expressed their dissatisfaction about the situation. They told me, "Those employees receive more generous allowances because they are obedient to Frank and help him cover up his misuse of Happy Life's resources. They help him conceal it in the financial statements."

One important point I was keen to investigate was the possibility of exist-ing practices to conceal Happy Life's sources of funding — especially those owned by the minors and safeguarded by the charity on their behalf — in the financials. So I requested a list of the major funds and grants during the previ-ous and current year along with a letter specifying the purpose of each grant. I asked for the budget that the government allocated to Happy Life and the company's actual expenses. I also wanted to see the bank confirmations and assurances for all the accounts. I was surprised that these bank confirmations had never been requested by the local government's finance department. It turns out one of the reasons was that there were no previous audits of Happy Life. When I started investigating the physical counts of inventory, cash and fixed assets, I noted that no physical inventory counts had even been con-ducted prior to our audit. However, they started a count during our visit.

I inquired into the internal audit function and asked if there was a fraud hotline for staff to communicate issues related to fraud and employee integ-rity. George informed me that a new internal audit manager had recently been hired, but he was reporting to the finance department. This was a red flag to me as it was not the appropriate chain of command for the internal audit function — the person holding such a position should report directly to the audit committee, but Happy Life did not have one.

Another important item in the financial statements was labeled *cash equivalents* and included expensive items owned by the children at Happy Life. When I asked about the internal controls on these items, which amounted to $220,500, Peter said he kept the goods at his home and admit-ted that some of it was missing. He did not allow anyone else to monitor the inventory and made no effort to store items in secure locations. The cash equivalents included gold and securities purchased for the children as an investment to help them when they were grown up. Some grants were offered specifically to talented children for their intelligence or participa-tion in international or local events.

Lack of Controls

I discovered major differences between the past two consecutive years when I compared the financial statements. In the second year, a large deficit appeared between the revenues and expenses. When I asked Peter for an explanation, he referred me to George. This was odd to me — it seemed that Peter's job performance was poor and George was dominating his supervisor in the finance department. When I asked George how the deficit was covered, he told me, "We receive generous grants and transfers from the government and major private-sector donations."

I asked why records of such transactions weren't included in the finan-cials I was given. George said, "No need for that. It is not one of our budget-ary accounts." He added, "The Ministry of Finance, which reviews the proper use of the resources, only looks at the budgetary accounts. We don't need to keep records of our grants and major donations. However, I can get you a list of them for the past two years."

I requested the supporting documents for all the grants received in the past two years and George told me, "Well, the papers for a major grant amounting to $326,530 are missing and the responsible employee was fired. Also, no fixed asset register is kept." I also discovered that employees used the money from one grant to take a trip abroad with some children — a complete misuse of Happy Life funds. At this point, I knew I needed to give Albert an update and request his approval to extend the audit to a fraud examination. I also asked that Michael D'Angelo continue to help me.

At the same time, Michael and I started to plan surprise counts of cash, inventory and fixed assets. We discovered that purchasing agents were given unsupervised access to a substantial amount of funds but their purchases were not monitored; there was no control in place to ensure they were made at fair market value. When I asked Jack Rodriguez about this, he simply said, "Everything is done with the approval of Peter and George." Jack hadn't asked about the proper controls over cash; his only concern was keeping the register in balance. And no one had performed a surprise cash count at Happy Life.

On a trip to take a sample of the inventory, I was surprised to find there was, in fact, nothing in the stores. We interviewed purchasing officer Jane McMillan and she revealed her doubts about the prices she had to pay for inventory and told us about thefts by employees. She provided documents that showed the missing inventory amounted to $54,000. I reviewed the purchase invoices to test the reasonability of prices and was surprised by the values. I asked George about them and he told me that sometimes the children requested expensive items from a specific supplier — not a valid justification. Also, no purchasing subsidiary ledger was kept for purchases.

I decided to make surprise physical counts of every asset during my routine examination to the financial accounts, and arrived at the same results — there was concealment, but the amounts were unknown because it was done off-book. I was informed by the inventory manager, Tomas Castillo, that he often received items but was told not to record them in the accounting system — an indicator of a skimming scheme. Tomas said he was told by Peter, based on Frank's instructions, to ship some items he received to the unknown vendors. When I asked Peter about it, he acted surprised and said, "We returned the items to the granters because we didn't need them."

I interrupted him to ask, "Why didn't you sell the items through proper channels and use the receipts from the sales as additional source of revenue?" He answered meekly, "It was Frank's decision."

I observed new grant shipments (computers, printers, etc.) distributed to employees and when I asked Peter why there were no records of the new equipment, he snapped at me, "Why should I keep records for items provided from sources outside our budget?" At that moment, I knew Peter was either stupid or a thief; I doubled my efforts.

One of the means Frank and Peter used to cover the deficit between actual and budgeted expenses was to conceal liabilities of Happy Life from other governmental entities. These were revealed when, after a few days, confirmations came from one of the major related parties that $136,054 was transferred to Happy Life as a liability — not a grant, like the financial statement indicated — to help cover the deficit in its budget. I discussed the issue with George, who became upset and insisted he was just executing Frank's instructions.

Tone at the Top

Next Michael and I interviewed human resources and payroll staff and learned that Happy Life paid excessive salaries to employees who essentially worked for Frank personally, not for the charity. Of course, we had to ask who hired these employees and authorized their salaries, although we already knew the answer — Frank.

We learned that most of the Happy Life employees were afraid of Frank, which allowed him to exert complete control over the company and its financial statements. My biggest surprise came when I obtained the original job offer made to Frank and compared it to the documentation Frank gave me. He added additional authorities to his job description in vague documents and attached them to the main resolution. This additional power provided a cover for his gross mismanagement and misuse of Happy Life's resources and assets.

Frank also seemed to enjoy passing off his dirty work to Peter and George. He controlled the release of information from Happy Life by insisting on personally attending all meetings with outsiders, such as external auditors, government inspectors, and so on. Also, if Frank was questioned by regulators, he would claim to be too busy to talk but would promise to send information as soon as possible. Another of his favorite excuses was that he didn't have enough employees to provide the financial statement analysis requested by stakeholders.

One day while I was walking around the Happy Life premises, I noticed Frank's luxury BMW. I returned to my office and requested a list of the cars that belonged to Happy Life. When Peter gave me the list, I immediately noticed that four luxury cars had been purchased with a grant worth $540,000. These cars were given to Frank and his favorite assistants. I asked Peter where the cars were parked after working hours, and he said Frank and his assistants took them home in case they needed to perform unexpected work in the evenings. Peter appeared pale as he told me this, and seemed to lose his concentration as he unsuccessfully attempted to describe Frank's responsibilities that could cause him to need a car in the evening.

The Outcome of the Investigation

I wrote all my findings in a report and forwarded it to Albert with the audit file and supporting documents. He consequently reviewed the issues in the report and communicated them to the chairman of CIGA. The chairman coordinated with legal counsel and higher authorities in the government, and they filed suit in court.

Frank Marino was fired, along with Peter, George, Jack Rodriguez and Tomas Castillo, for their roles in helping Frank conceal the asset misappropriations and misstatement of liabilities. Frank was ordered by the Court to pay full restitution. A new executive director was hired and Happy Life's internal controls were completely overhauled. The charity now has to undergo annual audits by CIGA and is required to submit periodic performance reports to government regulators.

Lessons Learned

This case clearly demonstrated to me how the absence of an anonymous hotline to receive complaints can delay the discovery of fraud and accounting irregularities. The staff members at Happy Life were working in fear of Frank Marino and had no protected way to express their concerns about his behavior. Also, organizations can successfully achieve goals but the output and gains can be stolen or misused by management and employees if internal controls are weak or not enforced. Auditors should exert due care in their audit assignments and try to ascertain the corporate culture.

Recommendations to Prevent Future Occurrences

We made the following recommendations to CIGA and the new management team at Happy Life:

- Examine the adequacy of the organizational chart with organizational goals.
- Establish and implement a proper code of ethics.
- Compare the actual roles of employees with their job descriptions.
- Establish a hotline to receive anonymous complaints.
- Establish the proper control environment.
- Assign audit staff to special reviews but also enforce job rotation.
- Conduct regular external audits to discover irregularities.

(continued)

- Compare internal records with third-party records to reconcile improper accounting of assets and liabilities.
- Establish an internal control department with skilled staff members.
- Form an audit committee to monitor the internal control function.
- Create clear channels of communication to enhance governance of the organization.
- Establish a board of directors consisting of outside, qualified professionals to monitor the activities of the organization.

About the Author

Tamer Fouad Gheith, CFE, CPA, CIA, is a Team Leader within the Business Risk department at the Abu Dhabi Accountability Authority (ADAA), UAE. Mr. Gheith has extensive work experience covering more than 13 years in the fields of financial audit, internal controls and fraud examination. He is an active member in multiple international organizations, such as the AICPA, IIA, ISACA and the ACFE.

27

A Very Merry Fraud

CLIVE TOMES

It was a call I could only have dreamed of. The phone rang during an extremely stressful time: I was finishing my last few weeks in the Jersey office of an international accounting firm while setting up my new accounting practice, and just a couple of weeks before Christmas. It looked like I'd fail, yet again, to get any shopping done before December 24.

"I've got a big job for you," said the voice on the phone. No niceties as always for straight-to-the-point Murdoch. I'd known him since our school-days, and he'd always been the same — blunt, no-nonsense, straight-talking Murdoch. He was almost on the verge of being rude, but he got results and I liked him.

"Be at my office at 5:00 P.M. You won't regret it," and that was all. No hello, no goodbye, no asking if I was available, and no clue about what this could be about — not that I cared. Any job would do as I desperately needed work in my new practice, and Murdoch was right — I didn't regret it.

I called my wife to tell her I'd be late, which fortunately she understood, knowing how important any potential piece of business was to both of us. I then made my way through St. Helier's busy shopping streets to Murdoch's office on the other side of town.

"At last," said Murdoch as I arrived at five on the dot. There were two men in his office, apparently businessmen judging by the suits and ties, looking even more stressed than I felt, if that were possible. "Let me introduce you, Clive. This is Dai Evans and Alex Marigold. Clive Tomes." Introductions over, business cards exchanged, hands shaken, we all sat down, and my biggest fraud investigation to date began.

"OK, here's the story," continued Murdoch. "Dai and Alex run a number of investment funds. Dai is the trustee and Alex is the investment adviser. Seven years ago they set up a new fund to take advantage of currency movements. Alex met a guy who turned out to be a fraud and con-man, Bartholomew Bluewood, who convinced him there was money to be made in the currency markets, and showed him a very convincing record of profits he had supposedly made in this market."

Alex interrupted, "I checked him out, and everything I found supported his claims. He also had the backing of SBL."

"SBL?" I queried.

"Secure Banking Limited, part of the international Walton banking group," answered Alex.

"If I can continue?" Murdoch doesn't take kindly to interruptions when he's in full flow. "Basically Dai and Alex are seriously concerned that the funds have all but disappeared, and we need you to investigate."

What an opportunity! There I was, about to open my new practice, and handed to me on a plate was what turned out to be, up to then, Jersey's biggest fraud ever. I couldn't believe my luck. I'd have to thank Murdoch later.

It was a long meeting. My notes covered more than ten pages, and my writing isn't large or untidy. It turned out there were two investment funds — one general fund and another with a higher risk strategy for the more sophisticated investor. And the money that was supposed to be there, more than $27 million, had all but disappeared; a rather unexpected situation, to say the least, for funds that had been reporting consistent and extensive audited profits for seven years.

We discussed strategy and how to achieve the end goals as quickly as possible. The main objective was to recover the missing money, but how to go about it? Murdoch's no-nonsense approach was instrumental at this stage. "We have to freeze Bluewood's personal and corporate assets as soon as possible — an injunction will do that for us. We also need to seize all his records before he has a chance to destroy them. For that we'll need a search order from the court, and we need them both as quickly as possible, to be served at the same time."

So it began. Murdoch got to work drafting up the required legal papers and arranging meetings with the necessary judicial authorities. I read up on the background from the papers Dai and Alex had given me. And my Christmas shopping plans were destroyed.

New Holiday Traditions

Christmas Eve was unlike any I had ever experienced before or since. We met at Murdoch's office at 7:00 A.M., planned the day, and set off in a couple of vans to transport everything we were to seize. Then we made the four-mile journey from St. Helier to Bluewood's mansion near Jersey's airport in St. Peter to knock on his door and demand entry at 8:00 A.M.

To give Bluewood his due, it must have been quite a shock to open his front door on Christmas Eve and find a group of professionals with legal papers demanding access. After his initial shock, he called his lawyer, and had to concede that he had no option but to allow us entry to review and seize everything in his house that, in our judgment, could be relevant to the investigation.

We spent the next few hours searching every cupboard and drawer, the attic and all the nooks and crannies for anything that could be relevant, not only about the investment funds but, equally important, about Bluewood's personal finances; at that early stage of the investigation we considered that to be the most likely place to find any money that had disappeared.

We didn't take everything; his wine stocks (which we would have loved to take), and the numerous designer watches and handbags, many still in the packaging in which they were purchased, would not be relevant, but we couldn't help noticing that Bartholomew and his wife's spending seemed to know no bounds.

Next it was back to St. Helier and Bluewood's offices or, more correctly, the offices of FX Advantage Limited, his private investment management company. The space turned out to be quite basic; apparently his liberal spending was limited to his personal life. Literally everything was taken from the offices, as we had no way of knowing the relevance of many of the papers and computer records, and the search order gave us the legal authorization we needed to take anything that could be important.

With the vans loaded with more than 25 large boxes and bags of papers, we checked one last time to make sure nothing was left in the offices that we might need and adjourned to the street outside.

Murdoch was in charge. "Right, I will not have time to look through all those papers; that's your job, Clive. You'd better start immediately and keep us all informed."

The bags and boxes were dropped at my new office, taking up all the spare room available, ready for me to attack after the Christmas break. My office was small enough as it was, and with all those bags and boxes in place, if I'd had a cat, it most definitely could not have been swung.

Oh yes, and Christmas . . . another disaster . . . no shopping done. By now it was well into the evening and, while I was organizing the storage of the papers in my office, most normal families were well into their celebrations. I just had my fingers crossed that my family would understand, and that my wife would have been able to prepare everything without my help.

New Year, New Investigations

Christmas passed without too many criticisms, to my great relief, and I was back at work. Fortunately I have always been well organized, and I started by numbering the bags and boxes and creating records of the contents of each. As I did so, I also identified the records that looked as though they would be of the most use. It wasn't an easy job to sort through mountains of documents but, after a few weeks, I completed the task, all the time reporting my progress to Murdoch and our clients.

It was fortunate that I had given that task such a high priority because soon after I'd finished, one of the investors made a complaint to the police and a criminal investigation began. In Jersey, as is probably the situation in most places, a criminal investigation takes priority over a civil case.

The police visited my offices and politely asked if they could have all the documents, although in truth I had no option but to comply. Fortunately they were very reasonable and allowed me a few more days to complete the photocopying, after which the papers disappeared into police hands. At least I could now consider investing in a cat, and the official investigation could properly begin.

Over the next few months, I could not have been busier. The records were suitably classified as accounting records, accounting reports and marketing documents, among other categories. My priority was to analyze the accounting information to identify what had happened and how, if at all, the funds had been dissipated.

Analysis and Exchange Rates

I pulled together everything we had been able to seize relating to Bluewood's personal finances during the relevant period because we suspected that he diverted funds for his own benefit. There wasn't all that much, considering we were covering a period of seven years.

Apart from bank and credit card statements, he didn't appear to have any financial interests in anything except his residential property, cars and, of course, all the wine and designer goods that we'd seen. Therefore, this part of the investigation was relatively simple; I reviewed all the available statements to identify any red flags, such as tracing funds elsewhere or finding investments that weren't evident in his home or office.

Bluewood only had two bank accounts — a basic checking account and a savings account, on which the balances were not particularly large, especially considering we were trying to find $27 million. I started looking for suspicious transactions in the accounts that might provide a clue about what had happened to the money.

The largest regular outgoings were the monthly direct debits of Bluewood's credit card bills, and they were often very significant amounts, sometimes in excess of $20,000. There were a few transfers between his accounts and receipts of his investment management fees into the account, but the initial review revealed nothing extraordinary, which I reported as such to Murdoch, Evans and Marigold.

So it was back to the detailed bookkeeping analysis. In those days, as a new practice with severe limitations on my resources, I had to make do with a spreadsheet for such exercises. Mind you, in my experience, most accountancy matters can be successfully analyzed by spreadsheet; the important thing is to plan it properly before starting to ensure that it generates the detailed information required.

In this case, the investment funds were supposed to take advantage of movements in foreign currencies. Bluewood was supposedly an expert in this field, and somehow was able to take advantage of movements in currency rates. To do this, most of us would need a crystal ball, but, as Evans and Marigold had told me, he had an impressive record of successful results. He seemed to have a rare talent or system that allowed him, at least most of the time, to correctly predict the direction of market fluctuations.

The approach seemed relatively simple. Bluewood only dealt in the major currencies, and his method was to convert large amounts of dollars into the other currencies, and after some time, convert them back. To do this profitably, when converted back, the dollars would have to have a higher value than the balance invested in the first place.

The operation only required bank accounts in the respective currencies, and analyzing the accounts would be a straightforward exercise. However, I also wanted to identify matching purchases and sales in each currency and identify the profit or loss on each trade.

For this purpose, each currency had its own section on the spreadsheet, with one column for the dollar amounts, a second for the foreign currency amounts and a third to highlight the profits or losses once the purchases and sales had been matched.

There's No Friend Like an Old Friend . . .

While I worked on what turned out to be an extremely long spreadsheet, Murdoch occasionally threw additional requests my way. For instance, one of Bluewood's strongest selling points when he was looking for new investors was the backing of Secure Banking Limited (SBL) and their audited results. Murdoch wanted me to look into Bluewood's relationship with the bank.

SBL was the Jersey subsidiary of a well-known and respected international banking group and was subject to regulation by the island's financial services commission. Clearly the security of their funds was an important factor for any investor, and SBL's support of Bluewood ticked that box. The audited results of the investment funds were disclosed annually with supporting audit reports — another major comfort to any potential investor.

Murdoch had been considering these factors and developed certain suspicions. He discovered that Bluewood had moved to Jersey with a special residency permit as an "Essential Employee." To obtain this permit, he would have had to have an employer, but he was self-employed. Murdoch found Bluewood's application for residency and saw that he listed SBL as his employer, which was clearly untrue.

In addition, Murdoch noticed that SBL's audit reports pertaining to Bluewood's investments were always signed by the same individual, a partner of one of the then Big Eight international audit firms. This related not only to the investment funds we were investigating, but to his results for many years before when he was operating from Bristol, England.

Murdoch asked me to look into these anomalies, examine the audit reports and provide him with a report on my findings.

Audit reports are usually worded in specific ways; in the UK the term "true and fair" is used; in the United States it is "present fairly." These terms are used partly because an auditor cannot check absolutely everything, and there has to be some generalizing. The interesting thing about SBL's audit reports was that they always stated the results were "complete and accurate"; a phrase that leaves no allowance for any error whatsoever. The auditor was claiming that he had checked and verified everything and the results were 100 percent reliable!

Further investigation into the auditor revealed that he was not actually an audit partner but specialized in taxes. I reported my findings to Murdoch and continued with my spreadsheet analysis by adding the exchange rates used in each transaction so that they could later be compared with market rates.

In light of the uninterrupted profits that Bluewood had been reporting, which had all been audited and confirmed to be complete and accurate, the results of my analysis could be described as somewhat unexpected. The exception is when you consider the fact that the investors' money had all but disappeared, suggesting that perhaps the reported profits didn't tell the whole story.

From very early in the lives of the investment funds, my analysis did not support the results reported by Bluewood. The vast majority of the foreign currency trades after the first year had resulted in losses, not profits. As a result, the invested funds were gradually whittled down to a relatively tiny balance.

In addition, my comparison of the monthly investment accounts balances, adjusted for any open foreign currency positions, with the records Bluewood submitted to investors and the audit firm was equally revealing. For the first year or so, they were reasonably similar, but after about fourteen months, the picture changed dramatically, and the negative differences increased every month thereafter. My first conclusion was that Bluewood's reported results were fraudulent. In addition, the audit was clearly not properly carried out, if done at all.

Bluewood might have reported nonexistent profits to maintain his reputation as a profitable currency trader, or he might have been motivated by ego. Regardless, the most important factor in our view was his remuneration.

Bluewood's company, FX Advantage Limited, had a management agreement with Dai Evans and his investment company, Magma Trustee Limited. Under this agreement, FX Advantage Limited received a management fee that was a percentage of the profits. There was no minimum fee, so Bluewood had to generate or create profits if he wanted to be paid.

Overall, Bluewood generated losses for investors, which reduced the total investment funds. In addition, each month he withdrew his management fee based on the fraudulently reported profits, which further reduced the funds. These two factors alone went a very long way in explaining the paltry assets that remained when Murdoch and I began our investigation.

Worth the Wait

Of course, this wasn't the whole story. The evidence that we had accumulated and provided to the prosecuting authorities, together with the results of their own investigations, ensured that, some five years after we had knocked on his door, Bluewood and his auditor were sent to jail to spend quite a few years at Her Majesty's pleasure.

We were satisfied with Bluewood's conviction, but it did little to help his victims, the investors. The question for us now was, could we somehow find a way to obtain compensation for the investors, some of whom had lost their entire life savings.

We had established through our work that Bluewood had not benefited except through his fees, which he used to fund his materialistic lifestyle, so there didn't seem to be a way to recover any funds from him. This left two other main players; SBL and the audit firm, both of which would undoubtedly have deep pockets.

There was a clear case of negligence against the audit firm, although they probably could have mounted a limited defense regarding the partner's lack of authorization to provide the audit service. We also considered what, if anything, could be filed against the bank. Murdoch knew that without SBL's support, Bluewood could never have attracted enough investors, and we were all hopeful that would be enough to bring SBL into the firing line.

With this new objective in mind, I revisited my spreadsheet analysis. One thing I had not yet done, as it wasn't required before this stage, was to compare the exchange rates that SBL applied to Bluewood's trades to the market rates. The vast majority of Bluewood's rates fell within the market ranges, so they could be ignored. However, a strange pattern began to reveal itself. Each month, two transactions had exchange rates that did not fall within the market ranges. These transactions always occurred very close to the end of the month, and always resulted in losses to the investment funds. Another interesting aspect about these particular trades was that the purchase and sale occurred on the same day in every case. In comparison, Bluewood's trading very rarely involved same-day purchases and sales.

In other words, these monthly transactions appeared very suspicious; they were different than Bluewood's normal trading, they fell outside market ranges, they always created a loss to the investment funds and therefore a profit to the bank, and they occurred at the same time every month.

My report to Murdoch was the last piece of the puzzle he needed. We approached SBL management and requested documentation for the trades in question. When the bank failed to provide the support documents, joint legal proceedings against it and the audit firm commenced.

In the end, both the bank and the audit firm settled out of court — neither wanted to risk the reputational damage of a court case. That was fine with us, as we just wanted the investors to be compensated. My role was to calculate a figure that would compensate each investor for his or her original investment plus a market rate of interest assuming the funds had been placed in a deposit account.

The investors received their fair settlements and Evans and Marigold received refunds for all the fees they had paid plus damages; SBL and the audit firm shared the cost of repaying the victims. In return, the legal proceedings were halted without any admissions of guilt or involvement in Bluewood's fraud.

Lessons Learned

This case taught me that fraud examiners must apply a degree of skepticism, perhaps even cynicism, to everything presented to us. It also taught me how valuable careful and detailed analysis is to any case; almost all the supporting evidence in the case came from my detailed transactions analyses.

The victims, their representatives, Evans and Marigold, also learned serious lessons. In particular, they learned to be suspicious of anyone who claims returns that seem to be too good to be true because they almost always are. Bluewood's reports never showed a single month of bad results, despite negative market fluctuations.

Recommendations to Prevent Future Occurrences

Investors should seek assurance that their money is being properly supervised. The trustee, Alex, didn't arrange to receive copies of the bank statements directly from the bank and was too trusting of the reported results. In mitigation, he did require an independent audit

(continued)

to be carried out, but then allowed Bluewood to appoint his own auditor rather than arrange the appointment independently. Do not be blinded by reputations. SBL and the audit firm were purportedly independent and reputable.

Verify the claims that people make about themselves before you trust them with your money. It wouldn't have been difficult to determine that the auditor was in fact a tax partner and had no audit experience or qualifications. Be careful and ensure that appropriate controls are in place for the protection of the parties involved. The underlying principles behind those controls can be summarized in two words — independence and segregation.

About the Author

Clive Tomes trained and qualified as a Chartered Accountant with one of the major international accountancy firms. In 1994 he created his own accountancy practice, one of his specialties being forensic work in support of several legal cases, including a number of fraud allegations. Clive became a CFE in 2003.

Missing Ingots

PRABHAT KUMAR

Tensions ran high as financial constraints began to choke the life out of Precision Casting Pvt. Ltd. (PCPL). After enduring another horrendous fiscal year, banks had refused the company's founder any sort of financial support and the company's financial position hit rock bottom. Bankruptcy seemed like the inevitable fate of the corporation.

Rewind 12 years and we'll see how PCPL came into existence. Ronald Lee had just graduated with a metallurgic engineering degree from the National University of Singapore. He already had a degree in management, and with his newfound achievement, felt that he was ready to take on the world. He returned home to Malaysia and married the daughter of a high-flying local businessman. His union with Sheryl came with its own benefits. Being married into a family with a sound business background, Lee soon became acquainted with big business and high-ranking government officers. In just a few short months, Lee had received approvals to develop land for his operations and to bring foreign workers into the country from Bangladesh. By January of the following year, PCPL was established as a small corporation that produced high-pressure aluminum die-cast parts for automobile companies. The quality of his products was unmatched by any competitor in Asia and within two years, PCPL had become the leading Asian supplier. However, nothing lasts forever. Lee was unable to handle the quick success and had developed the habits of an arrogant socialite. His attention to his work dropped severely and, as a result, the quality of the products declined and the profit margin dwindled. One year later, PCPL had begun sustaining severe losses and Lee had to liquidate 20 percent of the company's assets.

A Beacon of Hope

Yet now, as Lee sat in his high-rise office overlooking the Kuala Lumpur sky-line, a grin spread across his face. Out of the dark abyss that was about to engulf PCPL came a beacon of hope that could save the company — Ahmad Siddiqui and Yeo Ah Fatt had agreed to invest in PCPL. Ahmad Siddiqui was a manpower supplier in Malaysia who had made millions over the course of ten years. He was also the sole supplier of staff to PCPL and had developed a close friendship with Lee. Yeo Ah Fatt was an automobile spare-parts dealer who placed frequent orders with PCPL and was also well acquainted with Lee. However, the two new investors did not conduct due diligence and review any of PCPL's financial records before deciding to invest.

As a soft-spoken but shrewd businessman, Lee understood very well that Siddiqui's eagerness to invest in PCPL came from a desire to elevate his image from that of a labor supplier to an established businessman. This suited Lee just as well; his own extravagant lifestyle and ambition to be recognized in the high society of nouveau-riche Malaysians had opened many social opportunities for him. He could relate to Siddiqui's reputational concerns, and Lee had no qualms exploiting those concerns in his hunt for someone to boost PCPL's dwindling capital and prop up the failing corporation. Siddiqui was impressed with Lee's supposed business acumen and trusted him as an expert in the industry. Lee's other close business associate, Ah Fatt, wanted to invest because he hoped to establish a supplier at minimum cost in order to beat his competitors. Ah Fatt owned more than a dozen retail outlets and was too busy managing them to directly take part in PCPL's operations, but he trusted Lee's ability as a quality manufacturer with sound experience in the aluminum die-cast industry.

Siddiqui invested $4.5 million in PCPL and held 60 percent of the company's total capital in the name of his wife; they both became members of the board of directors of PCPL. Ah Fatt invested $2.5 million and gained control of 30 percent of the capital. Lee controlled the remaining 10 percent. Neither of the investors conducted proper financial due diligence. They trusted Lee's forecasts of future profits and audited financial statements from the past three years, which reflected only nominal losses but piled up creditors. The unsuspecting investors were convinced that the "minor" financial setback could be overcome by purchasing new machines with their investment. They firmly believed that with Lee's expertise and their investment, PCPL would start generating profits quickly. Since both these new investors were busy with their existing businesses, they allowed Lee nearly complete freedom in running the show as he had been doing for the past decade. Siddiqui, as one of the signatories of all the bank accounts, hardly raised any questions about payments being made to the various suppliers.

Since neither of PCPL's new majority owners participated in the company's day-to-day operational activities, they did not doubt the authenticity of the first few quarterly financial reports they were given — things seemed to be going smoothly. PCPL showed a net profit of $380,000, which was quite encouraging for new investors/owners.

Siddiqui was satisfied because his company was fulfilling all of PCPL's labor needs, and Ah Fatt was enjoying supplies at very competitive rates. What they did not realize was that there was something cooking right under their noses and it would completely destroy PCPL.

Declining Performance

During the second half of the following year, Lee called a board meeting to discuss certain issues pertaining to increased competition and a dwindling gross margin due to a variety of factors — all of which he convincingly explained. Both of his investors considered the problem genuine and vowed to provide full support to Lee. Siddiqui even agreed to extend a credit term of six months for payment of workers' wages and Ah Fatt agreed to a cash term for supplies made by PCPL.

Despite the support of the investors, PCPL's situation did not improve and a few months later Lee requested that Siddiqui and Ah Fatt lend him some money on his personal guarantee because the bank had already refused to increase his loans. Reluctantly they both approved his proposal, which opened a floodgate of borrowing. In less than eight months Lee had borrowed approximately $1.6 million to meet various liabilities at an interest rate of 24 percent. The financial results at the end of the year worried both investors but they were reassured by Lee that some big orders from two well-known customers would pull the company back to profit.

The next year produced a loss of $2.4 million with huge amounts owed to creditors and other mounting liabilities. This was the last straw for the investors. Ah Fatt met Siddiqui at his office to discuss the problem privately, and they decided to get to the bottom of PCPL's issues without letting Lee know about their concerns. They noticed that despite a 10 percent increase in sales, PCPL's consumption of raw material had increased by 26 percent — an alarming situation. The duo decided to recruit my fraud examination firm to investigate.

The Cost Analysts

With Lee in control of the entire operation and their investment at stake, Siddiqui and Ah Fatt did not want to scare Lee. So they introduced me to him as a cost analyst they hired to determine if any of PCPL's costs could be reduced. Since both of his major shareholders were firm about the decision, Lee had no choice but to allow our engagement.

My team and I had very little knowledge about the aluminum die-cast business when we accepted the assignment, so before we began the investigation, I spent about a week studying the industry and Lee's operation to get a fuller picture. I hired Alexander Tan to be our team's subject matter expert and had quite a few questions for him, such as:

- What is the average waste of aluminum when it is melted and used for die cast (known as *dross*)?
- What is the accepted level of impurity in standard aluminum ingot in terms of percentage?
- What is the productivity rate for a 200, 400, 600 and 1,000 tons PSI (pressure per square inch) machine?
- How and where is impure aluminum scrap disposed of and what is the current prevailing price for it?
- What is the normal rate of defect with die-cast products and what is the process for recovering aluminum from defective products?

The price of aluminum ingots is governed by the London Metal Exchange (LME) with a certain amount of premium, so I also visited the LME and other websites to obtain technical data and price movements of aluminum in the past 36 months. We gathered further information about other major players in the industry in Malaysia and prevailing market practices to know how the cost was derived, when a new die cast was needed and the mechanism of transferring the cost of the die to the customer for whom it was cast. This information-gathering exercise helped me to appreciate the genuine difficulties Lee would have maintaining records with complete accuracy.

After a week of research, armed with all the relevant information, I was ready to bring my investigation into a case that had been baffling the investors for more than two years. Since the issue concerned an excess consumption of the basic raw material compared to product output, my first objective was to confirm whether excess consumption actually existed.

The figure that reflected the purchase of raw aluminum ingots came from the general ledger and then we segregated all the purchase invoices because they would provide quantitative details for us later. Due to the fact that all the products were sold based on weight, we had some extra work on our plate to convert our figures. With the help of the marketing department's database and based on the standard weight for each and every product sold, all the sales quantities were converted into kilograms. We also determined the quantitative details of raw materials purchased, works in progress and finished goods. The results were both appalling and baffling — they suggested that an excess of 110 tons of aluminum had been purchased in one year alone. This, of course, profoundly affected the purchase cycle, production cycle and revenue cycle.

Working Hypotheses

After carefully studying PCPL's internal control infrastructure, I developed a few theories to account for the missing 110 tons of aluminum, taking into account the internal control weaknesses I had observed.

- The excess raw materials that Lee purchased never reached the factory but were debited to the purchases anyway.
- The raw materials had been received, and semifinished goods had been produced and sent to a third party for final processing, but they had not been returned to PCPL or been accounted for properly.
- Raw materials had been rejected and sent to outside parties for resmelting but had not been returned.
- More semifinished goods were sent out for further processing than the records showed, because Lee did not maintain quantitative records of defective and unfinished goods.
- Stated dross (waste) was higher than the actual quantity, and/or while disposing of the dross, quality aluminum had also been snuck out of PCPL's inventory.
- Finished goods had been shipped out to local customers and paid for with cash, hence no sale was recorded.

We tested these hypotheses one by one, and an examination of the purchase invoices confirmed that:

- Five different invoices that had been issued on different dates for the purchase of aluminum ingot could not be matched against entries in the inventory logs. If the materials had been delivered, they had not been entered into inventory.
- The supplier on these five invoices was the same — Ganesh Metal Industries — but it was not a regular industry supplier of ingot.
- The name of the truck driver on all five invoices was the same and the signatures were similar, but not exact matches. This suggested that it was not the same person signing each time.
- The five questionable invoices did not include a delivery time, but all of PCPL's other invoices did.
- There were no entries in the PCPL's guard book (maintained by security at the main gate) to confirm the vehicle numbers of delivery trucks for these five invoices.

The total weight of the aluminum on these five suspicious invoices equaled 66 tons, but we were looking for 110 tons of missing aluminum. This indicated that Lee, the one in charge of PCPL's books, had used more than one method to record higher consumptions and falsify the company's financial results. To confirm that the material had not been received but payments had been made nonetheless, I moved to the second stage of the investigation and guided my team to test the validity of our other hypotheses.

To gather evidence related to the five suspicious invoices, we thoroughly scrutinized journals and ledgers for any entries related to the purchase of raw material. For three of the five payments, the bank statement revealed payment was made with a check made out to cash, as opposed to a typical check with the supplier as the payee. Although PCPL's controller, Tina Khoo, insisted that cash checks had been issued to Ganesh Metal Industries upon its request, it was a highly unusual practice; we could find no other cash payments to suppliers at any point throughout the year.

After obtaining authorization from Siddiqui, I made photocopies of all the checks that had been used to pay suspicious suppliers and was able to confirm that the checks had been cashed by Lee — his name, signature and identification card number appeared on the back of the checks. In addition, we discovered three payments to a second company by the name of Multiple Construction, but the bank payment voucher and check stub reflected it was paid to Ganesh Metal Industries, which had supplied the aluminum associated with the five suspicious invoices.

Suspicious Vendors

We conducted background checks into Multiple Construction and Ganesh Metal Industries and discovered that Ganesh was a subsidiary of Multiple Construction, which had three directors, one of whom was named William Lee. Since the last name Lee is common and I didn't want to jump to conclusions, I approached the bank where the cash checks had been presented and was able to confirm that, although Ronald Lee was not a director at Multiple Construction, he was the sole signatory on the bank account. So Lee had, in essence, written a check to himself. We were still looking into the connection between William and Ronald Lee, but had not found anything conclusive yet.

Further investigations confirmed that Ronald Lee had used different methods to inflate the cost of production through bogus purchases, padded expense claims and payment of commissions to secure orders. He was the initiator of the scheme but had help from his trusty lieutenant, PCPL's controller, Tina Khoo, who was exceptionally skilled in her understanding of audit procedures and financial statements. She helped Lee keep the fraud concealed for almost three years. It seemed that Lee's manipulative objective behind the entire fiasco was to siphon off profits from PCPL for personal use to fund his lavish lifestyle.

Since my team was simultaneously testing the validity of other hypotheses, we were able to confirm that the goods that had been sent for resmelting were properly recorded and the recorded waste was not higher than actual. Cross-verification and recording of transaction did not provide any indication that these records had been manipulated. Interestingly, the company to which material was sent to be resmelted was Multiple Construction. In addition, PCPL's records regarding the aluminum sent to them were not satisfactory — the goods sent out did not reconcile with the total, re-smelted quantity that PCPL received back, after deducting the units that had been damaged during processing and those still being processed. The gap was substantial and a number of the relevant documents we needed to confirm the figures were missing.

My team and I turned our attention to the documents that indicated how much raw material was with Multiple Construction and compared the numbers with the invoices from the processor. It appeared that the amount of aluminum on the processor's invoices was more than PCPL received. The invoices did not include any supporting documents, but, despite such obvious red flags, Lee approved the invoices for the payment himself.

A visit to the factory with Siddiqui revealed that some processed material was packed in different packaging without labels and shipped directly to car-part traders. We could not locate records of sales to any of these traders.

We collected the daily production records generated during each shift for each of the nine die-cast machines Lee owned and compared them to those maintained by the production department. The machine records showed much higher production levels than the department reports. Our detailed analysis allowed us to clearly show that machines were in operation, raw material was consumed and goods were produced, but not all of the final material was moved into production. We discovered that those missing quantities were shipped to Multiple Construction and then on to dealers and customers, as per Lee's instructions. The sales were deposited in the designated account held by Lee and not recorded on PCPL's sales accounts — although the expenses of the transactions were well documented. William Lee at Multiple Construction received 10 percent of the sales for his help in the scheme.

To bring the case to a conclusive end we interviewed Ronald Lee and presented him with all the evidence. He readily admitted his fraudulent scheme to divert sales from PCPL and keep the profits to himself. He told us that William Lee was his cousin and that he had agreed to help with the scam for a percentage of the profits.

Currently both Siddiqui and Ah Fatt are negotiating a settlement with Lee to get their money back with interest, but they have both said if the negotiations fail, they will take legal action against Lee. To date they have not filed a complaint with the police because they are afraid that Lee, with his friends in high places, could make their report ineffectual and then they could lose the chance of recovery through negotiation.

Lessons Learned

- Siddiqui and Ah Fatt both learned not to trust people with their money without conducting proper financial due diligence. They trusted Lee as a business associate and friend, and let their

(continued)

(*continued*)

personal relationship cloud their professional skepticism. They also said if they could do it again, they would also have consulted with industry experts to look for any operational red flags already present in PCPL.

- Too much trust without proper control and supervision provided ample opportunity for Lee to show losses and divert profits from the business, which led his investors to believe that the die-cast business was not profitable.
- Ah Fatt and Siddiqui have also acknowledged the importance of accounting professionals and their role in providing invaluable services — especially when new investment is required. However, it was an expensive and painful lesson for them both to learn.

Recommendations to Prevent Future Occurrences

- Conduct proper due diligence before investing to check the financial history of the company and to see if it is operating with the normal range of the industry. Look for conflicts of interest among principals of the investment company and its vendors or customers.
- Professional skepticism is not just for auditors. Employees in a business should watch for red flags and report them to their supervisor or an anonymous hotline.
- Be active in your investments. If you hand over control with your money, you have no way of knowing what is happening to it.

About the Author

Prabhat Kumar, CFE, FCA and qualified forensic accountant, is Director and Senior Consultant with Alliance IFA (M) Sdn. Bhd, a company providing forensic accounting services in Kuala Lumpur, Malaysia. He has more than 18 years of experience in audit, accounting and financial expertise. For the past six years, he has focused his practice in financial information analysis and forensic accounting for the purpose of detection of fraud and to provide litigation support services. He has been instrumental in instituting a sound and effective internal financial control system for various entities, including multinational corporations.

When Silver Spoons Are Not Enough

A CASE STUDY OF FINANCIAL STATEMENT FRAUD

WALTER PAGANO AND DEBORAH KOVALIK

Manuel Consalado and Maria LaCosta were each born with silver spoons in their mouths, to families who lived in wealthy suburbs of Philadelphia. As is quite ordinary for children of wealthy parents, Manuel and Maria grew up with nannies, chauffeurs, tutors, maids, butlers and others to attend to their daily needs and seamlessly make their lives effortless and less burdensome. Manuel and Maria attended the best early learning and preparatory schools. They also attended the universities that their parents and grandparents attended.

As childhood sweethearts beginning in the eighth grade, Manuel and Maria were inseparable. They were articulate, friendly, intelligent, gifted and, indeed, very fortunate to have the positions in society that their families and social circles enabled them to have. Both of their families were involved in charitable and philanthropic causes and both were accustomed to always getting what they wanted. Manuel and Maria knew of no other existence.

Manuel's higher education and professional interests were in biology and life sciences, and Maria's were in accounting and finance. When they graduated from the University of Pennsylvania, they got married, rented an apartment in Rittenhouse Square in Philadelphia and continued their graduate education without having to work, because they were the beneficiaries of trust funds. Manuel completed his graduate studies with a Ph.D. in environmental sciences and Maria obtained her M.B.A. in finance and successfully passed the CPA exam shortly thereafter. They were young and the world was their oyster.

Manuel and Maria had no difficulty obtaining employment. They both had outstanding academic credentials, having graduated in the top 5 percent of their undergraduate and graduate school classes. The demand for them by prospective government and nongovernment employers was very strong. Also, the contacts — both professionally and socially — that each of their families had made over the years afforded them the opportunity to be very selective in accepting job offers.

Manuel took a position with a clandestine unit of the Central Intelligence Agency with an office in the Philadelphia area. The defense department was vigilant about biological, chemical and nuclear warfare and the United States was equally concerned about intelligence reports concerning biological and chemical agents. Of course, the "company" that Manuel worked for was merely a front for the highly secretive research work that he was doing.

Manuel impressed his military and civilian superiors from the very beginning of his employment. He was adept at understanding the interactions between organisms and the environments in which they propagated and lived and applying that understanding to combining chemical and biological agents with these organisms to conduct experiments and study the practical applications of his research.

Maria took an audit position as a staff accountant with a regional CPA firm in Philadelphia. Although she had no practical experience, her boss thought she had the potential to become a star because of her impressive academic achievement and because she had already passed the CPA exam before she was hired. Hopes for her success were very high.

Maria demonstrated a keen understanding of generally accepted accounting principles and auditing standards. Within two years she was promoted to manager and ran audits under the supervision of a senior manager and the engagement partner. To her credit, Maria required very little supervision. Her primary strength was assessing risk and understanding inherent weaknesses in internal control environments. She made excellent recommendations to management and boards at both public and private companies with respect to internal controls over financial reporting, mitigating risk and considering fraud in a financial statement audit. She became so highly regarded that she was a frequent presenter at the firm's continuing professional education programs.

Entrepreneurial Spirit

After spending almost five years in their respective fields, Manuel and Maria were ready to set out on their own. Manuel, having made numerous professional and political contacts, knew that his new company would receive government as well as nongovernment contracts in pursuing the work that he was so dedicated to. And Maria knew her way around a company's internal controls, books and records like no other.

So with the financial assistance of their families, Manuel and Maria Consalado established Environmental Life Sciences (ELS). ELS was formed to conduct research and studies for the scientific, educational and defense contracting communities with respect to the interactions between organisms and their environments, with application to the industrial defense complex. Manuel was ELS's chairman, CEO and president. Maria was chief operating and financial officer and vice president.

Over the next 20 years, the Consalados grew ELS from a fledgling company to one that employed 147 people and had global revenues in excess of $100 million. Manuel was not only one of the best scientific minds in the United States but, it turned out, a marketing guru.

Maria controlled all aspects ELS's business operations, taxes and financial reporting. She developed accounting, technology and internal control systems in such a way that the employees never fully understood that she had essentially devised ways to circumvent and override internal controls. ELS's outside auditors had no clue how she and Manuel had created an environment that had no real effective controls.

About 15 years after ELS was formed, a multinational company named Universal Sciences Group (USG) became interested in acquiring it for strategic reasons. USG was a portfolio company that owned many major players in and beneficiaries of the defense and military industrial complex. After negotiations, Manuel and Maria agreed to sell ELS to USG for $125 million in cash and had the potential to earn another $75 million in the succeeding five years based on ELS's performance.

Forming a Case Theory

I was working in my office on a sunny day in July when I received a call from an individual with whom I had never spoken. He said, "Hello, Walter, my name is George Roberts. I am an attorney representing USG, a company that is in litigation with the two individuals who sold ELS, a business that it acquired a few years ago. Craig Michaels, who is co counsel with me in the case, recommended that I consider retaining you as our testifying accounting expert to assist us in defending the lawsuit brought by the Consalados and in prosecuting USG's counterclaim against them."

George briefly summarized the case by stating, "The Consalados are suing USG for damages, alleging it mismanaged ELS subsequent to the sale and caused a reduced earn-out that the Consalados would have received had it achieved specific financial goals. USG is countersuing the couple, alleging they breached the representations and warranties in the stock purchase agreement that resulted in USG overpaying for ELS."

George explained the relevant sections of the complaint and characterized the case as classic financial statement fraud perpetrated by Manuel and Maria Consalado. He divided the alleged fraud into five categories: (1) fictitious or inflated revenues and accounts receivable, (2) concealed or improperly recorded liabilities and expenses, (3) improper recording and valuation of assets, (4) fraudulent or omitted financial statement disclosures, and (5) diverted revenue to offshore bank accounts. In addition, George said the complaint also alleged that the Consalados: (1) created fictitious business expenses, (2) concealed inventory, and (3) breached representations and warranties related to taxes, related parties and disclosures that they made in the stock purchase agreement.

I thought to myself, "Wow, this case sounds like it has all of the ingredients of some of the larger financial statement fraud cases I've read about."

After confirming that my firm did not have a conflict in the matter, I sent George an engagement letter and agreed to meet with him and his client, Andy Smith, USG's CEO, to begin reviewing the details of the case.

The following week my associate, Dee, and I met George, his co-counsel Craig and Andy in a very large conference room at George's law firm to begin the engagement. The conference room was filled with numerous boxes containing ELS's financial and accounting records, produced by the Consalados during the continuing discovery process. Dee and I listened as the lawyers and Andy explained why they thought the Consalados misrepresented ELS's true financial condition at the time of the sale to USG.

As I absorbed the lawyers' theory about the case, I could not help thinking that, despite fraud examiners' efforts to uncover fraudulent schemes, perpetrators of financial statement fraud and other financial crimes are usually not deterred by other people in their pursuit of unjust enrichment and unfair advantage at the expense of stakeholders and third parties. Over time, fraudsters perfect their "skills" until they have, in their minds, mastered the art of defrauding the unwary, unsophisticated or "it could never happen to me" crowd.

The hypothesis George presented, and asked me and Dee to confirm, was that ELS's financial statements were inaccurate, false, misleading and not in accordance with generally accepted accounting principles (GAAP), and that the Consalados breached the representations and warranties in the stock purchase agreement. I told the attorneys we would need to find evidence that the Consalados engaged in a pattern of behavior that spanned years, with the intention to misrepresent ELS's finances by recording inaccurate, false and misleading financial information. Specifically, I said the facts would have to show that the Consalados perpetrated the financial statement fraud by:

- Skimming gross receipts and diverting them offshore
- Concealing inventory
- Misrepresenting the true nature and purpose of expenses
- Misrepresenting the true nature of assets
- Covering up related-party transactions with the intent to strip ELS of its current and accumulated retained earnings and, at the same time, cause USG to overpay for ELS.

The Records Don't Lie

After my explanation, I asked George how many years we should investigate, knowing that federal and state statutes generally govern the relevant period of an investigation. George and Craig suggested we begin our investigation with the quarter immediately preceding the sale of ELS and work back seven years.

Dee and I planned to review, in electronic and printed format, ELS's books and records, including:

- All books of original entry
- Audited financial statements
- Tax returns
- Accounting, audit and tax work papers
- Correspondence
- Bank statements and canceled checks
- The stock purchase agreement (SPA)

The SPA among USG, ELS and the Consalados was relevant because it contained the representations and warranties made by the Consalados pertaining to financial statements, taxes, related parties and financial statement disclosures.

George and Craig and representatives of ELS provided Dee and me with the information and documents we requested and allowed us to speak to members of the accounting department to learn their processes and procedures. Once we had a clear understanding of who was responsible for specific tasks, what types of records were available at various ELS locations and where the information was stored, we began to review documents, ask questions, get answers, follow leads, ask more questions, follow more leads, get more answers and ultimately exercise the professional skepticism and judgment that all Certified Fraud Examiners, CPAs and forensic accountants are expected to exercise.

Dee and I started by carefully reviewing the first representation and warranty the Consalados made in Section 10.1 of the stock purchase agreement, which stated that "the financial statements of ELS (1) are in accordance with the books and records of the company, (2) have been prepared in conformity with generally accepted accounting principles applied on a consistent basis throughout the periods covered by the SPA, and (3) present fairly the financial position and the results of operations and changes in stockholders' equity of ELS as of the dates and for the periods indicated."

The first representation and warranty in Section 10.1 — that the financial statements are in accordance with the books and records of ELS — means that the financial statements include all transactions and adjustments made by the company and its auditors for the years represented.

The second claim in Section 10.1 — that the financial statements were prepared in conformity with generally accepted accounting principles applied on a consistent basis — means the financial statements were prepared based on a set of standards that is generally accepted and universally practiced by the accounting profession. The words "applied on a consistent basis" mean that ELS management applied the same accounting treatment to similar events in each accounting period.

The third statement — that the financial statements present fairly the results of operations — means that the financial statements have certain implied qualities, such as following accepted accounting principles that are appropriate for the circumstances. Another implied quality is that the transactions or events are qualitatively or quantitatively material to the financial statements.

Planning our investigation around these three claims, Dee and I were trying to prove that the Consalados skimmed gross receipts, misrepresented the true nature and purpose of expenses, concealed inventory or misrepresented the true nature of assets.

Dee noticed that accounts receivable were not integrated with the general ledger, so we examined the sales and accounts receivable journals and subsidiary accounts. Sales entries in the general ledger were input in batches rather than as specifically recorded transactions, and there were numerous credit memos and deletions offsetting sales. These were red flags to us, so we asked George for access to certain customers to verify the credit memo entries. George agreed and prepared the appropriate subpoenas. At the same time, George and Craig informed us that an ELS customer had come forward because he was suspicious about some unusual markings on his canceled checks. The attorneys did not elaborate on what the customer meant by "unusual markings."

We contacted the customers we wanted more information from and asked them to verify entries on the ELS books. Specifically, we asked them to provide us with copies of their canceled checks or credit memos. Our investigation uncovered numerous transactions covering almost eight years that demonstrated that the Consalados skimmed and diverted ELS cash receipts from several customers to foreign bank accounts. By examining the canceled checks and comparing them to entries in accounts receivable, Dee and I were able to determine that the customers issued checks to ELS for many of the transactions for which ELS allegedly issued credit memos or described as deleted. These payments contradicted the credit memos and the deleted sales entries in the books and were not deposited in any ELS bank or brokerage account. The "deleted" sales entries were another cover-up tactic employed by Maria Consalado to hide the fact that the payments were deposited in an overseas bank account not associated with ELS and not included in its accounts or general ledger.

Dee also uncovered a journal entry purporting to reduce sales and accounts receivable by $1 million that was similarly treated as a credit memo. When she asked for the documentation substantiating the item, Maria gave Dee a handwritten piece of paper that on its face substantiated an accrued expense payable — not a credit memo! Regardless of the fact that the journal entry was misclassified, we concluded that the substantiation was bogus and classified it as a fictitious credit memo because it too was used to cover up the diverted cash receipts.

We eventually determined that the Consalados diverted approximately $3.7 million from ELS into their private, overseas accounts and we began to think about the collateral consequences that the diverted cash receipts would have had on ELS's books. First and most obvious, cash balances were understated by approximately $3.7 million. Second, the bogus credit memos caused sales and accounts receivable to be understated by approximately $3.7 million. Third, the transactions reduced net income by an identical amount. And fourth, financial ratios, projections and EBITDA calculations were inaccurate and unreliable as a result of the understated cash, sales, accounts receivable and net income.

Next we discovered a fictitious expense scheme between a customer and the Consalados. The customer conspired with the Consalados for years to pay their personal expenses and deducted these payments from amounts he owed ELS. Dee and I became suspicious when we discovered that the customer benefitted from an unusually high number of credit memos; when we asked him for documentation for the credits, he admitted that they were fictitious and in reality were for the payment of $143,000 of personal expenses. This scheme reduced the net income of ELS and understated distributions to the Consalados by causing fictitious entries to be made to sales discounts and/or sales returns and allowances.

Many closely held companies like ELS lack adequate internal controls, so Dee suggested that we examine cash disbursements to determine whether the Consalados misrepresented any ELS expenses. A major factor in our decision to examine the expenditures was the fact that, for federal tax purposes, ELS elected to report its income and expenses as a pass-through or conduit entity. Essentially, each expenditure that was improperly classified as a business expense rather than as an asset or distribution to the Consalados reduced their individual income tax returns. Dee took the lead on this phase and did a fantastic job reviewing the accounts. She even discovered memos written by the Consalados that described the real nature of many such transactions. For example, we analyzed expenditures posted to a research account and found that approximately $425,000 had been diverted to pay for the couples' personal expenses, which resulted in an overstatement of research expenses and an understatement of distributions to the Consalados.

We also discovered that the couple concealed inventory from ELS's auditors. For one of the audit years, we noticed that a new firm audited the financial statements. In the notes section of its report, the firm stated that the balance sheet of ELS "has been restated from that previously issued primarily to adjust for understatement of inventory." The understatement was worth approximately $620,000. The effect of this adjustment caused total assets and stockholders' equity to be understated. We interviewed a senior executive at ELS who corroborated the auditor's report and shed light on other schemes. He testified that it was common practice for the Consalados to instruct their employees to hide inventory from the auditors by moving it from location to location and to sell products to foreign customers, cancel the invoices and divert payments to offshore accounts for their benefit.

Dee and I made numerous adjustments to ELS's financial statements with respect to those expenditures that were classified as business expenses when, in fact, they were the Consalados' personal expenditures. Overall, these schemes caused the financial statements to (1) not be in accordance with the books and records of the company, (2) not be prepared in conformity with GAAP, and (3) not present fairly the financial position and the results of operations and changes in stockholders' equity.

The Final Tally

Once Dee and I completed our investigation, I prepared a detailed written report explaining the documents and deposition testimony we reviewed and quantified our findings — worth approximately $12 million.

Category	Amount
Overstated Assets	$4,718,000
Overstated Liabilities	$1,000,000
Understated Distributions	$1,424,000
Understated Sales	$2,372,000
Overstated Expenses	$2,406,000

Based on the consistent pattern of behavior and conduct of the Consalados, I also stated that ELS's records probably contained more adjustments than those included in the report. From the adjustments in my report, a damages expert concluded that USG overpaid the Consalados by approximately 50 percent — $62 million. Subsequently, a jury awarded USG substantial damages, in the amount of approximately $24 million.

Lessons Learned

Dee and I learned so much from this case. First, collaborating with counsel helped us understand their case theory and how we, as accounting experts, could better assist them. Second, we found that our perseverance, tenacity and attention were essential, and they will serve us well in any complicated fraud case. Third, formulate a fluid plan, look beyond the evidence and think about additional or missing information and documents. Fourth, obtain sufficient information and documents and follow all leads before drawing any conclusions. Fifth, recognize that there are many faces of fraud so you can view the situation from different perspectives and consider all possibilities. Sixth, assess and understand the environment before embarking on a specific course of action. In the end, we learned not only that there were critical internal control deficiencies and weaknesses at ELS, but also that the Consalados intentionally caused them by manipulating numerous transactions to their personal advantage. The financial statement fraud was not isolated to a discreet account or issue. Rather, the fraud was spread across numerous balance sheets and income statements over many years.

Recommendations to Prevent Future Occurrences

Due diligence should never be sacrificed in an acquisition. It requires far more than cordial discussions and accepting at face value the information and documents you are provided. Examine the financial statements of a public or private company in-depth to understand its relationships, vendors, customers, processes, procedures, internal controls and risks. Banks are required to "Know Your Customer." The purchaser of a closely held business or a fraud examiner should also know his customer.

If USG's executives had conducted due diligence based less on the sellers' representations and more on analysis of the accounting and financial information, they would have uncovered the following red flags:

- The general ledger package was not fully integrated.
- Sales entries made in the general ledger were input in batches rather than by transaction.
- The sales journal contained numerous deleted transactions.

(continued)

(continued)
- The accounts receivable module contained unusual and unsubstantiated credit memos.
- Maria Consalados was responsible for and controlled the accounting department that failed the segregation of duties criterion.
- Numerous expenditures were bifurcated and posted to various expense accounts rather than to one account.

These red flags would have alerted USG's management that ELS's books, records and financial statements could not have contained complete and reliable information.

Certified Fraud Examiners should ask the right questions before sampling or testing accounts and not rely solely or exclusively on the assurances that financial statements purport to represent. Allow other companies' past irregularities and frauds open your eyes to all the possibilities of fraud and be your guide.

About the Authors

Walter Pagano, CFE, CPA/CFF, is the Litigation Consulting and Tax Controversy Partner in the New York Tax Group at EisnerAmper LLP.

Deborah Kovalik, CFE, CPA/CFF, CVA, CFFA, is a Litigation Consulting and Tax Controversy Director in EisnerAmper's New York Tax Group.

Deborah and Walter, both former IRS Revenue Agents, have substantial forensic accounting experience in conducting financial statement fraud examinations, investigating allegations of white-collar and tax fraud and critically analyzing financial data in complex commercial litigation cases.

CHAPTER

Sales Commission and Fraud Perpetration

A CASE STUDY OF FINANCIAL STATEMENT FRAUD FOR HIGHER SALES COMMISSION

TAREK EL S.M. EL MEADDAWY

Adam Berg was a 45-year old who had lived and worked as an American expatriate in Saudi Arabia for years. Adam graduated with a degree in commerce in the States and started a career in accounting. He was eventually enticed to Saudi Arabia with an offer to take over as the financial manager of a major branch of a refrigeration and air conditioning company called Zenda Company.

Adam was a talkative man and he always tried to convince people of his professionalism and responsibility. I believed this was due to a weakness in his experience and professionalism; he often spoke about himself as a solid asset for the company and how important his role was instead of proving these points through his work.

On my very first day at Zenda, where I was hired as the internal audit manager, I was warned about Adam. The previous internal audit manager said that Adam always tried to create problems during audits because he didn't want them to take place.

Adam's business cards indicated that he was a CPA but, after only a few interactions with him, I began to doubt his claim. I casually asked him about accounting standards and how he applied them in his work, and his answers gave me reasonable assurance that he could never have passed the CPA exam.

When I first met Adam, he tried to be nice to me and my audit team. He offered us his assistance during routine reviews and invited us to lunch every day. He even gave us a present once — famous Saudi dates. I was surprised by his gift because it seemed like he was trying too hard to ingratiate himself with us but, because it was the first time we met him, I believed it was his normal behavior.

However, his attitude changed drastically once we began our internal audit work and he realized he couldn't affect our work integrity with gifts. He launched his favorite attack against audits by creating problems for me and the auditors.

New Management

Zenda provided refrigeration and air conditioning services through branches in five countries in the Middle East (Saudi Arabia, Kuwait, Qatar, Bahrain and United Arab Emirates). Among the company's activities were trading the air conditioners and their spare parts as well as maintaining security systems. Zenda employed about 2,500 people in its different locations.

Zenda was one of 32 companies that made up a large family-owned group of businesses, including real estate, trading, hotels, contracting, manufacturing and refrigeration and air conditioning.

This group was owned by one of the most successful Kuwaiti businessmen until he passed away a few years ago and his family took on the responsibility of managing the group.

The family consisted of two sons and five daughters. The oldest son became the chairman and managing director, the younger son became the vice chairman and one of the daughters became vice managing director. Other family members had nothing to do with the business.

Sera, the daughter and the vice managing director, owned a reputable auditing and consulting firm and had earned an M.B.A. in finance; she was professional and highly educated.

As soon as Sera and her brothers took over at Zenda, she established a new professional internal audit department to serve the group and to submit internal audit services, because the previous internal audit department was not professional enough and focused on financial auditing only. The department members did not take into consideration the importance of internal controls for the reliability of the financial data. The previous internal audit manager was working on a part-time basis, so I was hired as the internal audit manager. Sera expressed to me her concerns about Zenda's internal controls and the integrity of the operations.

When I started, I found that there were chronic problems in Zenda, stemming from the absence of formal policies and procedures and a lack of proper documentation. I found that management was heavily focused on expanding the operations and growing the business, which made the lack of internal controls all the more troublesome.

In every country in which it operated, Zenda had a head office and several branches. A financial manager was responsible for every branch and the primary financial manager was responsible for overall activities in a country. Adam was the primary financial manager in the Kingdom of Saudi Arabia, which represented the biggest branch of Zenda.

All the financial data related to the country were gathered and consolidated in the head office and sent to the main corporate office in Kuwait.

Living the High Life

I was working with an assistant manager and two senior auditors on a preliminary survey of Zenda's Saudi Arabian branch's internal controls to assess their effectiveness in preventing and detecting frauds and errors. The first sign that worried me was the significant importance all the employees placed on the annual sales commission. I found through my audit that the employees' salaries were considerably low and I observed that their lifestyles exceeded their salaries. Most of them had luxury cars and prestigious accommodations.

I learned from employee interviews that most of them were not satisfied with their salaries but they were happy with the annual bonus and considered it the main source to finance their needs and their annual savings.

We also discovered that the country's sales director was also the country's general manager. He was a one-man show in the branch and he had the ultimate authority to make decisions and approve documents.

Along with this discovery, we noticed that Adam Berg, the primary financial manager in the Saudi Arabian branch, seemed to be enjoying a lifestyle well beyond his compensation package. He had a luxury car, wore a Rolex watch and lived in an expensive apartment.

All three legs of the fraud triangle appeared to be present in the Saudi Arabian branch:

1. *Opportunity* existed due to weak controls, a remote location far away from the main head office in Kuwait, improper monitoring from any party and improper segregation of duties.
2. *Pressure* existed due to low salaries, a high cost of living and the desire for many employees who were expatriates to save money while working in Saudi Arabia.
3. *Rationalization* existed due to Adam's feeling that he played a large role in the company's business and success.

Too Busy to Comply?

We believed that there was a high probability of fraud in Adam's regional offices because when we performed financial analyses on the financial statements, we found some odd ratios. In particular, the gross profit ratio was 17 percent higher than the previous year. We began an investigation to verify the effectiveness of internal controls and that the financial results were being fairly stated.

During our office visit we met with Samer Neama, a new accountant in the financial department who was responsible for a product called DSD — parts used in the air-conditioning industry — which the company distributed throughout the country.

Samer took over responsibility for the sales of DSD a year ago. Before Samer, Adam had been responsible for the sales. The company policy clearly stated that only the employee who was responsible for DSD sales was entitled to participate in the annual DSD sales commission program. This meant that in the previous year, Adam was eligible to earn the DSD commission, but since taking over the account, Samer was the only person entitled to the commission.

We documented the organizational chart and observed the working policies and procedures at Adam's branch — at the time there was no formal documentation of the regional office's activities. There were no official policies or an established work flow, so we had to create the documentation and standardize the processes as we went.

We observed that the accounting system used to track DSD sales didn't allow the sale to be entered without a corresponding entry for the cost of the sale, except in one case — if the user indicated that the sale was zero-cost, such as a bonus or a free giveaway.

After we performed the walk-through of the head office and checked the controls, we gathered the financial statements for the year and supporting documents for a proper sample of the accounting transactions.

Due to our concern about the gross profit ratios, I was worried about the sales and cost of sales. I asked Adam to give me a large sample of the branch's sales invoices and then tracked the invoices to their related documents, such as clients' orders, receiving reports from clients and payment checks paid by the clients. I found the transactions were accurate.

Then I asked Adam to give me the related accounting entries and to verify the cost of sales and the entries in the accounting system. "I don't know what you are looking for; I gave you all the sales invoices and you verified all the transactions. I think you want to make extra work but we're too busy right now. You should just audit the cost in another assignment," was Adam's response. I told him normal audit procedures included looking at the cost of sales with the related transactions to verify the accuracy of cost and that every period was completed. Still Adam refused to give me the cost of sales for the selected sample of the DSD transactions. He claimed he was too busy and told us to start another audit task. His attitude made me almost certain that he was concealing something. I told him if he didn't give me the requested data I would contact the head office for permission to complete my assignment.

Adam became very nervous and muttered, "Okay, I'll give you the cost of sales you requested."

Inflated Commissions

Once we started reviewing the DSD sales and cost of sales, we discovered the following:

- Adam recorded the revenue of the DSD sales and ignored a material amount of the related cost, which amounted to $600,000 and represented about 27 percent of the total cost of the year. His action guaranteed that he earned a larger bonus because he made a 10 percent commission on the ignored amount. We believed that this action was intentional because the system didn't allow the sales transaction without the related cost unless the person entering it manually claimed it was zero-cost for some reason.
- This fraud resulted in overstated annual sales of $600,000 for Adam to earn commission on.
- There was no proper documentation for the distribution of sales commissions at Zenda. Sales staff members were paid in an informal manner without any documentation based on instructions from the general manager of the region. We found that some employees didn't achieve the minimum target for the commission but earned it anyway, sometimes at a higher percentage than the formal percentage in the sales commission policy.

We mentioned the fraud case in the internal audit report we sent to the chairman and he issued a formal memo to establish a new organizational structure and maintain proper policies and procedures for the company, especially for sales commissions.

I discussed the matter with the chairman and the vice chairman and I advised them that there was a serious need to assign internal auditors in the remote branches because they needed regular verifications and audits. They agreed with me and decided to assign one internal auditor to each branch to report to me in the internal audit department at the head office in Kuwait.

The owners did not fire Adam because they feared that he kept much of the key branch information to himself. They worried that if Adam perpetrated this fraud, any severe disciplinary action could lead to higher losses to the company. But all the extra commission was paid back by the employees. Adam is not allowed to earn a bonus for three years, he has been transferred to another branch and he is not allowed to work with transactions that earn commission. He is permanently ineligible to hold the position of manager within Zenda.

Lessons Learned

We can learn from this case a good lesson concerning how sales incentives and commissions relate to sales figures and performance. It is a double-edged sword because this method provides a reasonable incentive to achieve sales targets but can make employees focus too much on the sales goals, which can lead to fraud if the employees don't hit their targets.

Segregation of incompatible duties is a very important and effective control in preventing frauds because the absence of segregation of duties can lead to manipulation with ease. In our case, if there was another accountant other than Adam responsible for the transaction entry and Adam was only in charge of posting the transaction, this case could be prevented from the beginning.

Remote locations need more monitoring from management and internal audit; otherwise the employees have the freedom to create their own rules that work against the best of interests of the company.

Standard policies and procedures are important tools for internal controls, especially for remote branches. Without them, a perpetrator could justify his action by saying that he didn't know what he did was wrong. The absence of policies and procedures allows every employee to create his own manual depending on his experience, personality and attitude.

Management can suffer if they leave essential information and responsibilities under the control of one person. Employee rotation is important so more than one employee has the skills to complete a job.

Recommendations to Prevent Future Occurrences

Regarding our report concerning the fraud case and the weakness in the internal controls the company took the following actions:

1. Assign an internal auditor in every location for the company branches.
2. Amend the sales commission policy to prevent fraudulent information concerning sales and cost of sales figures. We implemented a new commission policy that only pays on the collected portion of the performed sales.

(continued)

The monthly sales should be audited by an internal auditor who should verify the authenticity of the figures and check the accuracy of the accounting transactions for sales transactions.

3. Segregate incompatible duties. We hired a new accountant in the head office who is responsible for entering accounting transactions and signing them. The financial manager reviews and posts the transactions.

   The sales director is now responsible only for sales matters; all other managerial matters were transferred to the regional vice president.

4. Establish policies and procedures. Zenda established formal proper policies and procedures for all its departments and activities. These policies and procedures were communicated to the employees and they signed an agreement to adhere to them.

5. Send monthly reports to the head office. Several monthly reports have been identified to be sent to the head office on a monthly basis. They summarize the branches' activities and are audited by the main internal audit department on a quarterly basis.

6. Rotate financial managers. Zenda rotates its regional managers every three years, allowing them to work in a new branch with the regional staff. It provides a separate system of checks and balances and reduces the chance that a manager will develop too much sway over his staff members.

7. Conduct proper personnel checks. Full documentation should be gathered from potential employees before the hiring process takes place, especially proof of education and past work experience.

About the Author

Tarek El Meaddawy, CFE, CMA, CIA, CGEIT, has a wide range of experience in the field of audit and fraud deterrence. He started his career after graduating from Helwan University in Egypt. He is the head of internal audit in an international insurance company.

31

Like Two Sides of the Same Coin

PATRICK WELLENS

Kim Lee was a good-looking, 58-year-old, flamboyant extrovert who was full of energy. A self-made businessman, he was very successful and worked long hours to maintain the prosperous growth of his company. At 63, Jonathan was contrary to his younger brother Kim, who liked a posh, fast-paced life-style. Jonathan was the calm, introverted thinker of the family.

Both Jonathan and Kim went to the University of Hong Kong, where they graduated with honors in economics. Afterward they both attended several management training courses.

Jonathan had been married for more than 20 years to Dana, who used to work as a teacher, and they had one daughter, 28-year-old Kyla, who was studying in the United States to obtain a doctorate. Kim was married to Tamara, a homemaker, and they had two children, Tommy (27) and Sheila (26).

Kim worked his way up through a variety of sales positions (sales rep, district sales manager and regional sales manager) in a fast-growing consumer goods company before cofounding Sports Trading. Jonathan worked for years at a Big Four audit company, followed by stints in financial management positions until he decided to start his own company with his brother and act as general manager and CFO.

Kim had a great desire to be successful; he worked extremely hard but also liked status, authority and a posh lifestyle that included playing golf, driving around in a limousine, having dinners at fancy restaurants and wearing expensive clothing. Toward others he was charming, well groomed and pleasant. But it was difficult to really know what he was thinking. In public and toward employees, Kim was usually the mouthpiece of manage-ment. However, Jonathan was the real leader and silent force in the background.

Corporate Culture

Sports Trading (ST) was founded 30 years ago by the Lee brothers. To continue growing, about 15 years ago the Lees sold 50 percent of ST's shares to a European trader and, subsequently, to the sports company ISC. ST distributed, sold, promoted and advertised various brands and products in the Chinese market. The company signed various contracts with athletes and teams and was well regarded. Products were sold to the public via well-known warehouse, retail, third-party and closeout stores. ST employed 1,000 people at its headquarters and regional sales offices in China.

The communication and management style at ST were pretty much top-down; individual employees were not encouraged to take much initiative or ask probing questions. Rather, they were given detailed instructions and executed the orders given to them. I was also surprised to see most of the female employees wore uniforms. My initial thoughts of a sports company with young, dynamic, active employees were quite off base.

I worked as an internal auditor for ISC, the company that acquired 50 percent of ST's stock, and was the lead auditor conducting a routine audit of ST in China. After presenting the suggested scope and requesting specific input from executives at ISC, I was surprised to hear from the vice president of marketing (who also represented ISC on ST's board of directors) say, "There are some strange things going on — I believe the Lee brothers are defrauding the company."

"What brings you to that conclusion?" I asked. "What evidence can you give us?"

But the VP said, "I prefer that you form an opinion on your own."

It appeared that my routine internal audit was going to be far from what I expected and would probably take much longer than the three weeks I initially envisaged.

Contradictions in Sales Returns

Without knowing what frauds, if any, were occurring at ST, I decided initially to reconcile the balance sheet and profit and loss statement of the local accounts with ISC's central records and get explanations for any reclassifications and adjustments. Once I was confident that the central matched the local accounts, I performed an analytical review for the last four years. Apart from a small drop in the sales margins, I found no significant variances in sales or expenses. The company did not have major accounts receivable write-offs, inventory differences, large cash or goods in transit positions or any other accounts that would be red flags for fraud risk. Then I talked to the external audit partner and inquired about the company, related risks, state of internal controls, integrity and ethical conduct of senior management and the possibility of fraud at the company. He felt that senior management had integrity and said that in the past several years he had not raised major issues in his various management letters.

I started to investigate the revenue cycle and related internal controls. I met with the marketing manager to discuss our pricing strategy, our competitive position within the most important sports categories and the various discounts we gave to customers. I learned that we had volume and article discounts in place and additional special procedures could be authorized to ensure the remaining seasonal inventory would be cleared out. I learned more about the top ten clients and payment terms that were generally applied. Together with the sales manager I visited several shopping centers, wholesalers and retail outlets and learned more about the way they ordered their products; how ST tracked inventory and rotation levels; and how ST merchandisers had trained retailers to present our products (to distinguish them from our competitors' goods).

During my visits, Kim Lee seemed genuinely interested in helping me understand the business and facilitated the translation of some information we received from store managers. I had the impression that he tried his best to answer my questions; I certainly didn't think he was staging a show. I was aware, however, that due to my limited knowledge of Chinese, the explanations and translations I received were not firsthand accounts and could have been altered.

I also tried to understand how sales products were cleared out at the end of the season. I learned that the retail stores' objective was to sell merchandise while it was still in season. Three months into a season, products were discounted and the closer it got to the end of a season, the higher the discounts became. ST also had six factory outlets that sold products with small quality defects and heavily discounted merchandise from past seasons. Two out of the six factory outlet stores were owned by the Lee family and the other four were ST's. To ensure that the sales discounts were more or less identical among the six stores during a given period of time, I requested the sales records from all the outlets during the same period.

When reviewing reports from each, I realized that the two stores owned by the Lees consistently sold products for less than the other four stores — the ones owned by ST. I had been expecting to see some price variations on products from store to store, but it was disconcerting to see the Lees' stores constantly offering lower prices.

After obtaining detailed operational knowledge about sales and marketing, I started substantive testing of the general ledger accounts related to gross sales, price discount and credit notes. I obtained from the general accountant an explanation of what journals were posted automatically and what entries were made manually. After filtering, sorting and analyzing data, I was surprised to see many debit entries to the gross sales general ledger.

I selected for detailed testing many of those high-dollar entries, as well as requesting the supporting documentation for large credit notes and price discounts. Unfortunately whenever a credit note was generated within the accounting system, the field in which to insert a reason code was not filled in, so it meant that no statistics could be run and individual credit notes had to be retrieved and looked at in order to determine the reason. My surprise was great when I found out that wholesalers returned many goods, whereas the sales manager had just recently told me that generally did not happen. Indeed, within the accounting books, there was no provision for sales returns. Initial thoughts about the judgment and discernment of the external audit firm's partner crossed my mind.

Generous Contracts

I then asked the sales manager for the contracts with the major wholesalers, retailers and closeout stores to look for agreements relating to sales returns, volume discounts and payment terms. After this review (with the help of a translator and my colleague auditor who spoke Chinese), I realized that the accounts were not correctly stated and that consignment sales in lieu of gross sales should have been accounted for. To evaluate the accounting impact on the profit and loss statement for sales returns, we obtained detailed statistics of sales quantities and values by product for the past three years as well as obtained photocopies of all credit notes to manually determine the quantities and values. The total amount related to sales returns was less than $150,000.

To calculate an approximate impact on the profit and loss statement of the incorrect accounting of consignment sales, we needed to know what quantities and values were typically sold to each wholesaler and retailer as well as to understand the inventory turn rates. To do so, we spoke to the IT department and obtained a data dump. Then, for the 30 top-selling products, we analyzed the inventory transaction summary with detailed transactions of purchasing, sales by and sales returns data for these articles.

Next we obtained from the customer service department — which tracked the inventory levels of each wholesaler and retailer — the inventory-on-hand figures as well as the wholesaler/retailer sales information in all the stores. By merging and analyzing the various IT data, we could prove that, on average, goods were maintained for 15–20 days before being sold to final customers. As a result, net sales were overstated, approximately $10 million. I initially thought the internal controls might not have been working as planned, but I now started to look at ST from another viewpoint. I started to believe the vice president of marketing when he said, "I believe the Lee brothers are defrauding the company."

By showing the transfer of goods to wholesalers and retailers as sales instead of consignments, local ST management was capable of showing better-than-budgeted working capital targets and reporting higher-than-actual inventory turn rates.

I interviewed the marketing manager and learned how the local marketing budget supported the company's business strategy in addition to the regional and worldwide strategic initiatives. I asked how the marketing budget was assigned to events: camps for kids, TV advertising, radio advertising, athletes/teams, merchandising and other expenses, and I got an understanding of how some of these expenses were tracked to project codes in the accounting system. I then inquired how suppliers for marketing services were selected, how competitive bids were obtained and in what cases purchase orders were filled out. Furthermore I wanted to know how services provided by third parties but not yet invoiced were captured in the accounting system since these expenses should be reflected in the books at month-end. Unfortunately, the marketing manager was not able to demonstrate to us how these liabilities were reflected; she did not understand this accounting concept at all. As a result I concluded that there might be a potential risk of understatement of expenses and liabilities.

I then looked into the accounting books for a general ledger account called "invoices in transit," but could not find such an entry. I performed a search for unrecorded liabilities by reviewing all supplier invoices that came in after month-end and verified whether they related to a previous accounting period. This resulted in an understatement of expenses for tens of thousands of dollars at the end of the quarter. "This internal audit report is not going to be well received," I said to myself.

I then requested copies of the contracts with teams, clubs and athletes in various sports to get an understanding of what bonuses become payable to them and under what circumstances. Most of the contracts were structured to be performance oriented. Athletes would typically be reimbursed when they won a major event, and team owners would be paid based on the team's ranking in its league. As part of the sponsoring/promotion contract, athletes would receive a number of T-shirts, shoes and other ST products. Since the performance bonuses were substantial and, given that ST had many contracts, I wondered whether the company had a database that included details like the starting date, ending date, termination clauses, bonus payments due and so on. Unfortunately ST did not have such a database, but I was given Excel files containing most of the information I hoped to find. Not surprisingly, when we analyzed 30 randomly selected contracts we found differences between the contractually agreed performance bonus and the accruals recorded in the accounting books.

From the marketing and sales expenditures, we selected high-dollar transactions in the general ledger accounts and traced them back to contracts to see that they were properly authorized. Many contracts with sports federations and athletes were not signed by the marketing manager, as specified in ST's delegation of authority, but by the sales manager. It turned out that an instruction from the marketing manager to all ST employees in English, informing staff that he alone could approve sponsorships, was translated into the local language as "all sponsorships with athletes and teams must be signed by the *sales* manager."

And the List Goes On . . .

As I reviewed the aging of receivables, I was surprised to see large balances that had been outstanding for more than one year. ST's provision for bad debts did not take into account a discount to reflect the current value of receivables older than a year. Again, I learned that expenses were understated and started to doubt the accuracy of the books. I couldn't help but think, "What has this external auditor been doing the last couple of years?"

After I finalized the sales and marketing cycle, I was going to focus on expenditures (travel and entertainment, procurement and payroll) and was wondering what else I would find. To review the travel and entertainment expenditures, we familiarized ourselves with the company's travel and entertainment policy, the company car policy and the list of employees with credit cards. We decided to review the expenses of the general manager, sales manager, CFO and marketing manager as well as a random selection of sales reps since these staff members were responsible for the bulk of the travel and entertainment expenses.

By reviewing the monthly credit card statements and a representative sample of travel expenses for our chosen staff, we discovered that the supporting documentation for expenses was often missing (leading to quite high non-tax-deductible expenses). In many cases simply a credit card slip was attached to the claim for the expenses; the detailed expenses (restaurant bill, list and function of participants, etc.) were generally missing and the name of the business/establishment in which the credit card transaction took place was not easily identifiable. Moreover, the general manager and sales manager were claiming and being reimbursed for private expenditures. The VP of marketing was shocked when we told him; he had no idea because he had never conducted a review of travel and entertainment expenses.

In addition, we investigated the purchase-to-pay cycle. Initially we familiarized ourselves with the procurement policies (selection and evaluation of suppliers, obtaining different bids for purchases over a certain value, when purchase orders were used, etc.). Then we followed up with the procurement staff to get a better understanding of what activities they dealt with centrally versus those decided by the department heads of individual cost centers. By downloading supplier master data, supplier invoices, credit notes and payments from the accounting system, we learned better what suppliers and supplier categories represented the major expenses. We investigated trends, duplicate payments, breaks in numerical sequence, different suppliers with the same VAT numbers, those with the same bank account details as employees and suppliers with PO addresses.

Additionally I requested whether senior management and purchasing and sales staff needed to sign annually a written conflict of interest statement declaring not to have shares or interest in competitor companies with which ST did business. The personnel manager told us that no such policies existed.

I asked a person from the ST Finance Department to search whether the Lee family members had interests in other companies and learned that they had participations in or control over five others. Not surprisingly, ST was buying products from two of these companies. After I performed a quantitative analysis of what we were buying from them and comparing these with market prices, I found out that the Lee brothers were charging ST above the market rate. The annual impact of these purchases on ST was $300,000.

Another big chunk of expenses was payroll since the company employed nearly 1,000 people (including various regional offices). We performed a walk-through of the recruitment process, learned how personnel data was entered into the human resources and time card systems and learned how the information interfaced with payroll data. We looked at actual versus budgeted personnel expenses by cost center, internal controls around the creation and deactivation of employees in the payroll system, access controls over changes to remuneration components and the controls when salaries were paid out.

We also tested for ghost employees by reviewing whether employees were part of the time registration system and the telephone list. Regarding some of the employees who did not appear on either the telephone list or the time registration, we were told that they were regional sales employees. We asked whether they signed an application form for a corporate credit card or mobile phone; when all these answers were negative, we asked the HR manager for their personnel files, résumés and annual evaluation forms. We came to the conclusion that ghost employees existed and the HR manager and Lee brothers knew about it.

Legal Advice

Once I had a relatively strong indication of fraud, I contacted the head of legal at ISC, Adam Kowalski, who joined us in China. After he looked over the initial evidence, we discussed the next steps in my auditing process and stayed in daily contact. Although Kowalski did not enter the premises of ST, while in China he talked to various lawyers to get their opinions. Supporting the case and showing the lawyers some of the evidence firsthand meant we had to make a lot of copies. Kowalski also attended our exit meeting presentation to the Lee brothers.

When we explained the findings and accusations to the board of directors (which included the Lee brothers), they responded with silence. Even after I directly asked them what they thought of the situation, they did not say anything. The ISC board of directors bought the remaining 50 percent of the shares of Sports Trading soon after the audit concluded. No criminal charges were filed by ISC's senior management.

Lessons Learned

As part of this fraud investigation, I learned that when embarking on a joint venture in Asia it is important to have strong governance principles, ethics and controls agreed upon between the parties. Although the shareholder agreement between ISC and ST stated that both would be represented in the board of directors and contained all the necessary legal clauses, it did not say much about how the company was going to be managed and what controls ISC would like to implement at ST. The shareholder agreement was made in full trust and said very little about ethics, governance and compliance. I assume that both parties respected each other and probably never had a discussion about it. In hindsight, that was a big mistake.

Recommendations to Prevent Future Occurrences

The following recommendations can easily be implemented:

1. In the case of ISC and ST, ISC's representation on the board of directors was limited to the VP of marketing, who did not speak Chinese. This resulted in him signing documents he did not fully understand and, more importantly, he was not very effective in controlling whether the guidelines he issued were put into practice. One must realize that in the Asian culture, employees do not immediately come forward when they see irregularities, but strongly rely on the authority of their direct supervisor.
2. When acquiring a company, besides conducting financial and legal due diligence, it is also important to perform "forensic" due diligence, where business practices, ethics and the like are reviewed. Had ISC done so, some of the accounting issues and unethical practices might have been discovered earlier.

(continued)

3. In Asia it is quite common that employees are linked through family with other companies; conflicts of interest can exist. They have a different understanding than the U.S./European concern about such matters.

4. Although we want to trust our external auditors to find irregularities, internal control systems cannot rely solely on them. The fact that the VP of marketing, representing ISC in ST, did not understand the differences between consignments and sales, did not speak the local language and was not familiar with Chinese culture definitely contributed to some of the issues we encountered.

5. Initial findings by internal audit that might have indicated fraud could turn out to be false alarms. Legal evidence is quite different from what internal audit considers evidence, and it is important to work with local lawyers to get their opinion on the facts.

6. ST did not have a whistleblowing hotline in place. I believe that an anonymous hotline for employees would have helped us find out about irregularities and/or deviations from corporate policies, especially because ST's management style and corporate culture did not allow employees to openly question their leaders' decisions.

About the Author

Patrick Wellens is a Senior Manager of Forensic & Dispute Services at Deloitte in Switzerland. He previously worked as CFO and Internal Audit Manager. He obtained a Master's in Economics, Master's of Finance and an M.B.A. and is a Certified Fraud Examiner, Belgian Registered Forensic accountant and Certified Internal auditor.

CHAPTER 32

A President Illuminated

THEODORE G. PHELPS AND CINDY PARK

Sue Chadwick was a presence. When she walked into the room, you couldn't help but notice. She was tall and attractive, with thick white hair that was neatly coiffed and suited her oval face and piercing eyes. Her age did not show through her sharp personality and the confident manner in which she spoke and moved. This woman was clearly in charge.

Sue had worked hard to get where she was and she did it on her own. After graduating high school, Sue opted to head straight to work instead of attending college. She started in the secretarial pool at Phoenix Construction, one of the state's largest construction companies, and rose to the position of executive assistant to the president. She keenly observed every facet of the business and absorbed every tidbit of knowledge.

To say Sue was savvy and conniving would be an understatement. Sue wasn't like most women her age. Being in the workforce meant everything to her — she was not content to stay at home, join a bridge club or work on her tennis serve. Sue was more than ready to leave Phoenix Construction and take over the reins of Sue's Lights, the company her husband, Gene, had quietly run for the past ten years. In fact, Sue was likely the driving force behind Gene's semiretirement. When she took over as president, she took everything she had learned during her years at Phoenix and put it into practice. And she wasn't alone — her only child, William, had been working at Sue's Lights since graduating high school. Now in his late 20s, William was Sue's faithful, willing and loyal servant and was available for any task she wished to execute.

Then, there was the ever-present Tinkerbelle — a toy poodle with a striking white coat that matched her master's. Tinkerbelle was Sue's companion and confidant, even sharing Sue's large glass-topped desk in her office. One could walk in and watch as Tinkerbelle snoozed or ate among piles of papers, files and construction blueprints. Tinkerbelle had full command of the office, much like her master. She was small but mighty and wore a jeweled collar. Two small bells dangled from her sparkling collar and gave constant announcement of her comings and goings.

A Bright Future

Sue's Lights was an electrical subcontractor that performed most of its work for schools, universities, ports of call, airports and railroads. Minor sales came from electrical maintenance contracts with apartment complexes, grocery chains and retail stores. Sue's Lights had an impressive client list and vendors were anxious to conduct business with the growing subcontractor. Sue had guided the once tiny, ten-year-old company into status as a major player in the commercial construction business with sales of $13 million and assets of $5 million during her five years as president. She had garnered several achievement awards from small-business groups and women-in-business associations. Her list of contacts was wide and deep, and her dominance and influence were almost mesmerizing to those she encountered.

Sue had been shopping around for a new banker at the end of the year. Bravo Bank, the small-market bank she selected, was eager to extend her credit considering her presence in the industry and her business accolades. She told the bank that Sue's Lights had taken on several multimillion-dollar projects at the same time and was in need of additional working capital. The bank conducted a standard review of the submitted financial statements and job profitability reports and was impressed. Early the next year, the bank extended $2.2 million in various credit facilities to Sue's Lights along with a personal guarantee from Sue. The cash infusion was a relief to Sue — she had plans.

The bank required monthly financial statements and job profitability reports from Sue's Lights, but Sue was chronically late getting the information to the bank. She was always able to provide a reasonable excuse and employed her cunning social skills to successfully obtain reporting extensions. Sue's Lights had spent 100 percent of the line of credit and loan proceeds within a month of being issued the loans, and had made only two loan payments in six months. Bank executives applied increasing pressure on Sue to make payments. No amount of sweet talk could keep the bank at bay — the loan officer was closing in on Sue. She spent the majority of her days behind closed doors on the phone.

The bank declared Sue's Lights in default on her loans only seven months into their life and a couple of months afterward placed the company into a court-ordered receivership. Sue was out of cash and forced to shut down her business in the midst of several large, ongoing projects.

An Unorthodox Executive Team

My boss at Fraud Busters, Inc., Ted, called me from his field location, while I was putting the finishing touches on my latest embezzlement investigation. "Did you bring your umbrella today?" he asked and then continued "I just came from court and have been appointed receiver over at Sue's Lights. We are going to meet with the owner as soon as you can get out here; I'll be waiting. The address is. . . ." I hung up the phone and quickly grabbed my fraud examination plan and the research I had already done on Sue's Lights. Ted and I had been waiting for the court appointment and now we could start examining the books and records.

It was still pouring rain when I arrived at Sue's Lights. Ted waved to me from the front entrance. Before he opened the door he paused and said, "You know we need to move quickly on finding all of the assets, especially what happened to all of the cash. The bank loans are only nine months old. No telling what's been going on here, but the bank is suspicious of Sue Chadwick and her close relationship with several vendors." I nodded in agreement as the rain twirled off our umbrellas. We pressed through the front door out of the deluge and into cold, darkened offices. I looked up and there was Sue, standing rigid with her arms crossed just outside of her office. Tinkerbelle stood at attention by her legs.

Sue remained by her office door while Tinkerbelle pierced the silence with her short, sharp barks and raced toward me and Ted. Instinctively, I knelt down to greet the noisy companion. "Her name is Tinkerbelle," Sue stated. "I'm glad you like dogs." I looked up to an extended hand "I'm Sue. My lawyer told me you both were on the way. I can't believe the bank did this to me." And with that, Sue launched into a tirade about the bank, Sue's Lights' cash-flow problems and how one of her main suppliers, Downtown Lights, was the main culprit in the company's financial demise. Ted and I patiently listened as we sat in Sue's office and, when she was finished, Ted briefed Sue on how a court-appointed receiver operated.

Ted and I had just broached the request for Sue's Lights' books and records when a very well-dressed gentleman entered the room. The conversation stopped as Sue stood up and said, "Ted, Cindy, this is Peter, my new VP of Operations." Peter nodded his head and responded, "That and I am also the VP of Finance for Twilight. We've been providing wholesale electrical supplies to Sue's Lights for years."

Without skipping a beat, Peter led Ted and me into a conference room with binders and folders stacked on a table and proceeded to open and explain each of the sets of documents. Peter too revealed his dismay with Downtown Lights and their role in the closure of Sue's Lights.

As Ted continued to converse with Peter, Sue returned to her office and I quickly surveyed the documents spread out on the conference table. Peter watched me and said, "I think I assembled everything Sue's attorney said you would need; is there anything else?" "Yes," I replied. "I would like all of the company bank statements going back the last two years." Peter quickly responded with an enthusiastic "No problem!" and turned on his heel and vanished from the conference room.

Ted and I stood together stunned and alone in the conference room. We looked at each other and grinned . . . Red Flag #1. I could see why the bank was so suspicious. Ted and I would be taking a close look at Sue's Lights' transactions with Twilight. Peter's employment with both companies was unusual to say the least.

Peter returned to the conference room with a stack of binders in his arms. Sue was behind him and holding two black binders. "Peter has brought you the bank statements and I have the check registers for each of the accounts. You see we have a half-manual, half-computerized accounting system that I will need to explain to you. In addition, our computers crashed and you won't be able to access them. All of the accounting reports are printed and in large binders at Carol my bookkeeper's desk." Sue proceeded to explain how the manual register was integrated with the computerized check runs.

When the phone in Sue's office rang, she stopped mid-sentence and darted out to her office. Peter and Tinkerbelle trailed behind her. I heard her office door close. Ted picked up his umbrella. "I'm headed out to one of their construction jobs in progress. I need to secure all of their equipment and vehicles. I'll be back later to see what we've gotten ourselves into."

The conference room occupied a corner of the building and ceiling-to-floor windows filled two of its walls. I sat down looking out to the front street. The wind was blowing the trees lining the street to and fro and forcing the rain in heavy doses down the window I was staring through. I opened up one of the binders and started my work.

I saw curious transactions as I flipped through the pages of the manual check register. The register showed large deposits from Twilight *and* Downtown Lights; some were several times a month over the entire two-year period. I also noticed large and even payments to Sue and other individuals, some as high as $150,000. I didn't recognize these individuals' names on the vendor list or the accounts payable aging reports. I also noted even weekly payments of $500 to $2,500 to the IRS and the state. "Could it really be this easy?" I thought as I noted each of the questionable transactions into a spreadsheet.

In Plain Sight

The bells on Tinkerbelle's collar started to clank and I could hear her heading in my direction. Tinkerbelle soon paraded into my line of sight, and Sue strode in the conference room behind her. "Can I have the accounts payable ledger?" Sue asked. Without waiting for an answer, she picked through the binders to find the accounts payable ledger. "One of the bonding companies is on the phone. I need to confirm how much we owe all of the vendors, especially my big ones, Twilight and Downtown Lights. Since Bravo Bank so graciously shut us down, the bonding company is taking over all of our projects and needs to know how much each vendor should be paid. I'll return it to you." Sue shouted back to me on her way to her office, Tinkerbelle tucked under her arm. She shut the door behind her.

I thought to myself, Sue appears anxious to make sure the bonding companies pay her vendors, including Twilight and Downtown Lights, the same entities making large, questionable deposits back into the Sue's Lights' accounts. I walked over to Carol's abandoned desk. The work area appeared as if someone was going to return at any moment. Binders with reports and ledgers, stacks of mail and various documents littered the desktop along with a partially full coffee mug. I picked through the financial mess and located the large thick binder containing the current year's detailed general ledger.

Selecting one of the largest amounts from my questionable transactions spreadsheet I attempted to locate a suspect deposit from Downtown Lights in the detailed general ledger. No luck. I tried one from Twilight, but nothing. In fact, I was unable to locate any of the deposits from either vendor in the detailed general ledger. I wasn't surprised; I knew something was up. I could hear Sue's lowered voice still on the phone inside her office. I gently knocked on her door.

"Come on in," Sue answered.

"I apologize for the interruption. Could you tell me where the CPA's financial statements and tax returns are filed?" I slowly entered the room.

"Open that credenza file just behind you, they should be in the top drawer," Sue spoke as she cradled the phone between her neck and shoulder. "Hold on," Sue said into the receiver. Peter sat quietly in the chair opposite Sue's desk.

I could feel their eyes penetrating my whole body as I thumbed through the hanging files to locate the past three years' worth of CPA-issued financial statements and tax returns. "Thanks," I said looking straight into Sue's eyes and she into mine in complete silence. Even Tinkerbelle, laid out atop Sue's desk, had her head cocked up staring intently at me. I smiled, turned and walked out the door, closing it behind me. Sue's muffled conversation continued.

These must be the financials they want me to see, I thought, as each accounts' ending balance roughly matched the CPA's issued financial statements and tax returns.

I decided to briefly check out the payables to Downtown Lights and Twilight and reviewed Carol's accounts payable detail. Each page listed invoices by vendor and then in chronological order an invoice number followed by the underlying purchase order and invoice amount. As I flipped through the Downtown Lights detail, I noticed they used a six-digit invoice number. But I was also seeing a collection of five-digit invoice numbers associated with two different purchase orders. My train of thought was interrupted by the opening of Sue's office door, and Tinkerbelle rushed at me and issued a short bark. I looked up at Sue and Peter.

"I'll keep you posted," Sue told Peter as he walked toward the front door.

"It was nice meeting you," Peter nodded to me as he turned and left. I never saw or spoke with him again.

"Sue, I was wondering if you could show me where the rest of the business records are located?"

"Sure . . . well, you know there are some corporate records in the credenza in my office and I've already shown you Carol's desk, so let me go through the rest of the offices."

We completed our tour of the office at the door leading out to the warehouse.

"Do you really think you'll need to access any files from our warehouse?" Sue queried me.

"Do you mind?" I responded.

"Okay, so long as you know that I have no idea what is in most of this stuff, so don't ask me any questions . . . okay?"

"Okay," I answered. The back of the warehouse was filled to the ceiling and width of the building and 20 feet deep with storage boxes. I was literally dwarfed by brown, corrugated boxes. "Okay," I uttered again. We walked back to the main offices. Sue's cell phone rang.

"William!" Sue exclaimed while walking a fast clip back to her office; the door closed fast behind her. Tinkerbelle barked at the closed door and then looked rather indignantly at me.

I headed to the office where the purchase orders were kept. The bells on Tinkerbelle's collar jingled as she followed me. This office had been kept neatly organized so I easily found the purchase order binder. I paged through the sequentially numbered, white, original portion of the three-part form looking for the two Downtown Lights purchase orders referenced in the ledger. Interesting . . . the two purchase orders were missing.

I sat down and started looking through all of the drawers when I came upon a thin gray binder labeled "Downtown Lights" and a pack of loose pages from Sue's Lights' accounts payable ledger. I went through the pack searching for the same unusual grouping of five-digit invoice numbers I had seen before. I found them and the invoices had been highlighted with an incredible message: "These invoices need to be inflated!" Another paper in the pack was a memo indicating the need for the (inflated) invoices to be organized since the invoices were accumulating. Curiously, the memo urged the inflated invoices to be hand carried by William, instead of mailed. The memo had been signed by Sue.

"Wow," I spoke out loud as I sat back in the chair just staring at my newly found evidence. I finished searching the rest of the office for the missing purchase orders without luck, but I walked out with far more than I hoped for when I entered.

Back at Carol's desk I pulled out a drawer in search of the missing purchase orders and I saw a large unlabeled white binder. The inside first page was labeled "Special Transactions." I sat down and started going through the binder. I temporarily put my suspicions of Downtown Lights on the back burner and now was focusing on some sort of scheme involving Twilight. A portion of an e-mail thread in the binder said:

> Sue:
> You need to send a purchase order to me and reference any project name you want and then I will send an invoice to you for the purchase order.
> Peter
>
> Peter:
> That sounds good. Just remember to put a delivery date on it, let's say in 30 days, and a delivery address and payment terms so it looks real. And use my cell number instead of the company business number.
> Sue

The Special Transactions binder also had summaries of loans, interest and invoice amounts along with purchase orders, invoices and copies of checks — all involving Twilight and Sue's Lights. What was going on? This scheme must be related to the large Twilight deposits into the Sue's Lights account.

A substantial amount of funds were coming in from Downtown Lights and Twilight and being disbursed to Sue Chadwick and other unknown parties. I wondered where Sue had been spending her time in the past few months. Before the day ended I headed over to the paid-bills files and started looking for credit card statements (a great way to see where one is spending their time) and pulled out a bulky file for a gas credit card. Everything looked normal up until two months prior to the court-ordered receivership, when gas charges started appearing in Arizona, an adjacent state.

I headed over to make some copies from the Special Transactions binder and the gas credit card statements, and just as I started copying some of the gas credit card statements, Tinkerbelle started barking incessantly and jumping on my leg. Her bells clang loudly as I hurried to finish my copying.

"What is going on?" Sue shouted over Tinkerbelle as she emerged from her office and crossed over to the copy machine. I slowly placed the copies from the binder face down over the credit card file.

"Tinkerbelle has been missing you; I am just a sorry replacement," I said while bending down to try to calm the dog. I picked her up and placed her in Sue's arms, and continued making copies while chatting nonchalantly with Sue.

On my way home I called Ted and updated him on the day's affairs. I contacted the two bonding companies involved and urged them to hold off on any payments to Twilight or Downtown Lights until I completed my review. I conveyed my general concerns and promised to get back in touch with them later. The rain stopped and the setting sun was trying to pierce its rays through the heavy cloud cover. What an interesting day it had been.

Out of the Rain

When I got back to Fraud Busters' offices the next day, Ted and I started pouring over the copies of Sue's Lights bank statements and canceled checks Ted had requested from the bank. We compared actual withdrawals with the notable disbursements I had scheduled out the previous day. It appeared the manual check register accurately reflected the deposits and disbursements on the bank statements. We also closely examined the endorsements and the institutions where checks were being deposited.

I stopped and smiled when I saw the Community Desert Bank endorsement on the back of one the checks made out to Sue Chadwick. "Ted? I think I have a lead. Remember those gas credit card statements I had been reviewing and the sudden gas charges in Arizona?" As Ted walked over to my worktable piled with documents and files, I waved the canceled check copy in the air. He examined the endorsement and left quickly for his office to make a phone call. Ted returned "I've got a guy on the ground in Arizona checking out the account. We'll see."

As Ted continued to track the cash, I returned to make sense of my copied pages from the "Special Transactions" between Sue's Lights and Twilight. The scheme became clear as I laid out the documents. Sue's Lights was past due on payments to Twilight but was in dire need of cash to keep projects running. Twilight needed additional working capital. Together they worked out a rather complicated scheme.

Twilight loaned money to Sue's Lights. Sue's Lights fabricated purchase orders and Twilight issued phony invoices back to Sue's Lights for the amount of the loan plus considerable interest. The "new" invoices increased Twilight's factored accounts receivable borrowing base satisfying Peter's need for additional capital. The binder had a reconciliation of the scheme showing loan repayment amounts and dates. The reconciliation also indicated that Sue had not repaid Peter at the same rate that funds had been loaned. This explained Peter's sudden position with Sue's Lights and his extraordinary knowledge of Sue's books and records — he had been protecting his own cash position.

I needed to head back to Sue's Lights to find more documentation. I spent the next several days digging through the Sue's Lights warehouse chock full of boxes. My search was fruitful.

Almost immediately I found a box filled with not one, but three different versions of the financial records for Sue's Lights. The first set was a computer print-out, the second was a set of records called Sue's Reports and the third set was old-fashioned accounting green sheets wherein every account was manually tracked month to month, with tick and tie marks throughout. It was a cornucopia of financial data likely representing the real state of affairs for Sue's Lights.

The large Twilight deposits noted on my first day were recorded in the manual records as accounts payable to Twilight. Twilight had loaned Sue's Lights $1.9 million over a period of only six months and the entire amount had been concealed from the financial statements.

The best part of the box was the unbelievably frank correspondence among Sue, Carol and Ollie (Sue's Lights' CPA). Carol sent correspondence to Ollie using phrases such as "these are not the real numbers," "we fudged the numbers last month" and "the bank or the bonding company doesn't know this." The weekly correspondence confirmed Ollie's strong role in all of the deception since he provided the professional guidance on how to record the fraudulent transactions.

I delved further. The curious Downtown Lights deposits were also found in the manual records. They were asterisked and subtotaled off to one side of the sheet. I followed the asterisks through to a sheet of adjusting journal entries (AJEs). It appeared the funds deposits to Sue's Lights were initially recorded as sales but were then adjusted through a maze of accounts such as construction underbilling, construction overbilling, shareholder loans, depreciation, payroll expense, miscellaneous and even retained earnings. The AJEs made no sense whatsoever and had absolutely no basis in generally accepted accounting principles (GAAP). These documents were incredible and it was just about to get better.

Filed with a mess of mismatched financial documents was a letter from Sue to Wilbur, the president and founder of Downtown Lights. The letter mentioned inflated purchase orders and real purchase orders for a large project. They were the same two purchase orders referenced in the payables ledger that I had been pursuing. This had the telltale signs of a kickback scheme. Sue was evidently responding to Wilbur's claim that she had not paid enough sales tax on the "inflated" invoices. He was advising her that she owed him more money. Sue was supplying Wilbur with her own calculations and had concluded that he owed her money. The letter could have been labeled "There is no honor among thieves." Could it get any better? Yes . . .

Among the boxed files of the Downtown Light's project of interest were several notebooks filled with a complete summary of the entire scheme along with the original purchase orders, the inflated purchase orders, original invoices, inflated invoices, check copies, correspondence showing Sue's son William's involvement and more. Indeed it was a kickback scheme wherein Downtown Lights inflated invoices on a time-and-materials contract. Excess funds were kicked back to Sue after Wilbur had covered his company's invoices on the current project as well as on several previous projects with Sue's Lights — a fraud investigator's dream!

I felt a bit like a pinball bouncing from one fraud scheme to another. It was time to tie everything together.

Sue had managed to pay off the entire $1.9 million to Peter at Twilight, but not without a fight. Peter had filed and recorded a lien on Sue's personal home for a remaining portion. By the time the receivership had been put in place, Peter was getting his final payments and releasing the lien on Sue's personal home.

In the Downtown Lights scheme, Sue's Lights had inflated the invoices by $1.88 million resulting in $1.37 million in net kickbacks to Sue. Sue's true debt to Downtown Lights and "extra income" on the project were not reflected in the financial statements.

Approximately $3.6 million in liabilities was concealed from the financial statements, including the Twilight scheme, the Downtown Lights scheme, loans to friends and business associates and unpaid payroll taxes.

Only one of the two bonding companies responded to my concerns regarding Downtown Lights and Twilight. Construction Bonding Company sent out their counsel, Robert Kaplan to meet with Ted and me to discuss Downtown Lights.

We presented all of our findings and walked through the details and documents of the kickback scheme. Robert possessed a keen sense for the fraud and the accounting manipulations and must have been convinced since Construction Bonding Company held off on making any payments to Downtown Lights.

Ted and I had our final meeting with Sue as she and her attorney were scheduled to meet at our offices to discuss the receivership. Sue strode into our conference room with the same air of confidence displayed on the first day we met her. During the meeting we presented our findings. Her counsel continually silenced her verbal outbursts. Sue kept her hand placed over her mouth. After the presentation, they slid out of the office without uttering a word.

The findings during our investigation resulted in two separate civil litigations: one between Bravo Bank and Ollie's CPA firm and the other between Construction Bonding Company and Downtown Lights.

Lights Out?

The CPA firm settled out of court with Bravo Bank based on the damning evidence uncovered during our examination.

Robert Kaplan skillfully negotiated a settlement during mediation with Downtown Lights, resulting in substantial savings for Construction Bonding Company since only half of the vendor's claim was paid. Ted and I presented evidence at the mediation. After the mediation, Wilbur looked down and shook his head, "I knew I should have never gotten involved with that woman. . . . I just couldn't help it."

What happened to all of the cash? Truthfully, we'll never know. The bank accounts were closed as soon as we could track them down. We think Sue stashed some away for herself and William.

However, life for Sue was not going to be easy. Bravo Bank repossessed her personal home and business real estate and the receivership closed down all of her accounts. We heard Sue and her husband divorced and surmised that Sue and her son were off living together somewhere.

Lessons Learned

"I didn't think you were really going to look at all of the documents," is a statement we hear on almost all of our fraud examinations. Keep digging if there are enough red flags.

As hindsight is 20/20, we should have started tracking the cash immediately. I believe we could have outsmarted Sue with that approach, but she left us with so much to discover.

The investigation involved an overwhelming amount of documentation, and it was absolutely crucial to stay focused and remain objective. We had to constantly remind ourselves of this, as the drama provided by Sue and Peter was intentionally distracting.

Who knows, Sue could be in your town setting up shop now. I can see it clearly — her, William and Tinkerbelle back in business, just waiting for a future fraud investigation. Be sure to carry pet treats.

Recommendations to Prevent Future Occurrences

Our practice does a significant amount of work with financial institutions. As consultants we understand the cost of performing due diligence prior to granting credit facilities. It is a delicate issue. However, upon completion of our investigations, the institutions always query us on how they could have prevented the fraud. For this case in particular, we responded as follows:

(continued)

(*continued*)

1. Banks and financial institutions need to consider the cost of NOT performing front-end due diligence that could ultimately reduce the incidence of fraud.
2. Failure to obtain required financial reports in a timely manner signals a problem.

About the Authors

Theodore G. Phelps, CFE, CPA, CIRA, is the CEO and founder of PCG Consultants. He has over 30 years of experience working with financially distressed companies, most of which have been middle-market and closely held businesses. He is a Diplomat of the American College of Forensic Accounting, studied engineering at the United States Naval Academy and completed his education at the University of Southern California with a degree in Accounting.

Cindy D. Park, M.B.A., CFE, CICA, is a fraud investigator and forensic accountant. She provides consulting services in the areas of fraud, internal controls and business enterprise improvement. Ms. Park is a graduate of Indiana University and has twenty years of fraud and auditing experience in a wide range of industries.

CHAPTER 33

Trouble in Tallahassee

DR. TIM NADDY

The phone rang. A quick check on the caller ID showed me it was the company's former in-house legal counsel. I didn't want to answer it. It had been a busy holiday season and I had just got my son settled into the park swing for the first time in quite a while. Heck, it was probably the first time in a couple months that I had felt the sun's warmth on my face instead of watching it come and go through my office's Venetian blinds. During this time of year, though, I have to answer the phone. Holiday pleasantries are a superficial necessity and a quick "Merry Christmas" or "Happy Hanukkah" was not going to kill me.

"Hey, Ben. What's up?" I answered.

"What's going on in Tallahassee?" he started. Hmm . . . this was different. Usually when he calls we spend the first few minutes throwing around innocuous, machismo-laced jokes. Not today.

"What do you mean?" I asked while letting my subconscious rhythmically push the swing.

"Jim's been fired. Haven't you heard?"

"News to me. What for?"

"I thought you'd know; that's why I'm calling you . . . ."

James Young, known to his friends as Jimmy and his colleagues as Jim, appeared to be a guy who had it all together at the age of 27. A father of three little girls, he had been married to his trophy wife for seven years and lived quite the lavish lifestyle. I mean, why not? At 24 years old, he founded the latest Internet darling, PayYerWay.com, an online payment processor that was going to revolutionize the way consumers paid for their online purchases. As president of the company, his job was twofold: to be in control and to exude confidence.

Now it seemed that something was amiss in Tallahassee. Apparently, the well-manicured James was let go, or rather told to leave town, and

PayYerWay.com was placed in the unfortunate position of trying to figure out exactly what he did. Management had shifted into crisis mode after a whistleblower within senior management noticed certain elements were not matching up.

How much was at stake was easy to appreciate. In less than two months, the fledgling tech startup company was scheduled to hold a critical meeting with an international retail giant looking to assimilate PayYerWay.com's operations into its own to better streamline its Internet purchasing abilities. But, if the potential purchaser received wind of Jim's alleged fraudulent behavior — the president of the company — the news alone would surely usurp any negotiations that could take place. So management did what only management could do . . . bury the issue and bury it quickly.

Why I got called I don't know. I hadn't worked for PayYerWay.com for at least three months when Ben called. Since I had decided to resign my position for cash-flow reasons in September, I hadn't performed any oversight duties for PayYerWay. In fact, I had already taken another job across town in a completely different industry that required all of my time. But, to receive an unexpected call on that day in December made me think that somehow my name had been brought up in conversations to which I was not privy. Why my name was included and in what context it was used I just didn't know. What I did know was that it was time for me to find out just what the hell *was* going on in Tallahassee.

Starting Early

Jim was a B-average college student who hadn't taken a single business course. He lacked natural confidence, but was able to teach himself how to project an image of a confident self-promoter. In reality he strived for acceptance throughout his life. Childhood was rough for Jim and he was picked on often for being clumsy. Adolescence wasn't much kinder to him — he was mediocre at sports and not too appealing to the ladies, but he did begin to develop a knack for getting what he wanted. He even managed to experience his 15 minutes of fame in high school. As the only sophomore sitting on his south Florida high school's honor court, he helped craft a decision regarding a senior classmate's unethical behavior in the school lunchroom. Jim's admonishment was quoted in his school newspaper as, "I guess bad things do finally catch up to you. And for him, they did."

In college Jim took a part-time job to make ends meet. Luckily, being in Tallahassee meant there were many student internships within the many departments of state government in which one could begin learning the necessary skills for a budding career in public service. He held several state jobs, bouncing around departments as opportunities presented themselves for him to climb the ladder. As a college senior, he tried his hand at his first sales job for a regional chemical company called Kill 'em All Exterminators, where he quickly rose to the position of top salesman in the state. By the time Jim graduated, he had broken the southern territory sales records and was told he could have a great career in the exterminating business if he so chose. However, Jim had other plans.

Jim began developing his idea for an Internet business when he noticed that many of his fellow exterminators found it difficult to save money for vacations. During a conversation with his territory manager, Jim suggested that Kill 'em All Exterminators should establish a special savings account into which employees could deposit a percentage of their paychecks — like a 401(k) account for vacations. Then when they were ready to take a vacation, they could simply withdraw the funds and be on their way. The idea was put into practice and Jim ended up developing a concept for a vacation travel website designed to allow employees to manage how much they took out of their paychecks to save for vacations. They could pay their way, or "PayYerWay." During this time, he met his cofounder and eventual CEO of PayYerWay.com (PYW), Sam Watkins.

After the idea garnered some investor capital, PYW became a target of a local Tallahassee benefactor who started working his extensive rolodex to assist with its launch. Money from investors poured into the company and PYW looked to be on the path to success. Notably, it was also around this time that Jim's unusual behaviors began to surface. It has been said that money doesn't change you, but rather accentuates the person you were before you had money. If that was the case, then Jim had some serious issues when he was a poor college student that were only exacerbated when his wallet started getting fat.

With each investor he landed, Jim's confidence soared. Built atop his successful background in sales, his new, sharply honed corporate confidence made him deadly in the investor pitch. It seemed no one could say "No." It also seemed he couldn't say "No" either. Jim became extremely concerned, close to neurotic, about making sure people perceived him to be more sophisticated than he really was. He developed expensive tastes but had insufficient income to support them; however, that did not stop him from living the old-fashioned American dream. On his $150,000 annual salary, Jim somehow managed to live in a $1.4 million home and maintain a $400,000 vacation home. He also owned two $50,000 Range Rovers, had an affinity for $1,000 Mont Blanc pens (that he frequently lost), wore $100 designer t-shirts and toted numerous men's Gucci briefcases and luggage. To top it all off, he never left his home without his limitless credit card. Yes, he was the embodiment of conspicuous consumption and loved the fact that everyone could see his wealth.

It was only a matter of time until his personal issues would come to the forefront. Jim developed a predilection for cosmetic surgery to help trim down his body to fit inside his expensive designer suits. His drinking became excessive, as did his Las Vegas casino partying sans wedding ring. PYW had to weather multiple alleged sexual harassment claims from both inside and outside the office walls; however, each was conveniently settled out of court (and paid for by the company) and Jim never admitted wrongdoing. While he saw himself as the Don, everyone around him saw him slipping deeper and deeper into dangerous territory. At the same time, Jim's credit card company saw him slipping deeper and deeper into debt. People started noticing his ostentatious ways and whispers were beginning to get louder that Jim may be more than just a businessman. Word was . . . Jim was a conman.

Top-Heavy Organization

For all intents and purposes, PayYerWay.com was an interesting business concept. In the age of instant gratification, where ballooning credit limits and rising consumer debt seemed to fuel the insatiable desires of the American Dream, a couple of guys decided to go against the grain and devise a way for consumers to shop responsibly. Essentially, PYW was a startup Internet company that provided consumers a way to pay for things via the Internet in anticipation of the purchase. PYW was bucking the trend of credit-based purchasing by giving consumers an online payment alternative that could be managed responsibly within the consumers' personal budgets.

This responsible approach garnered PYW positive press within the media for being an advocate for the consumer. Their catchphrase was "Buy what you want. Pay what you can." In fact, the company couldn't have hit the market at a better time. Consumers throughout the United States were heading toward a credit crisis that would eventually grind the economy to a halt when the creditors tightened the screws on cardholders. PYW won numerous small-business awards for the company's proconsumer stance. However, it should be noted that much of the success was based on very good marketing and manipulated statistical data; not revenues. This was a concern for many astute investors; however, the positive press kept current investors at bay and allowed PYW to attract new investors.

PYW's management was typical for an Internet startup. Internet startups typically must prove themselves to investors by beefing up their management team with high-quality professionals who are usually near the top of their respective industries when tapped. Naturally, with the egos that are involved, many startups develop a top-heavy hierarchy because these recruited professionals want to be decision makers — well-paid decision makers. PYW's management team was no exception. Of the 40+ PYW employees, ten of them were designated as upper management and each of them demanded annual salaries in excess of $90,000; six of them in excess of $125,000. Mind you, this is a *startup company with no conceivable revenues.* Thus, this team was being paid by investor cash.

The top of the management pyramid was dominated by a two-headed monster — two people acting as the boss. In this case, one was acting as CEO and the other acting as President. Since both gentlemen were cofounders of PYW, they both wanted to be in charge. Jim Young was the original CEO and Sam Watkins was the president. However, several investors were concerned with Jim's youth and preferred that Sam, age 41, take over as CEO of the company. So, reluctantly, Jim gave up the CEO title, but maintained his authority in the company. They actually made a pretty good team because Jim was a great salesman and Sam had a great marketing mind.

On the next rung of the ladder sat Keith Ferguson. Hired as CFO, Keith was originally approached by Jim and Sam because of his well-known contacts. They both knew that without a person experienced in investor relations, PYW would have difficulty raising the necessary capital to launch the company. The only issue was that Keith had no credentials for serving as CFO. He was a former Division II-A NCAA football coach who made many friends during his coaching tenure. With those friends, he became an investment manager for a large brokerage house, but had never actually run a company, let alone drafted corporate financial statements. He was known for saying in investor meetings, "I'm not a numbers guy, but I know an opportunity when I see one." That did not instill much confidence in the potential investors' minds.

On the bottom of the management pyramid were four young VPs (information technology, strategic relations, finance and analytics) and a few seasoned directors. PYW did not have a formal board of directors, which, according to Jim and Sam, was beneficial because then "the Board can't tell us what to do."

The tone at the top of the organization was Fun, with a capital F. Lax, youthful leadership breeds a lax, youthful environment. Internet companies seem to pride themselves on their relaxed work environment because they say it keeps the creative juices flowing. PYW believed in the same mantra. Many of their line-level employees were young (early 20s) and had either just graduated from college or were still in school. When college-age kids work long hours together in close proximity it's safe to assume that normal office decorum is not commonplace. Thus, it should not be surprising that the office conversations included a lot of sexual innuendo; the type of things employees learn not to say in an established company. In addition, with their youthful banter came youthful business ideas; however, no wisdom from experience was there to help make them fruitful. Marketing and promotion were the best products pushed by the PYW team because all of the employees were of a particular type: extroverted and competitive.

Overall, PYW had a lot of flair externally but had no real organizational substance to deliver the service.

Youthfulness and inexperience abounded, and money was seen as easy come, easy go. Jim and Sam spent money unwisely on things that were routinely questioned by the investors who were paying for them. Jim and Sam had no real sense of budgeting or accounting, but had a firm grip on their corporate credit cards. With new investors lining up to buy membership units, there was no limit to their extravagance. Even though the company had not yet turned one dollar of profit, they kept spending money as if PYW was making millions. For $60,000 they sponsored an Indy Car racing in the Indianapolis 500 (that wrecked during qualifying). Another $50,000 bought them co sponsorship rights for a NFL Poker Party at the Playboy Mansion. $40,000 was spent by Sam, the marketing head of the two-headed monster, on a brand new black Corvette upon which a small PYW sticker was affixed to its back window for "marketing" purposes. (This same Corvette would be sold by the company to Sam a year later for $26,000, well below market value.) In addition, $45,000 collectively was spent to purchase prepaid, two-year leases on a Range Rover and a BMW 7 series for use by Jim and Sam, respectively.

The culture of the company could be summed up in one word: carefree. The attention to appearing successful was important to leadership so they could continue to sign investors. Additionally, PYW's youthful and inexperienced culture made it a risky investment, but that risk would not see the light of day until the appearance of success finally started to fall apart.

What Happened in Vegas

The event that began the unraveling of this scheme was when VP of Strategic Relations, Bill Michaels, went to Las Vegas to represent PayYerWay at an NBA poker event. While there he ran into someone he had met a while back in Chicago during an Internet seller tradeshow. This gentleman, Guy Seo, was a prominent executive in the transaction-processing department of a very popular Internet search engine. He had been approached by Jim with the offer of coming on full time with PYW due to his expertise in the field. During the discussion, Bill gingerly asked Guy if he had received any compensation arrangements for his upcoming employment. He said yes, but that the president had arranged for everything so there should be nothing to worry about. In addition, Guy mentioned to Bill that he had just brought in two investors in the amount of $75,000. These two investors had not received any verification of their subscription documents, although they had already sent their money to PYW. These comments were of particular interest to Bill because he knew that PYW was experiencing serious financial hardships and he had not been paid his salary for the past month or so. The information did not make sense.

So Bill, curious about the newly arranged hiring of a soon-to-be well paid executive, went back to Tallahassee and started asking questions. Bill's questions were not well received by the management and he was told to stop messing around in business that wasn't his. Jim specifically told Bill that his nitpicking was not appreciated and damaged his trust in him. Shortly thereafter Bill was fired from PYW.

Welcome Back

This is right about the time I came into the picture. I had previously left PYW for another job, but I periodically kept up with certain colleagues with whom I had built relationships. However, I was thrust right into the middle of this ordeal because apparently my name was never removed as VP of Finance from the company's website, making me the de facto guy for investors to go to for financial answers. The timeline of events drawn out below is a good reminder that time is of the essence during fraud investigations. The investigation developed as follows.

January 6

During the afternoon, I received a concerned call from Guy Seo regarding the president's recent termination and how that decision would affect his potential employment with PYW and if there might be something wrong with the investments made by the two investors he brought into the company. It was the latter of the three concerns that piqued my interest. I asked Guy to explain a little more about what he meant when he said something may be wrong with the investments. Guy gave me the quick and dirty on how his buddies paid their investment monies back in November but had not yet received their investor documents. He asked if I would look into the issue and I agreed to. Guy sent me a few e-mails that originated from Jim Young with a set of financial documents attached. Upon reviewing the attachments, I noticed immediately that these were not the financial documents I had created when I was employed as VP of Finance, and could only guess that they must have been created by someone at PYW.com (my presumption was Jim). Guy asked if I would speak to his investors and I told him to have them call me directly.

Around 3 P.M., the fraud investigation officially began. I spoke briefly with Liam Fitzpatrick, one of the investors brought in by Guy Seo. He told me that he had reviewed the financial package given to him by Jim and had followed Jim's instructions to wire the money to a Farmers Merchants Bank account. I informed Liam that I was unfamiliar with that bank account as it did not exist when I left PYW in September of the previous year. He told me that he had wired the money in October. This was interesting because at that time PYW employees had not been paid for weeks due to the cash crunch; however, it appeared now that the company was, in fact, receiving investor money. Liam sent me all of his financial correspondence with Jim, and with the financial information from Guy I began searching for answers. A quick comparison of Liam's financial package with the financial statements I had created for the prior year's third quarter told me everything I needed to know. He was a victim of financial statement and investor fraud.

Jim fraudulently removed $1.8 million of expenses in the doctored financial statements while increasing the revenues by $500,000 (a total of a $2.3 million swing in a company that didn't make more than $18,000 in the previous three years of operations.) So, in effect, he made PYW appear profitable, which it was not, and that it had a stable and climbing revenue growth percentage, which it did not. With the doctored financial statements, he persuaded Liam and two others that I knew about (although there were probably more) to invest in PYW. As President, Jim had the authority to open a bank account in the company's name, and then he diverted the investors' cash into the new account. After the cash was received, Jim would have the cash put into his own personal bank account; thereby showing a zero balance at month's end. Yes, the activity would have shown up in the bank statements, but the bank statements never made it to the company for review. Of the amount discovered, $125,000 was absolute; however, per discussion with others who saw the bank statements, this amount is actually upwards of $900,000.

I recorded all discrepancies and forwarded them to Guy and Liam for their files.

At 6 P.M., I sent an e-mail to inform the CEO, Sam Watkins, as well as other pertinent parties, that I believed a fraud had occurred and suggested they seek legal counsel and attached the evidence of wrongdoing. This served to inform the management team that Jim was allegedly involved in financial statement and investor fraud. An emergency meeting was held that night with interested parties to discuss a plan for containment and resolution.

January 7

I was invited to a meeting at PYW's offices by Fred Schwartz, investor and father of David Schwartz, VP of Analytics, to discuss the observations I sent to PYW management the night before. From my understanding, Fred was acting as internal counsel for crisis management. (He later became a manager of the company and then vanished just as quickly as he came in.) Fred asked me to discuss my observations with a CPA friend of his, Ted Westerlik, who was flown in from Texas specifically to help sort out the accounting mess. During the conversation, Ted took notes and for some reason did not seem to be all that surprised by the points I was laying out for him. I found his cavalier attitude somewhat unsettling. After speaking with him, I went down the hall and sat in the conference room where Sam Watkins, a silent co founder named Paul Askew, and several other employees were discussing the issues at hand. Sam looked distraught, but again it felt . . . fake. Before I left, I went to speak to the VP of Technology, Jack Nimble, in his office and he said that he believed the company was covering up something, but didn't know the details. I told him about the things I found and Jack decided to give me the QuickBooks file that supported the prior year's third quarter financial package on a thumb drive. That was the last piece of evidence I needed.

The Case Builds

Remember that uneasy feeling that I had during my meetings at PYW? Well, my gut was right. I did not like the interviews that took place the day before and left the company thinking management was hiding something. So, I retained legal counsel to determine how and to whom I should report this. As instructed by my lawyer, I initiated no further contact with the company after this date.

A couple of weeks later, on January 23, I received an e-mail from the VP of Analytics on my personal e-mail account asking for assistance with the company's Capital Maintenance Log. Since I was the one who built the log, they needed assistance trying to figure out what was going on. However, once again there was something suspicious. In the body of the e-mail the words *implicate* and *book-cooking* were thrown around in a nonchalant manner. I forwarded the message to my lawyer and, under his instruction, decided to report the fraud to the Florida Department Law Enforcement (FDLE). That same day I met with an FDLE investigator. I explained the entire timeline to him and showed him the evidence binder I had pulled together on the advice of my lawyer. The investigator was intrigued and set me up to meet with the agents in charge of white-collar crime.

On February 12, more than a month after the fraud had been discovered, I finally got a formal meeting with the FDLE agents in charge of white-collar crime investigations. I met with Agents John Langston and Philip Runyan at the FDLE. For all intents and purposes, it was a routine discussion. They took my statement and I walked them through the evidence binder and timeline. I gave them my evidence to make copies. After the interview, a funny thing happened — the agents asked me if I would be able to perform the fraud investigation for them since the FDLE was currently short staffed. After a short pause, I explained to the gentlemen that it would be improper for me to perform the investigation as it is a clear conflict of interest and any work that I did would probably be thrown out of court. They concurred.

On February 19, I received an e-mail from Agent John Langston stating that he had made a copy of my binder and I could come pick it up from the FDLE office. He went on to write, "I documented the info you provided in my report to reflect your concerns. After the legal review, we decided there were no victims at the time to pursue charges. If the investors who put up the money decide to pursue anything at a later date we can possibly look at a scheme to defraud." Thus, the investigation was at a standstill until the victims came forward and since I was not a victim, my information was not enough. I couldn't believe that I proved a fraud occurred, but the investigators were not going to pursue it.

It took over a month for Victim 1 to come forward. On March 24, I received a call from victim Robert Hardy. He wanted the information for my lawyer and the FDLE agents, so I sent it to him and to Guy Seo. It took another couple of weeks for Victim 2 to come forward. On April 10, I received an e-mail from Webster Andrews. It appeared that he also wanted the information for my lawyer and the FDLE agents, so I sent him the same information.

Then, silence. Three months went by before anything was heard from the company and when the silence was broken, it came from within. On July 2, I received a blind carbon copy of an e-mail from a former PYW employee, Chris Mariucci, who worked in the PYW design department. Chris had been brought over to PYW because he had worked with the CEO for several years before PYW started and was one of the original PYW employees. He left the company after not receiving his salary a few months in a row, due to a shortage of investor funds. Coincidently, shortly after his departure, PYW received investor money and paid their employees. The scorned CEO decided that since Chris had left before that check was received, he was not entitled to his paycheck. Angered by this deception, Chris decided to write a tell-all e-mail and sent it out to the entire PYW address book, both past and present employees. This e-mail helped highlight the culture of PYW during Chris' two+ years there.

On July 9, Sam's former executive assistant secured legal counsel to recover thousands in back pay. Before securing a lawyer he sent an e-mail to me stating that due to his close proximity to the CEO he knew things that could be damaging to the company, Jim Young and Sam Watkins. However, once he lawyered up, that conversation thread died.

And in the End . . .

In brief, nothing ever happened. I was in one sense shocked that Jim was able to get away with this crime, but in another sense relieved that I would not have to deal with this over the next couple of years until I needed to testify at the court proceedings.

In late July, the FDLE denied the investigation. After hearing that all three victims came forth with complaints, I tried to follow up with Agent John Langston to see if he needed anything else from me. He stated somewhat bluntly that the FDLE was not going to pursue the investigation. In fact, when Victim 3 came forward Agent Langston told him, "we've written 12 reports on this investigation and nothing is going to come of it." I was shocked that he was so callous, but I guess he sees this kind of stuff all the time.

In August, with FDLE deciding not to pursue the investigation, I reported the fraud to the chief of staff of the Florida Attorney General. He informed me that white-collar crime is dealt with at the Office of Financial Regulation (OFR). So on August 20, I met with Inspector Justin Reynolds, an investigator at the OFR. I gave him a statement and also gave him the evidence binder for his staff to copy. It must've been lost in all the other evidence binders on his desk because I never heard from him again.

Then, during an ACFE fraud seminar in early September, I met Talla-hassee Police Department (TPD) investigator Ally Gates. I briefly explained the scenario to her and duly made a copy of the evidence binder for her as well. Nothing happened.

Nothing came of the investigation because all parties involved appar-ently thought that some other agency would conduct the investigation. Because of limited time, resources or possibly interest, Jim is currently using his ill-gotten gains as feeder money for more Internet companies (energy, credit reporting, etc.) that don't have any tangible products. It will not sur-prise me if he attempts this scam again.

Lessons Learned

Fraud is rampant. Examiners who are in charge of the books must be cognizant of their surroundings. They need to place trust in their gut instincts because most times, if things don't feel right, they probably aren't and need to be investigated.

When in doubt, get out. If those in management will not listen to the financial expert's perceptions and observations, then it's time to leave. Especially, if their observations lead the examiner to believe improprieties are afoot. Examiners must be proactive and never let cir-cumstance and anxiety overcome their sense of judgment. Examiners are well trained and have a knack for uncovering these things. They must investigate, understand and take action.

CYA — Examiners need to document *everything*. It's the only way they can save themselves from being a scapegoat for those unscrupulous types.

Examiners should not be surprised if law enforcement does not pursue the alleged fraud. In this case, the evidence was brought to four different law enforcement investigative bodies and *none* of them pursued it. Why? The best guess is that on the surface it wasn't big

(*continued*)

(*continued*)

enough to warrant attention. This experience taught me that fraudsters do get away with fraud often, but that should not deter examiners from being any less vigilant.

Recommendations to Prevent Future Occurrences

Examiners should not allow anyone in upper management to have access to the financial statement's raw data. Only the CFO or the controller should have that information. Segregation of duties is important and would have caught this type fraud.

Examiners should *pay attention to the warning signs.* If they're there, fraud is probably occurring.

About the Author

Tim Naddy, D.B.A., CFE, CPA. Integrate, educate and elevate are words that embody Tim's work ethic. According to Tim, nothing teaches humility nor preaches integrity like his three little boys who remind him daily that ivory towers are best suited for fairy tales and that passion is reserved for those who dare to dream.

Glossary

5300 Call Report a regulatory financial and statistical report

Amortization the systematic expensing of the cost, less any residual value, of an intangible asset over its estimated useful life

Audit committee a subcommittee of an organization's board of directors that is charged with overseeing the financial reporting process

Backlog a term in the construction industry for the value of the projects that a contractor expects to be completed in the near future

Cash larceny the theft of an organization's cash after it has been recorded in the accounting system

Collateralized debt a loan that is secured by a specific asset; if the borrower defaults, the lender takes possession of that asset as payment

Concealed liabilities and expenses a type of financial statement fraud scheme in which the perpetrator(s) intentionally understates or omits liabilities and/or expenses from the organization's financial statements

Corruption fraud schemes in which an employee uses his influence in a business transaction in a way that violates his duty to his employer for the purpose of obtaining a benefit for himself or someone else; examples include bribery, extortion and conflicts of interest

Criminal conspiracy an agreement between two or more people to commit an illegal act

Davis Bacon rates wages set by the federal government and based on job title and geographic area to ensure that employees on government contracts are paid fairly

Debt rating a measure of the credit worthiness of a corporation's or government's debt issues

Debt servicing costs the cash flow required to meet the organization's interest expenses, principal payments and sinking fund requirements during a specific time period

Depreciation the systematic expensing of the cost, less any residual value, of a fixed asset over its estimated useful life

Double-pledged assets assets mortgaged to more than one lender

Embezzlement the wrongful taking or conversion of the property of another for the wrongdoer's benefit

Fictitious revenue the recording of sales of goods or services that never occurred

Fiduciary duty certain duties, imposed by law, that people in a position of trust — such as officers, directors, high-level employees of a corporation or business and agents and brokers — owe to their principals or employers; the principal fiduciary duties are loyalty and care

Financial statement analysis an examination of the relationships among the amounts on the financial statements using techniques such as horizontal, vertical and ratio analysis

Financial statement fraud the deliberate misrepresentation of the financial condition of an enterprise through the intentional misstatement or omission of amounts or disclosures in the financial statements to deceive financial statement users

Forced reconciliation a method of concealing fraud by manually altering entries in an organization's books and records or by intentionally miscomputing totals

Foreign currency swap investment strategy in which funds are converted from one currency to another to take advantage of changing conversion rates

Fraudulent disbursement a scheme in which an employee illegally or improperly causes the distribution of funds in a way that appears to be legitimate

Fraudulent write-off a method used to conceal the theft of assets by justifying their absence on the books (e.g., as lost, destroyed, damaged or scrap in the case of inventory, or as bad debts or sales returns/allowances in the case of accounts receivable payments)

Ghost employee an individual on the payroll of a company who does not actually work for the company

Grand larceny larceny of property whose value is greater than a specified amount; the amount varies depending on the laws of the jurisdiction

Impaired asset an asset whose fair market value is determined to be less — and expected to remain less — than the value recorded on the books

Improper asset valuation the fraudulent misstatement of the recorded value of an asset (usually inventory, accounts receivable or fixed assets)

Improper disclosure the fraudulent omission or intentionally misleading wording of any of the narrative disclosures, supporting schedules or other such information required to be included in the financial statements

Intangible asset a nonmonetary asset that is not able to be seen or touched, such as a patent, trademark or goodwill

Internal controls policies and procedures designed and implemented to ensure the organization's operational efficiency and effectiveness, reliability of financial reporting and compliance with laws and regulations

Lapping the crediting of one account through the abstraction of money from another account, typically to conceal the theft of incoming payments

Letter Rogatory (letter of request) court-issued document to a foreign court requesting that the foreign court: (1) take evidence from someone within the foreign jurisdiction or serve process on an individual or corporation within the foreign jurisdiction, and (2) return testimony or proof of service for use in a pending case

Liability/expense omission a deliberate attempt to conceal from the financial statements a liability or expense that has already been incurred

Long-term debt liabilities that are not due for more than a year

Management letter a letter issued by management to the auditor declaring the sufficiency, completeness and appropriateness of the organization's financial statements

Money laundering the disguising of the existence, nature, source, ownership, location and disposition of property derived from criminal activity

Overstatement type of financial statement fraud in which one or more amounts on the financial statements are reported as greater than the actual amounts; revenue and asset accounts are the most common subjects of overstatements

Qualified audit report an auditor's report stating that "except for" the effects of the matter(s) to which the qualification relates, the financial statements are presented fairly in all material respects

Related-party transaction a transaction that occurs when a company does business with another entity whose management or operating policies can be controlled or significantly influenced by the company or by some other party in common

Revenue cycle the business process that begins when a sale is made and ends with the collection of the related sales revenue

Short-term debt liabilities that are due within a year (also called *current debt*)

Skimming theft of cash prior to its entry into the accounting system

Tangible asset an asset that is able to be seen, touched and/or physically measured, such as cash, inventory and equipment

Tax avoidance the use of legal means to reduce a taxpayer's tax liability

Tax evasion the intentional use of illegal means to reduce a taxpayer's tax liability

Tax shelter any method used to reduce a taxpayer's tax liability; such methods can be either legal or illegal

Timing differences a method of financial statement manipulation in which revenue or expenses are intentionally recorded in an improper period

Tone at the top management's personal integrity and attitude toward internal controls

Understatement type of financial statement fraud in which one or more amounts on the financial statements are reported as less than the actual amounts; expense and liability accounts are the most common subjects of understatements

Unqualified audit report an auditor's report stating that the financial statements are presented fairly in all material respects

Wire fraud the use of electronic communications to perpetrate a scheme to defraud a victim of money or property

Index

Printed and bound by CPI Group (UK) Ltd, Croydon, CR0 4YY

23/04/2025

14660909-0003